Improving the Software Testing Skills of Novices During Onboarding Through Social Transparency

Von der Fakultät für Elektrotechnik und Informatik
der Gottfried Wilhelm Leibniz Universität Hannover
zur Erlangung des Grades

Doktor der Naturwissenschaften
Dr. rer. nat.

genehmigte Dissertation

von

Dipl.-Math. Raphael Pham

geboren am 10. April 1987 in Berlin

2016

Referent: Prof. Dr. Kurt Schneider
Korreferent: Prof. Dr. techn. Wolfang Nejdl
Korreferent: Prof. Dr. Michael Felderer
Tag der Promotion: 20. Oktober 2016

Bibliografische Information der Deutschen Nationalbibliothek

Die Deutsche Nationalbibliothek verzeichnet diese Publikation in der
Deutschen Nationalbibliografie; detaillierte bibliografische Daten sind
im Internet über http://dnb.d-nb.de abrufbar.

ISBN 978-3-8325-4385-3

Logos Verlag Berlin GmbH
Comeniushof, Gubener Str. 47,
10243 Berlin
Tel.: +49 (0)30 42 85 10 90
Fax: +49 (0)30 42 85 10 92
INTERNET: http://www.logos-verlag.de

Raphael Pham. *Improving the Software Testing Skills of Novices During Onboarding Through Social Transparency.* PhD thesis, Gottfried Wilhelm Leibniz Universität Hannover, 2016.

Dedication

Behind personal projects of this size, there is a story of personal growth. And growth—I believe—is driven by the people who surround us, day by day. I wish to take a moment to express my gratitude to those who have made my story of growth possible!

I am grateful to Prof. Schneider who has given me the opportunity to do research in the first place and who has never ceased to support me. Under his supervision, the Software Engineering Research Group at Leibniz Universität Hannover has been a productive and welcoming environment to me.

To Leif I owe a great deal of the way I think about things nowadays. Lunches at "Spandau", old-man walks and coffee breaks were the highlights of my day. Slowly, one captivating discussion after another, I learnt a little bit of the way of Leif.

Stephan always had a sympathetic ear for my many worries and knew how to cheer me up. I will gladly return for sleep-overs in pajamas and video games.

Olga and I did our PhD studies during the same time and shared a lot of worries. Valuing all of her great advices, I found her professional competence inspiring. Without her, Stephan, and Leif, my academic endeavors would not have been possible.

As a researcher, Tobias impressed me with his vigor, precision and his keen eye for details. Oliver and I have spent several great summers swimming in the Altwarmbüchener See. Both Tobi and Olli, I could always count on—even when moving homes on a Sunday morning on Christmas.

Anna finished her PhD thesis long before me and joined the software industry. She provided me with an important glimpse of life 'after the thesis'.

Mario taught me to take a step back, gaining a bigger and less hectic view on things. I treasured our tea sessions and I am looking forward to the next one.

Naxi, Nicco and Fred—I know—will always have my back, come what may. I can only hope to one day be able to demonstrate my loyalty to them the way they have shown me time and time again.

Grandmother knows how to put events into perspective, especially regarding family matters. I only wish I could visit her more often.

And when life gets complicated and drama-ridden, I find calm and serenity in my partner Marie. Being the smartest person I know, she made me answer the right questions at the right time. With her at my side, I look forward with confidence in mind and happiness at heart.

Everything is well.

Berlin, November 2016   *Raphael Pham*

Abstract

Systematic software testing is a fundamental part of software engineering, however, inexperienced software developers have difficulties practicing it. They have little hands-on experience with testing, misconceptions, and are unable to implement their theoretical testing knowledge. Although being aware of the benefits of systematic testing, they do not practice it vigorously.

Newcomers—such as fresh graduates from university—enter the onboarding phase of their first job position underprepared. They quickly need to adapt to the company's developing culture while overcoming their own testing deficiencies. Practitioners have developed coping strategies, but taking care of this lack of testing skills increases the costs of the onboarding phase. Not taking care of it early on hinders the newcomer's progress in becoming a high-quality engineer.

This thesis qualitatively defines the lack of testing skills and identifies main causes for this situation. It employs Everett M. Rogers' Theory of Diffusion of Innovations to analyze how the innovation of practicing systematic testing is perceived by inexperienced developers. Using this theory, this thesis makes predictions on how to increase the adoption of systematic testing in the onboarding situation.

Two empirical Grounded Theory studies give an in-depth understanding of the testing behavior of students just before joining the engineering workforce as well as the testing behavior of newcomers during the onboarding phase.

This thesis proposes a three-part approach to overcome the lack of testing skills in newcomers. It is tailored to the needs of newcomers in the onboarding situation and targets to help newcomers adopt systematic testing more easily and quicker. Inspired by insights from a third empirical Grounded Theory study about the testing behavior on a social coding site, it employs social transparency to increase observability of testing activities in a development team, thereby increasing the newcomer's testing activity. Lastly, tool-support as well as evaluations are presented.

The approach presented in this thesis enables software companies to leverage the effects of an increased social transparency on the onboarding process in a systematic manner. Helping newcomers in overcoming the testing skill gap lowers the cost of onboarding and ultimately improves the hiring situation for both newcomers and practitioners. For newcomers, the overall onboarding experience is improved. Their individual lack of testing skills is taken into account and they are enabled to implement and extend their testing knowledge better.

Keywords: Systematic Software Testing, Onboarding Process, Theory of Diffusion of Innovations.

Zusammenfassung

Systematisches Testen von Software ist ein fundamentaler Bestandteil des Software Engineerings. Unerfahrene Entwickler haben jedoch Probleme zu testen: Wenig praktischer Erfahrung, Vorurteile und Missverständnisse erschweren das Testen in kommerziellen Projekten. Obwohl die Vorteile von Testen klar sind, wenden sie es nicht an.

Diese unerfahrenen Entwickler (z.B. Universitätsabsolventen) beginnen die Anlernphase ihrer ersten Position als Software Ingenieure unzureichend vorbereitet. Dort müssen sie schnell die Entwicklungskultur übernehmen und zusätzlich ihre Lücken im systematischen Testen überwinden. Praktiker haben Strategien zur Überwindung dieser Testlücken entwickelt—jedoch verlängert und verteuert dies die Anlernphase. Ein Nichteingreifen gefährdet den professionellen Werdegang des Neulings.

Diese Arbeit definiert die Testlücken von unerfahrenen Neulingen qualitativ und identifiziert Hauptgründe für das Entstehen dieser Problemsituation. Dabei wird die Theorie der Diffusion von Innovationen von Everett M. Rogers eingesetzt, um zu analysieren, wie unerfahrene Entwickler die Praxis des systematischen Testens wahrnehmen, wenn sie zum ersten Mal damit konfrontiert werden. Mithilfe dieser Theorie werden Voraussagen und Vorschläge zur Verbesserung des systematischen Testens in der Anlernphase gemacht. Zwei empirische Studien erklären ausführlich das Testverhalten von Studierenden kurz vor Studiumsabschluss und von Neulingen direkt bei Berufseintritt und unterstützen die Hypothesen der theoretischen Analyse.

Der drei-geteilte Ansatz dieser Arbeit ist speziell auf die Bedürfnisse von Neulingen in der Anlernphase zugeschnitten und soll ihnen helfen, systematisches testen leichter durchzuführen. Angeregt durch Ergebnisse einer dritten empirischen Grounded Theory Studie über das Testverhalten auf einer sozialen Coding Plattform, verwendet dieser Ansatz Social Transparency: die Sichtbarkeit von Testaktivitäten des Teams wird gezielt erhöht. Damit soll der Neuling zu mehr Testaktivitäten angeregt werden. Implementierungen samt Evaluationen der hier vorgeschlagenen Konzepte werden ebenfalls vorgestellt.

Der hier vorgestellten Ansatze hilft Software Firmen gezielt die positiven Effekte von Social Transparency auf das Testverhalten in der Anlernphase einsetzen. Dies verringert die Kosten der Anlernphase und entspannt die Arbeitsmarktsituation für den Neuling und den betroffenen Praktiker. Die Verbesserung der Anlernphase geschieht aus Sicht des Neulings und verhilft ihr zu besseren Testfähigkeiten und besserem Testwissen.

Schlagwörter: Systematisches und automatisches Software Testen, Anlernphase, Theorie der Diffusion von Innovationen.

Contents

1 Introduction

There is a distinct gap in the testing skills of fresh graduates' and industry's expectations. While the existence of this gap has been reiterated in a multitude of different settings worldwide, qualitative and descriptive information has been missing. Practitioners have recognized this lack of testing skills and have derived costly onboarding strategies to cope with it. Mentoring and taking care of a newcomer's testing skill gaps impacts a team's productivity negatively.

Academia and research proposed numerous improvements to testing education, gaining only little widespread adoption. This thesis systematically supports industry in handling the continuing testing skill gap newcomers. This gap is qualitatively defined, its root causes are uncovered and systematic improvements to onboarding are presented.

Anecdotal Accounts of Practitioners. Practitioners have criticized the education of computer science graduates in general and in regard of systematic testing specifically. In 2002, Richard Conn [35], software process engineer at Lockheed Martin, demanded a more real-world oriented approach to software engineering education. In 2003, Eric Brechner [23], director of Development Training at Microsoft, identified five areas in computer science education, which needed improvement in order to meet industry needs. In more detail, these included better testability and automated testing. Assessing current testing practices in 2006, five well-known practitioners [68] described university training in software testing as "widely second-rate", criticizing that most testers were self-taught while a universally agreed-on terminology and testing body of knowledge was missing. Considered individually, such re-tellings are anecdotal and non-generalizable.

Problematic Testing Skills of Graduates. In 2013, researchers Radermacher et al. [127] conducted a systematic literature review [92,94] in order to identify knowledge deficiencies of computer science graduates, pinpointing areas in which graduates do not meet both academia's and industry's expectations. Among other topics, they identify *systematic testing* as a recurring knowledge deficiency across numerous publications, reporting on graduates' inability to use coverage tools [28], lack of testing vigor [72], and problems in debugging [15]. Radermacher et al. criticize that most studies state the *existence* of a lack of testing skills, but do not provide enough descriptive information for a qualitative understanding. They note that some of the 30 included studies are up to 20 years old.

In this thesis, a qualitative understanding of the testing skills of nowadays' graduates is presented (cf. section 4.1).

Continued Need of Testing Skills in Industry. In 1997, Byrne et al. [25] interviewed practitioners in Ireland for desired topics in curricula and compared the results to the '91 curriculum [150]. Even back then, systematic testing was the second most wished for topic by practitioners, noting that *"students had read about these subjects [software testing] but only a few had a real appreciation of the practical issues involved"*.

In numerous instances, practitioners were surveyed on a larger scale using lightweight questionnaires. The topic of *systematic testing* was almost always voted one of the most 'important topic in practice' and 'in need of improvement in education'. Usually, practitioners are presented a set of educational topics (for example, SWEBOK [1]), asking them to chose topics that are most relevant in practice and topics that need improvement in education. Such studies were conducted as early as 1998 and worldwide (e.g. North America, Canada, England, Finland, ...), covering a multitude of working environments, domains, and educational settings.

Lethbridge et al. has conducted several such studies, engaging active practitioners from North America and Canada [101–104]. 'Systematic testing' is one of the top topics that practitioners missed in education and learnt to value in working life. Lethbridge et al. notice a *"clear knowledge gap and a reliance on on-the-job learning for topics related to software processes, people skills, and human-computer interaction"* and propose these topics for *"new-hire training and increased university coverage"* [104].

In 2005, Kitchenham et al. [93] repeated the surveys by Lethbridge et al. with computer science alumni in England. Testing was voted among the top ten topics of practical importance with participants reporting a distinct knowledge gap.

In 2014, Deak et al. surveyed computer science alumni in Norway in a similar manner and compared their results to a prior study from 2007 [44]. In both surveys, alumni voted systematic testing among the top ten topics that needed more attention in education.

In 2007, Surakka et al. conducted a similar study, this time questioning a more heterogenous population of software practitioners, computer science professors and students in Finland [146]. Comparing their results to the studies by Lethbridge et al., systematic testing was—again—voted very high in importance by all subject groups.

The use of questionnaires allows for a large number of practitioner participants and researchers use statistical means to demonstrate the significance of their results. However, such lightweight analysis is quantitative and only shows *that* practitioners demand better testing skills in graduates. A deeper, qualitative understanding is not provided.

Systematic Testing Heavily Underrepresented in Education. In 2010, Astigarraga et al., researchers of IBM, sharply criticized academia for a lack of in-depth testing education, even accusing educators of paying only lip service to industry's need for better test-educated graduates [5]: Due to the fact that *"software engineers hired directly from universities have had no formal training in software testing"*, industry had to deal with *"lower productivity, additional training costs, and a lower quality of testing, which ultimately results in higher development and support costs"*. After looking at two North American universities[1] and finding only one test-related course, they analyzed the cur-

---

[1]Carnegy Mellon University and Stanford University

ricula of 27 top-voted North American universities for coverage of systematic software testing. While three fourths of computer science programs covered 'test' to some degree in their software engineering courses (note: one fourth did not at all), only seven of 27 institutions taught testing in a dedicated testing course. The researchers found little to no test-related content in undergraduates coursework.

Astigarra et al. went on to assess both curricula standardization initiatives (Curricula 2001 [149] & 2008 [29], SE2004 [6]) and test certification programs (ISTQB[2], and others), criticizing them for giving systematic testing far too little attention while not requiring any demonstration of practical testing capabilities. In Curricula 2001 & 2008, only four out of 47 courses included any reference to software testing, while SE2004 allocated a total of only 27h of 495h (6%) to teaching testing principles.

Also in 2010, Garousi et al. [61] conducted a similar analysis of current computer science curricula in North America and Canada, coming to similar results: systematic testing is heavily underrepresented in computer science education and taught as a side-topic among a wealth of other software engineering topics. Testing is often limited to JUnit while using artificial and too small (under 80LOC) applications under test.

1.1 Approach

The *main goal* of this thesis is to facilitate a quicker adoption of testing culture by newcomers during onboarding, resulting in more test writing. Besides leveraging the positive effects of social transparency on testing behavior, newcomers are supported in overcoming gaps in technical testing skills. The approach of this thesis achieves the following *subgoals*:

> *Subgoal 1:* the team's testing culture is made visible, motivating the newcomer to engage in systematic testing,

> *Subgoal 2:* technical barriers of test writing are lowered and the newcomer is enabled to learn more easily from senior developers in a real-world setting,

> *Subgoal 3:* the newcomer is supported in overcoming testing knowledge gaps independently.

Implemented Strategies. The concept of *social transparency* is employed for making other team members' test activity (testing culture) visible (subgoal 1). While parts of this thesis may resemble *gamification* strategies, it is not based on gamification theories.

Concepts of *code recommendation* and *example-based programming* are used for helping newcomers overcome technical barriers when engaging in testing (subgoal 2), leveraging insights from empirical studies of newcomers' needs and testing behavior.

Strategies from *knowledge management* are used to help newcomers to overcome gaps in testing knowledge independently during onboarding (subgoal 3). A detailed design for a tailored test tutorial base is presented.

---

[2]www.istqb.org

3

Underlying Theoretical Analyses. The tripartite approach presented in this thesis is tailored to the testing-related problems and needs of inexperienced developers. A theoretical analysis of the educational situation of systematic testing identifies main causes for these problems and needs. It establishes an understanding of how these problems emerge and how they carry over to the industrial onboarding situation. Employing Rogers' Theory of Diffusion of Innovations [130], this analysis provides an understanding of how inexperienced developers perceive systematic testing, allowing to make predictions on how to increase the adoption of systematic testing in the onboarding situation. Indicators for the validity of the theoretical claims made in these analyses are provided in two empirical Grounded Theory studies. These studies give an in-depth understanding of the testing behavior of students *just before* joining the engineering workforce as well as the testing behavior of newcomers *during* onboarding.

1.2 Research Methods

Two of the three proposed strategies of this approach are implemented as Eclipse IDE-plugins and have been successfully evaluated with graduates. These implementations stem from collaboration with two students during their Master's theses, which the author of this thesis proposed and supervised.

The strategies proposed in this thesis are rooted in real-world insights stemming from three extensive empirical studies. One Grounded Theory study examined the testing behavior on a social coding site and the influence of a high degree of social transparency on it (cf. chapter 11). In order to be able to make informed design decisions and to gain a better understanding of the needs of newcomers and practitioners, two additional Grounded Theory studies were conducted, answering the following research questions:

1. What are the testing skills of graduates and are there any problems? (cf. section 4.1)

2. How do practitioners perceive these problems and how do they cope with them? (cf. section 4.2)

Implementation Study: Communicating Testing Culture. Making other team members' testing activity visible and getting newcomers to adapt this behavior is a main strategy of this thesis (cf. chapter 6, p. 83). Collaborating with Jonas Mörschbach through the course of his Master's thesis, the author of this thesis and Mörschbach engineered six dashboard-like monitors that display other team member's testing activity in the IDE of a newcomer, dubbed *Testing Displays*. During development, paper prototypes were evaluated with students to ensure understandability and correct effect on inexperienced developers. Two quantitative, cross-designed evaluations with Bachelor- and Master students indicated that inexperienced developers wrote more tests when exposed to testing displays. An extensive qualitative evaluation with a whole university course (36 student participants) gave insights into how novices perceived these testing displays. This approach and its evaluations can be found in chapter 9, p. 105.

Implementation Study: Enabling Easy Technical Adoption. The second strategy of this thesis proposes to lower barriers for technical adoption by newcomers (cf. chapter 7, p. 89). This strategy is implemented by providing suitable test code examples to newcomers, facilitating quick copying & pasting for an easy start. Collaborating with Yauheni Stoliar through the course of his Master's thesis, the author of this thesis and Stoliar engineered a test code recommender system that provides newcomers with working test code examples in their IDE, dubbed *Test Recommender*. During development, a paper prototype was used to qualitatively evaluate understandability and practicality regarding inexperienced developers. A quantitative, cross-designed evaluation indicated that students were quicker in writing tests when using the IDE plugin. This approach and its evaluations are described in chapter 10, p. 131.

Empirical Study: Testing Skills of Novice Developers. In order to better understand the struggles of novices when testing, the author of this thesis and a dedicated research group explored the enablers, inhibitors and perceptions of testing in novice software teams. They interviewed 97 soon-to-be Bachelor graduates about their testing behavior after finishing a practical software engineering project. This Grounded Theory study provides a qualitative understanding of the specific testing needs of newcomers just before they leave university and apply for engineering positions in industry. These insights are used to tailor the approach proposed in this thesis to these needs of newcomers. The main findings of this study can be found in section 4.1, p. 39.

Empirical Study: Practitioner's View on Testing Skills of Inexperienced Developers. In order to judge the relevance of the findings regarding testing skills of soon-to-be graduates, the author of this thesis and a dedicated research group conducted another Grounded Theory study. This time, the target population was practitioners who handled the onboarding of such inexperienced developers. This study provides a qualitative and deep understanding of current onboarding practices in industry and the impact of low testing skills in new hires. It also influenced the design of the approach of this thesis, making it lightweighter with a focus on industrial applicability. The main findings of this study can be found in section 4.2, p. 54.

Empirical Study: Testing Culture on a Social Coding Site In this study, the author of this thesis and a dedicated research group examined the testing behavior on a popular social coding site and found the positive effects that a high degree of social transparency can have on it. This study provides inspiration for potential solutions, as well as different strategies and influences for effectively diffusing a testing culture to a newcomer. The most influencing findings of this study are described in chapter 11, p. 137.

1.3 Scope & Assumptions

Scope. This thesis lies at the intersection of academia and industry, focusing on the lack of testing skills of graduates. While it uncovers systemic issues in testing education (and hindering attributes in testing itself), it does not propose improvements in testing education. Academia has implemented different improvements over the years (cf. section 12.2.1), however, practitioners are still struggling with low testing skills of newcomers (cf. chapter 4.2). Instead, this thesis proposes to adapt to the status quo and to support industry in handling newcomers with low testing skills better. Therefore, the contributions of this thesis target the industrial onboarding phase.

While there are many ideas on how to improve the discipline of testing for the general software engineer (mostly targeted at senior developers), this thesis focuses on newcomers shortly after their testing education and at the beginning of their working life. This is a particular subgroup of the active software developer community that will always be present and that needs support in accomplishing their engineering task.

The approach is tailored to the needs of newcomers and is not transferable without changes to other software engineering disciplines (cf. section 13.4).

Assumptions. A key part of this thesis is the communication of a team's testing culture, facilitating the adoption thereof. If the development team does not exercise any testing activities and if *de facto* there is no testing culture, this approach cannot support the newcomer. This thesis assumes regular testing activity in a development team.

The approach of this thesis focuses on written and automated testing. Manual execution of tests is not considered. It is designed to be applied to onboarding processes of co-located development teams. Onboarding remotely or to a remote teams introduces different requirements and is not in the scope of this thesis.

1.4 Target Audience

While direct recipients of this thesis' contributions are the newcomer and the practitioner working with the newcomer, the audience of this work is broader. Insights of this thesis can be useful for organizations that employ novice software developers and want to improve how they train them. By understanding why novices do or do not adopt testing practices, process managers can actively remove barriers and facilitate desired testing behavior.

Researchers can use this thesis' contributions to guide the creation of new tools and practices that support novices in adopting good testing practices. On the one hand, it uncovers technical challenges for which better tool support is needed. On the other hand, research into policies in software development can benefit from findings regarding attitudes towards testing.

For educators, this thesis documents testing-related preconceptions that they might encounter in their own students. It describes weaknesses in current education that—if addressed—would help prepare students better for careers as software developers and managers.

2 Fundamentals

An in-depth understanding of the Grounded Theory methodology is beneficial to the reader but not mandatory. A description can be found in the Appendix, p. 169.

Systematic Software Testing. High software quality is achieved, if the AUT satisfies the requirements posed by the customer. Systematic testing helps to check if the AUT satisfies its requirements.

> **Definition** *Quality* is the totality of characteristics of an entity that bear upon its ability to satisfy stated and implied needs. (EN ISO 8402)

> **Definition** *Application under test (AUT)* is the software application that is currently being systematically tested by the developer.

> **Definition** *A failure* is reached the when the AUT does not behave as expected and does not meet its requirements.

A failure occurs dynamically when the AUT is executed and the observed *actual behavior* diverges from the *expected behavior* (as stated by requirements). A failure is the result of a defect in the source code of the AUT.

> **Definition** *A defect* is the static cause in the source code for a failure of an AUT. Often, a defect is also called a *bug*.

Defects are unintentionally implemented in source code by the developer because of developer errors. It is also possible, that developers introduce defects due to carelessness or inattention.

> **Definition** *An error* is a misconception or misunderstanding by the developer that leads to implementing a defect.

A wrongly implemented paper-printing method with a wrongful variable assignment (defect) leads the AUT printing in duplex when single-page printing is selected (failure). The user requirement of a duplex- and single-page-printing feature is not met. Systematic testing helps to detect such failures.

> **Definition** *Systematic testing* is the execution of an AUT with the goal to uncover defects.

A *test run* implementing systematic testing encompasses preparation, guided execution and some form of documentation:

- carefully finding the best[1] *input values*, and

---

[1] Here, *best* describes the highest potential to uncover defects.

- finding the corresponding[2] *expected* AUT behavior (or output values),

- preparing the AUT (for example, bringing it into a required state for the test run),

- executing the AUT,

- comparing the *actual* AUT behavior, and

- documenting the results in a test report.

Input values can also be a specific *interaction sequence* with the AUT, for example with the GUI of the AUT. For example, pressing the "Print"-Button (input value) should open the print-dialogue window (expected behavior, output value).

Systematic testing clearly differs from a quick exploratory execution of the AUT to "see if the newly implemented feature works". Such an exploratory testing is defined as *manual smoke testing* (or *smoke testing* for short).

> **Definition** *Smoke testing* is the unguided execution of the AUT to quickly check if a feature is working.

Smoke testing is done by a developer right after a small feature is implemented, executing the AUT and manually interacting with its GUI. With little preparation and input values (or the interaction sequence with the GUI) chosen spontaneously, there is no consideration for its effectiveness in finding defects and no result documentation.

Two modes of systematic testing: *manual* and *automated* systematic testing. Manual systematic testing includes every step defined in the definition for systematic testing being executed by a developer *by hand*: The developer executes the AUT, interacts with the GUI in a pre-defined sequence and manually checks if it behaves as expected. Manual testing differs from smoke testing in that it is a deliberate and systematic effort: While manual testing is done in a prepared manner, checking whole interaction processes, smoke testing checks only one specific feature.

Automated systematic testing includes every step of the definition of systematic testing but is executed automatically by a computer. The computer starts the AUT, prepares its test setup if necessary, interacts with it according to the pre-defined test sequence (for example, inserting input values or interacting with the AUT's GUI automatically), compares the AUT's reaction and records successes and failures. The developer has to write specific *test code* that calls the AUT and executes it according to the current test case and automatically compares actual and expected behavior. Automation is usually enhanced by using a *test framework*, which provides essential testing tools (e.g. easy comparison of values and objects). Examples are the JUnit-Framework[3], Java's Robot class[4], and Selenium[5] or Bredex's Jubular GUI Dancer[6] (capture-replay tools).

---

[2]Which AUT behavior is expected by which input value is defined in the requirements.
[3]http://junit.org
[4]https://docs.oracle.com/javase/7/docs/api/java/awt/Robot.html
[5]http://docs.seleniumhq.org
[6]https://www.bredex.de/guidancer_jubula_en.html

Testing Culture of a Software Development Team   The term "testing culture" is difficult as "culture" is elusive and laden with multi-facetted meanings[7].

> **Definition** *Testing Culture of a Software Development Team* is the team's way of engaging in systematic software testing, the entirety of the team's testing-related ideas and customs, and associated social behavior during a software development project.

This definition of testing culture helps members of the team to decide what testing behavior they will tolerate and what testing behavior they will reject. It explains *what* it means to be engaging in systematic testing as a member of this team and *how* to do it. This way, the expression of the "newcomer adopting the team's testing culture" expresses that the newcomer starts to behave as the rest of the team.

Social Translucency   [8] In contrast to physical interaction, digital interaction lacks social information and context of communication partners. Erickson et al. [54] propose to make participants and their behavior more visible to one another and define three characteristics that influence digital interaction: *visibility, awareness, accountability*. Making social information *visible* gives us the chance to become *aware* of our conversation partner's context and act according to our cultural social rules—otherwise, we could be held *accountable* for our misbehavior. For example, seeing a coworker intently programming, we will not disturb that colleague. In the company's chat room application, the coworker's situation may not be comprehensible to other coworkers. The chat status "do not disturb" can convey such social information.

Real-world interaction is additionally governed by the existence of constraints of the interaction and the space in which it is being held. The *individual's awareness* of these constraints and the *group's shared understanding* of these constraints shape our interaction. For example, being aware that others around are subjected to the same physics lets us chose an appropriate volume when we speak with each other. Erickson et al. [54] identify three approaches convey socially salient information in systems: realistic, mimetic, and abstract conveyance. Realistic (*every* facial expression is conveyed) is problematic because of little technical abilities to capture all of it. Mimetic approaches try to "mime" the real world through consciously manipulating avatars. Abstract systems convey social salient information through text, pictures, and diagrams—specifically designed for conveying certain socially salient information. Testing Displays presented in chapter 9 are an example of that.

Social Transparency.   Stuart el al. [144] introduce a framework for the concept of *social transparency* of collaboration in groups or online communities, building upon social translucence. They adapt the concept of being aware of another collaborator's actions to modern, digital collaborations—such as social networks, global software engineering

---

[7]In the appendix, a practical and triangulating approach to defining the term "testing culture" is presented—it is not mandatory for the remainder of this work.

[8]This section was published in a similar form in [121] which the author of this thesis authored together with Jonas Mörschbach and Kurt Schneider.

or social coding platforms and define: social transparency is the availability of social meta-data surrounding information exchange.

They identify three dimensions of transparency and discuss their first order effects (immediately visible) and possible second order effects (long term effects): *identity, content, and interaction transparency*. *Identity transparency* is "the visibility of the identity of the sender and/or receiver in an information exchange". Being identifiable is likely to heighten a collaborator's sense of accountability.

The origin visibility and history of changes to an information (also artifacts) is defined as *content transparency*. A high content transparency lets developers view changes to the artifact and understand its evolvement better by supporting the creation of a mental model. For example, SVN revision history and visualization thereof can help a developer understand the evolvement of a written test suite better and facilitate a narrative of the workflow. Stuart et al. hypothesize that content transparency can increase productivity when creators of artifacts know that their actions are visible. However, a high content transparency can also increase stress on the creator's side.

Interaction transparency refers to the visibility of third party access on an information exchange between two partners. For example, how easily a developer can see that other users are interacting with or accessing an artifact, such as a specific readme-file. A high interaction transparency lets users judge popularity of an information exchange and even make inferences about normative behavior within a group. For example, in online communities, newcomers learn from the exchange between senior members and eventually adapt community norms [97].

3 Theoretical Analysis of Why Novice Developers Reject Systematic Testing

Communication scholar Everett M. Rogers introduced the Theory of Diffusion of Innovations in 1962 (DOI theory for short.). This theory tries to explain the adoption process that takes place when an innovation is introduced to a population of potential users. An innovation can be an idea, a method to solve a problem or a kind of tool that is perceived as new[1]. Introducing a new innovation to a population of individuals and facilitating overall adoption is a complex process. Even though an innovation promises well-known advantages over the current state of the art, it may not be adopted in practice. *Practicing systematic software testing* can be regarded as one such innovation. In this chapter, Rogers' Theory of Diffusion of Innovations is applied to systematic testing.

DOI Theory in Software Engineering. The DOI theory has its roots in social sciences and has been developed through many studies in this field. As software is developed by humans and teams of humans, one could argue that this theory is directly applicable to situations encountered in software engineering. There are several instances where predictions made using Rogers' theory were confirmed in the field of software engineering, further confirming its applicability in this field.

For example, in 2013, Leif Singer [139] constructed parts of his PhD thesis using DOI theory with the goal of systematically raising the adoption of software engineering methodologies. In 2014, Xia et al. [154] used DOI theory to explain how secure development tools—which they identify as preventive innovations—are adopted in development. In the early 90's, DOI theory was used to explain the adoption of CASE tools among developers [80, 125].

As early as 1989, Raghavan et al. [129] addressed the problem of technology transfer in software engineering. Even though there were a lot of new ideas, only little of found application in industry. Research attributed these problems to *"management pressures that interfere with the use of software-engineering practices or to general apathy and resistance to change on the part of potential users"*—but this was judged to be a dangerous oversimplification. Raghavan et al. advocated to understand and apply DOI theory to software engineering methods to get a systematic understanding of the diffusion process: *"We strongly believe that studying and adapting Rogers' framework to the software engineering context could significantly enhance our overall understanding of the*

---

[1]It does not have to be objectively new, it just needs to be perceived as new by the individual.

diffusion process and help us develop effective strategies to successfully diffuse software engineering innovations."

DOI Theory in This Thesis. First, the DOI theory is applied to the situation when the innovation of systematic testing is first diffused to the population of inexperienced developers. One common example of such a situation is the classroom setting of computer science undergraduates at a university (cf. section 3.1). This provides the reader with a theoretical understanding of

- how inexperienced developers first perceive the innovation of systematic testing,
- why they form a dismissive mindset towards systematic testing,
- what attributes of systematic testing make its diffusion in education particularly difficult, requiring a later re-diffusion in industry (testing-inherent attributes),
- why the current educational setting is not suited to convey the innovation of systematic testing (environmental attributes).

These insights help to explain the so-called *Knowledge-Attitude-Practice-gap* (KAP-gap [130]) often found in students and inexperienced developers: They have knowledge about systematic testing and even sport a favorable attitude towards quality assurance but still fail to apply it with vigor. An understanding of how inexperienced developers perceive the innovation of systematic testing is fundamental for guiding and designing an approach to overcome this KAP-gap. This understanding provides a *baseline* to work with and enables strategic application of improvements presented in this thesis (cf. chapter 5).

Next, Rogers' theory is applied to the first situation when the innovation of systematic testing becomes *practically* relevant to the inexperienced developer and when she needs to overcome the KAP-gap quickly. This is the onboarding situation when she enters working life in a new developer team. Even though her situation has changed, her attitude towards testing stem from the educational situation. Using the terms of DOI theory, changes in important situational factors are uncovered and both situations are compared. This way, the diffusion of the practice of systematic testing from its first introduction (educational situation), over its non-application (KAP-gap), to its first moment of actually being needed (onboarding situation) is traced. DOI theory allows to propose strategic changes for overcoming the KAP-gap and better facilitation of the adoption of systematic testing.

3.1 Choosing the Setting of this Analysis

For many software engineers, the situation in which the innovation of testing is first introduced to them is similar to lectures commonly found at universities. This situation lays the groundwork for the emergence of the testing KAP-gap—whose effects then carry over to the onboarding situation (cf. section 4.3, p. 70)—making its in-depth analysis necessary. In context of this thesis, four different models for such an *educational situation* are distinguished, differing in their effectiveness in conveying testing.

No Testing Education: The newcomer did not attend any kind of educational software engineering program before entering the onboarding phase. Her understanding of systematic testing is non-existent, which increases onboarding effort greatly.

Education: The inexperienced developer attends an educational program before entering the onboarding phase. This program involves lectures held by a teacher role, which are accompanied by exercises to deepen the understanding of concepts. Examples of this setting are lectures held at universities.

Education with Practical Projects: This situation is similar to the prior situation *Education* with the addition of one or more instances of practical software engineering courses. These courses differ from exercises in that they put the student in the role of a software engineer in a software development project for a limited time. Examples of this situation can be found at universities worldwide [24,107]. Not every university provides this kind of project, though. Students are encouraged to participate in internships at companies. However, it is unclear how regularly this occurs.

Education with regular Practice: There are educational models that are intertwined with commercial practice, so-called *cooperative studies* or *dual studies*. During these studies, the student is partly working as a software engineer while attending lectures as well. This is effective in conveying a practical sense of working as software engineer and in diffusing the innovation of systematic testing. However, compared to the other models, this education model is the least common (c.f. section 13.3, p. 163).

These models do not cover all possible variants of educational setting on software engineering worldwide, however this thesis assumes the educational settings *Education* and *Education with Practical Projects* to be the most prevalent worldwide, : Astigarraga et al. [5] and Garousi et al. [61] have both found systematic testing represented as only a 'side-topic' in current curricula, if at all. Specialized testing courses were very rare, making the *Education* setting most likely for a majority of developers. On the other hand, hands-on testing experience can also be gained (to some degree) in students capstone projects, collaborations with industry even [24,60,73,95,107,119], leading to the inclusion of *Education with Practical Projects*. To what degree systematic testing is enforced in these projects is not always clear.

3.2 The Theory of Diffusion of Innovations

In this section, definitions and constructs of DOI theory are illustrated by and applied to the educational setting of *Education with Practical Projects*. Exemplary, it is modeled after a real lecture course on software engineering at the Leibniz Universität Hannover in Hanover, Germany. It covers the main constructs of a lecture held by a lecturer (e.g. a professor), rounds of practice-focused exercises and a practical project. Assumptions made for this model can be applied to similarly modeled educational settings using similar constructs.

> **Definition** *The diffusion of innovations* is the process in which an innovation is communicated through certain channels over time among the members of a social system. ([130], p. 5)

> **Definition** *A social system* is a set of interrelated units engaged in joint problem solving to accomplish a common goal. ([130], p. 23)

> **Definition** *A change agent* is an individual who influences clients' innovation-decisions in a direction deemed desirable by a change agency. ([130], p. 27)

Applied to the educational situation: A student is an *individual* (or unit) in a *social system*, comprising or her classmates. The students' *goal* is to learn about software engineering and the lecturer's goal is to teach systematic testing and convey its benefits. The lecturer takes the role of a *change agent* while the *change agency* is both the software engineering community as well as society in general. Both wish to educate aspiring software engineers who will join the software engineering community.

> **Definition** *Norms* are established behavior patterns for members of the social system. They define a range of tolerable behavior and serve as a guide [...] for the behavior of members of the social system. ([130], p. 26)

Applied to the educational situation: A social system has norms. In classroom, students know how to behave and what is expected of them, learning from the lecturer. They follow lessons and take part in exercises. Alone or in groups, they solve homework to practice systematic testing.

> **Definition** *An innovation* is an idea, practice or object, which is perceived as new by the individual. ([130], p. 12)

An innovation can be *new* to an individual in different ways:

- Knowledge about the innovation itself: The individual is introduced to the existence of the innovation for the first time.

- Persuasion about the innovation: The individual has known about the innovation but has not formed an attitude towards it.

- Regarding a decision towards or against adoption of the innovation: An individual has known about an innovation, formed an attitude towards it but has not taken any action to decide to adopt or reject it yet.

An innovation does not need to be objectively new—it only needs to be *perceived as new* by the individual. In the context of this thesis, it is assumed that students have not been introduced to systematic testing nor practiced it. That is why this thesis focuses on the first kind of newness: first knowledge about the innovation. Rogers categorizes knowledge that an individual gains about an innovation into three categories ([130], p. 173):

- *awareness-knowledge*: information that an innovation exists, answering the question "What is the innovation?",

- *how-to-knowledge*: information that is necessary to use an innovation, answering the question "How does it work?",

- *principles-knowledge*: information that explains the functioning principles of an innovation, answering the question "Why does it work?".

Applied to the educational situation: In lectures, students are first introduced to new methods of assuring software quality, including but not limited to how to write automatic tests. This way, students gain *awareness knowledge* about systematic testing. The lecturer explains the core ideas and principles of systematic testing and thusly provides students with *principles-knowledge*. In exercise lessons and homework, students work through examples in order to apply their newly gained principles-knowledge, gaining *how-to-knowledge*.

Rogers identifies attributes of an innovation that influence its adoption rate. He categorizes these attributes into groups and views them as determining variables of the dependent variable "rate of adoption" ([130], p. 221). According to Rogers, the first group is most important for the adoption of an innovation: perceived attributes of an innovation.

first group:

- attributes of an innovation as perceived by the individual

second group:

- type of an innovation,
- nature of communication channels,
- nature of the social system,
- change agent's promotion efforts.

3.2.1 Perceived Attributes of an Innovation

A potential adopter perceives an innovation along different attributes, which can influence her reaction to it. These are *"subjective evaluations of an innovation, derived from [an] individual's personal experiences and perceptions, and conveyed by personal networks."* [130], p. 223. These attributes are: *relative advantage, compatibility, complexity, trialability,* and *observability.*

Relative Advantage of Systematic Testing

According to Rogers, the level of perceived relative advantage is the strongest predictor of an innovation's rate of adoption and it is influenced by the expected costs.

> **Definition** *Relative advantage* is the degree to which an innovation is perceived as being better than the idea it supersedes. ([130], p. 229)

Individuals assess the *"ratio of the expected benefits and the costs of the adoption of an innovation."* [130], p. 233. Especially the initial costs of adopting an innovation influence its rate of adoption—higher initial costs may be a barrier to adoption and lead to less adoptions.

There are different possible dimensions for the measure "better", depending on the context of the situation. Rogers suggests five the dimensions ([130], p. 233): economic profitability, increase of social status, decrease of discomfort, saving time and effort, and immediacy of reward. These are also applicable to the innovation of practicing systematic testing.

Applied to the educational situation: In class, students learn about the *advantages* of practicing systematic testing and it is possible to measure this innovation using these dimensions[2]:

- Written tests can automatically and programmatically check if the AUT complies with the requirements formulated in these tests. A quick execution of a test suite reports if a previously working function is still working. This *saves time and effort.*

- When collaborating with other developers, tests can serve as a form of contract of behavior of the system under development and encourage confident changes to the system. This promises to *decrease discomfort* when collaborating.

- The feeling of having a "safety net" of written tests can *increase comfort* when developing production code, reducing the discomfort of unknown side-effects.

- Lecturers look at systematic testing from an economical perspective and highlight its potential to *save costs.* Even though practicing systematic testing is costly, it bears the potential to find critical defects in AUT early on. There is a sweet spot between preventive quality assurance costs and overall defect removal costs.

According to Rogers, assessing an innovation is essentially a process to determine whether or not an innovation brings benefits in *one's own* situation. The students' educational situation is a big influencing factor in this assessment, leading to the following hypothesis:

---

[2]The dimensions 'social status' of practicing systematic testing are discussed in more detail later in this chapter (cf. section 3.2.3).

Hypothesis: *In the educational situation, students assess the relative advantage of practicing systematic testing as low.*

There are many aspects of the educational situation supporting this hypothesis: Students are only *told* about these advantages—instead of experiencing them first hand[3]. In the educational situation, the student simply *does not need* any of the benefits yet—their situation demands only passing the exercises successfully. Systematic testing is not important for their livelihood or money earning. This makes it difficult for them to appreciate the benefits that systematic testing promises.

Additionally, the *immediacy of reward* is not given. The benefits of *saving time and effort* and an *increase in comfort when changing things* only appear in later phases of development—if at all[4]. This makes the costs of testing stand out more and clearly perceivable by students. As argued by Rogers, individuals tend to focus on the benefit-cost ratio of adopting an innovation. This leads to a negative view on testing.

Compatibility of Systematic Testing

According to Rogers, a perceived high incompatibility is a strong blocker for adoption.

> **Definition** *Compatibility* is the degree to which an innovation is perceived as consistent with the existing values, past experiences, and needs of a potential adopter. ([130], p. 240)

Socio-cultural values and beliefs, individual needs or previously introduced ideas can influence and determine compatibility. Previously introduced ideas form the individual's current understanding of a technology and *"are the main mental tools that individuals utilize to assess new ideas and give them meaning."* [130], p. 243. Individuals assess new innovations based on their current knowledge and understanding of previous ideas.

Applied to the educational situation: Usually, students have not worked on complex software projects before and have little experience with systematic testing. This thesis assumes that they have *no clear beliefs and values for or against* systematic testing and *their personal experience* with it is limited. However, students may have *other, not directly related values* that interfere with their willingness to practice systematic testing.

Hypothesis: *Students perceive a low compatibility with the innovation of practicing systematic testing.*

One such value supporting this hypothesis is an *over-assertive self-view*: for example, students may be convinced that their programming skills are, in fact, "so good" that they do not make any mistakes and do not need any extra quality assurance, like systematic testing. Additionally, the lack of experience with testing makes it difficult for students to relate to the benefits that testing brings as well as *the needs* it fulfills. They

---

[3]As will be argued in later sections, exercising systematic testing techniques in university exercises is not enough to fully *experience* its benefits, cf. section 3.3.2.

[4]Lecture exercises do not focus on a project's progression and the role of systematic testing in later phases but rather exercise isolated application of certain testing techniques.

have never worked in an environment that required automatic tests, simply because the projects they were involved with—if any—have not been complex enough to warrant any extensive testing.

Complexity of Systematic Testing

A perceived high complexity can be a strong barrier for adoption.

> **Definition** *Complexity* is the degree to which an innovation is perceived as relatively difficult to understand and use. ([130], p. 257)

The attribute complexity takes into account the time it takes to master an innovation. The more complex an innovation is perceived and the more time it takes to apply it successfully and receive its benefits, the less likely a widespread adoption becomes.

Applied to the educational situation: Real-world test suites can rival production code in size and are in their essence small programs themselves. However, the complexity of how to actually implement test code is dialed back in an educational setting, leading to the following hypothesis:

> **Hypothesis:** *Students perceive the innovation of practicing systematic testing is perceived with a low complexity.*

Lecturers focus on conveying the core concepts first and technicalities second, programming exercises are designed accordingly. It is not uncommon for exercises to be specifically engineered for a classroom setting—instead of being taken from a real-world project, without simplifying changes. In this setting, students perceive the *complexity* of practicing systematic writing of tests as relatively low. The learning curve for applying these techniques is also kept low.

Trialabilty of Systematic Testing

A higher trialability increases the rate of adoption.

> **Definition** *Trialability* is the degree to which an innovation may be experimented with on a limited basis. ([130], p. 258)

When considering a new innovation, an individual wants to know: "How does this innovation help me *in my situation?*". Being able to try an innovation without consequences reduces uncertainty and facilitates learning of the innovation.

Applied to the educational situation: At university, the innovation of practicing systematic testing is presented in a manner that provides a high degree of trialability.

> **Hypothesis:** *At university, students perceive the innovation of practicing systematic testing as highly triable.*

In exercise lessons, students can try it without significant consequences. Their income does not depend on the success of the exercise software or the quality of the tests they write. Consequences comprise of negatively graded exercises. Commonly, these exercises are designed to facilitate exercising and experimenting for a deeper understanding and provide a high degree of trialability.

Observability of Systematic Testing

Visibility of others applying an innovation stimulates discussion with peers, which often facilitates the exchange of evaluation insights. *"The easier it is for individuals to see the results of an innovation, the more likely they are to adopt."* [130], p. 16.

> **Definition** *Observability* is the degree to which the results of an innovation are visible to others. ([130], p. 258)

When individuals observe their surrounding peers in their social system applying an innovation and being successful with it, they are more likely to adopt.

Applied to the educational situation: In the educational situation, students act within a social system of other students. With different configurations of student interaction and team-work in exercises, it is difficult to assess how *observable* the testing actions of other students are to a student.

> **Hypothesis:** *At university, students can perceive the innovation of practicing systematic testing with a normal degree of observability (neither low nor high).*

Depending on the structure of the lecture and exercises, a student may or may not be able to observe other students being successful with practicing testing:

- if every student solves the exercise at home, little observability is given.

- if students solve exercises together in small groups, higher observability is given.

- in class, students observe the lecturer demonstrate how to write tests and observe the lecturer's success with it. Other students may demonstrate their exercises.

It is important to note that the lecturer's role is different from the students': the lecturer acts as an active change agent and is not part of the social system of the students. The lecturer has a different social status than the students which can impede communication and its power to influence the behavior of students. Individuals tend to communicate more effectively when they are more alike. Rogers calls this the *heterophily-gap* and states that it is inherent to the process of diffusion of innovations. *"When [individuals] share common meanings and a mutual subcultural language, and are alike in personal and social characteristics, the communication of new ideas is likely to have greater effects in terms of knowledge gain, attitude formation and change, and overt behavior change."* [130], p. 19. Ultimately, students tend to be more influenced by the behavior of their peers—other students in class—than by the lecturer's behavior. In this sense, the first two situations are regarded as more important to the assessment of observability of systematic testing in the educational situation. While both situations represent extreme cases (no communication to other students vs. tight collaboration),

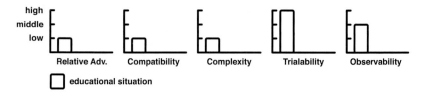

Figure 3.1: Assessment of five attributes of the innovation of systematic testing by students in the educational situation (for illustrative purposes only).

this thesis assumes that the relevant level of observability in educational practice lies in the middle of these ends.

This thesis assumes that students perceive only a small feeling of success when observing their classmates: Students are not working on a project together but simply solve the exercises given to them. There is no project context or personal involvement: The student's income is not directly dependent on these exercises. Even though observability given in the educational situation, it does not improve students' perception of practicing systematic testing.

3.2.2 Assessment of An Innovation's Attractiveness

The previous section introduced five attributes that students perceive testing by. Hypotheses about how students either assess an attribute as *low, middle* or *high* were made and explained in detail. Using these assessments, the state of how students perceive testing when they are first introduced to it is captured, using an ordinal scale[5]. Assessments for one attribute cannot be compared to an assessment for another attribute. "Low" for relative advantage is not the same as "Low" for compatibility. However, two different assessments for the same attribute may be compared to each other if taken at different points in time. Fig. 3.1 shows the first assessment of the attributes of systematic testing as perceived by students in the educational situation (cf. previous section 3.2.1). These *attributes' assessments* of systematic testing demonstrate

- how systematic testing is perceived when students are first introduced to it,

- how this perception changes when students enter working life (e.g. the onboarding situation, cf. section 3.5) and finally,

- how the approach presented in this thesis improves assessments of certain attributes (cf. section 3.6).

---

[5]For all attributes except complexity, high is better than middle, middle is better than low. For complexity, the reverse is true.

3.2.3 Remaining Attributes of An Innovation

Type of an Innovation. There are different types of decision to adopt an innovation: *optional, collective* and *authority decisions* ([130], p. 28). An optional decision is made by the individual, a collective decision is made in accordance with the rest of the social system (such as a public voting) and authority decisions are made by small groups and imposed onto the social systems (such as laws).

Applied to the educational situation: In the educational setting, the decision to adopt the practice of systematic testing is *optional*—it lies in the hands of the students. There are no control mechanisms to ensure that a student adopts systematic testing in subsequent projects.

Communication Channels. The diffusion of an innovation in a population is accomplished by communication between individuals. Rogers differentiates two types of channels for this communication ([130], p. 204): *mass media* channels and *interpersonal* channels. The former use mass mediums like radio and reach a larger audience. Often, they operate as broadcasts, create knowledge and are primarily able to change weakly held attitudes. The latter enable face-to-face communication between one or more individuals and are more powerful in their ability to influence attitudes. *"[Interpersonal communication channels can] persuade an individual to form or to change a strongly held attitude. The role of interpersonal channels is especially important in persuading an individual to adopt a new idea."* [130], p. 205.

Applied to the educational situation: The educational situation—by Rogers' definition—is interpersonal: a typical classroom setting is a face-to-face communication between one or more individuals. However, the classroom setting displays some attributes of a broadcast situation. Even though there is the possibility of opening a back channel (a student asking a question), it is mostly the sender that broadcasts to the population (e.g. the lecturer presenting). Interaction between the lecturer and students may not increase to a more interpersonal communication level for the following reasons:

- a student may be too intimidated by the lecturer to ask a question,

- a student may not want to embarrass herself in front of other students,

- the lecture is not designed to take care of questions.

For these reasons, the classroom setting is attributed aspects of what Rogers calls mass media channel: the classroom setting can create knowledge and change weakly held attitudes. Practical exercise lessons in smaller groups, on the other hand, do fit the interpersonal channel description better. Here, the level of interaction is typically higher, which facilitates a two-way exchange about practicing systematic testing.

Nature of the Social System. The social system's *norms* and the *interconnectedness* of the communication network can influence an innovation's rate of adoption ([130], p. 222). Norms determine whether a new idea is looked upon with favor and or frowned upon. Does its adoption raise the adopter's social status, such as prestige? Is the new idea compatible with normal behavior of the social system?

The degree to which the communication network structure is interconnected has an impact on communication patterns. If little exchange between individuals is promoted, communication about the innovation and its benefits may be impeded.

Applied to the educational situation: By assumption, students have little experience with systematic testing and as such, in the classroom setting, practicing systematic testing *is not normative behavior.* Also, its vigorous adoption is not specifically associated with any *change in social status* and there is no increase in prestige. This is due to the lack of a project context that would connect all students as team members. In the classroom setting, students are not working on a project together but in isolation—none of their quality assurance efforts in class culminates in a well-executed product development nor produces any associated feeling of accomplishment or observation of benefits (e.g. income, etc). When they solve the given exercise, each student is rewarded his or her studying points and that is all. Collaboration and the effectiveness of practicing systematic testing is not part of these exercises.

The degree of *interconnectedness of the communication* in the student social system is hard to estimate. There may be very little communication between students or very much. It is not clear if practicing systematic testing is a topic students talk about. As a practical measure, a middle level degree for interconnectedness is assumed—such as sporadic communication in smaller groups when students solve exercises together.

The Change Agent's Promotion Efforts. In the educational setting, the change agent is the lecturer who teaches systematic testing to students. These promotion efforts of the change agent are regarded as very high as educating is one of the main tasks lecturers have devoted themselves to.

3.2.4 Preventive Innovations

According to Rogers, even though an innovation is advantageous to the potential adopter, it does not sell itself—its adoption is not guaranteed. This is especially pronounced with so-called *preventive innovations.*

> **Definition** *A preventive innovation* is a new idea that an individual adopts now in order to lower the probability of some unwanted future event. ([130], p. 233)

The relative advantage of preventive innovations is inherently difficult to *demonstrate* for a change agent and to *perceive* for an individual. On the one hand, change agents try to persuade potential adopters with advantages that *may* materialize at *some point* in the future—however, this is not guaranteed. On the other hand, the prevention of an unwanted event is *difficult to grasp* for adopters. It is the absence of an event and as such it is hard to count or quantify.

Relative advantage is a main factor influencing an innovation's adoption rate but with preventive innovations, this advantage is not clear cut and difficult to recognize.

Additionally, the *immediacy of the reward* is not given, which lowers the perceived relative advantage (cf. relative advantage, p. 16). Rogers concludes: *"the individual's motivation to adopt a preventive innovation is relatively weak"* [130], p. 176.

Applied to systematic testing in general: The activity of systematic testing is a preventive innovation—and it is a good example at that. The reasons for practicing automated testing in software development project are manifold. Commonly, it is introduced in order to find existing defects and to detect newly introduced defects (regression testing). Before automatic tests can help in finding software defects, a developer has to invest a considerable amount of time and effort in writing them. The initial costs are clearly visible. However, the benefits of practicing systematic testing are not easily quantifiable. The number of defects that writing tests will prevent in later development is unclear at the time of adoption. Writing tests *now* may help in finding defects *later* on—but it is not guaranteed that there will be any defects at all or that practicing systematic testing will uncover them. Now, an experienced developer will quickly throw in that defects are bound to happen in any given software development project of a certain size and complexity. From this point of view, writing tests now will very probably be beneficial later on. But a novice developer has not have come to this insight yet.

3.3 The Knowledge-Attitude-Practice Gap and Systematic Testing

Even though an individual has formed a positive attitude, adoption and implementation of an innovation is not guaranteed. Rogers points out, that *"formation of a favorable or unfavorable attitude toward an innovation does not always lead directly to an adoption or rejection decision."* [130], p. 176. Rogers calls this discrepancy between attitude and implementation the *KAP-gap* (knowledge, attitudes, practice). According to Rogers, the occurrence of the KAP-gap is especially pronounced with preventive innovations.

Rogers proposes that the KAP-gap can—in some cases—be overcome by so-called *cues-to-action*, *"an event occurring at a time that crystallizes a favorable attitude into overt behavior change"* [130], p. 176. These cues-to-action can happen naturally or can be strategically introduced by change agents.

One main contribution of this thesis is the insight that the preventive innovation of practicing systematic testing is prone to facilitate a KAP-gap in the testing behavior of inexperienced developers[6]:

> **Hypothesis** *Inexperienced developers, upon learning about the practice of systematic testing, often do not implement it even though they have developed a positive attitude towards it.*

This hypothesis is based on insights gained from uncovering *inherent attributes* of the innovation of practicing systematic testing and *external, situational context* (in which this innovation is introduced to inexperienced developers) that hinder its adoption. In section 3.6, ideas for cues-to-action to overcome this KAP-gap are introduced.

---

[6]This contribution is underlined by empirical data from two empirical studies (cf. chapter 4).

1. **inherent attributes of systematic testing (described in section 3.3.1):**
   - systematic testing is a preventive innovation
   - the perceived attributes of systematic testing make it unattractive when it is first introduced to students
   - systematic testing requires a real project context to demonstrate its benefits

2. **external, situational context (described in section 3.3.2):**
   - the educational situation is not suited to convey the benefits of testing

3.3.1 Inherent Attributes of Testing hindering its Adoption

As a result from the analysis of how systematic testing is introduced in the educational situation, three influencing factors emerged.

Preventive Nature. First, the innovation of practicing systematic testing is a preventive innovation with clear up-front costs and not-guaranteed benefits. Additionally, these benefits cannot be quantified easily.

Appears Unattractive. Testing is perceived as unattractive. In the educational situation, most of the five innovation's perceivable attributes take unfavorable configuration (cf. Fig. 3.1). Complexity and trialability are initially assessed as low and high, increasing attractiveness of the innovation of testing. However, both attributes of testing are kept *artificially* low, respectively high. When students are asked to perform real-world implementation of testing practices, they are confronted with the actual high complexity of testing.

Needs a Project Context. Testing requires a complex-enough *project context* and *personal involvement in the project* to demonstrate its benefits and usefulness. Developing a software product in a team of developers provides such a context. Within the project context, an inexperienced developer is able to observe some aspects of testing (this is not a complete list):

- Complexity demands testing: The more complex a project grows, the more the need for testing increases. Developers cannot overview the whole application every time they change something. Testing manually becomes infeasible.

- Benefits of regression testing: During and in later phases of the development, an automated test suite supports the development process by enabling regression testing. Anytime a developer changes the application under test, she can automatically check if previously working parts still work.

- Tests support collaboration: When collaborating with other developers, other team members' code needs to be integrated constantly. Automated tests help to do this more quickly and confidently.

Practicing testing in a project context is that this *reveals its true complexity*: Testing in a project context demands a lot of technical and contextual knowledge. For example, there may be knowledge needed on how to precisely mock objects in this project or how to acquire correct test data for a certain situation.

Personal involvement in the project is important to fully appreciate the benefits of systematic testing. Being involved and caring about the success of the project increases the developer's care for the quality of the code. For example, the developer could be dependent on the success of the project. In this situation, quality assurance methods are welcome and especially systematic testing can produce a feeling of "being saved of big trouble" if it catches a critical defect. This can act as a cue-to-action and can increase appreciation for systematic testing.

When systematic testing is first introduced to inexperienced developers, this complex-enough project context is often excluded for the sake of conveying its principles first (principles-knowledge). This, however, hinders its adoption and can support a dismissive attitude towards it.

3.3.2 Educational Situation not Suited to Convey Testing

The innovation of systematic testing is difficult to convey. The educational environment in which it is first introduced is not suited for this task. Two factors hinder the educational setting in conveying systematic testing more successfully:

- focus on conveying awareness- and principles-knowledge, little how-to-knowledge, and

- the educational environment lacks real software project context in which the innovation of systematic testing could demonstrate its benefits.

Lack of How-To-Knowledge. The educational setting provides students with *awareness-knowledge* and *principles-knowledge* about systematic testing—but lacks *how-to-knowledge*. Lecturers only have a limited frame of time. They focus on the ideas and principles of systematic testing, rather than on technicalities or technical trends—those change fast, but ideas and principles prevail longer. Also, testing is often not mandatory in the students' curriculum. If it is taught, it is only taught for a short time—among other important software engineering topics [5, 61]. At some universities, it is also possible for students to skip classes with testing entirely, thus not coming into contact with it at all. The how-to knowledge (knowledge of how to actually apply systematic testing) provided to students is limited. This, however, is very problematic regarding systematic testing: *"[...] when an adequate level of how-to knowledge is not obtained prior to trial and adoption of an innovation, rejection and discontinuance are likely to result"* [130], p. 173. Systematic testing is such a complex innovation and according to Rogers, those require extensive of how-to-knowledge. The how-to-knowledge conveyed in lecture and exercise *is not deep enough for an innovation of this complexity*. A practical software project course (e.g. providing the students with opportunities actually experience systematic testing in a real project context) is not guaranteed at every university. Such a practical opportunity to actually implement systematic testing would require and facilitate how-to-knowledge greatly.

No Project Context. The common model of education (featuring a lecture with accompanying practical exercises) does not offer the student any *project context* in which she could apply the innovation of practicing software testing. This is problematic: Without it, students have difficulties *perceiving* the benefits of systematic testing and *understanding* its complexity.

Testing is experienced in isolation and not in context of a real project. The complexity of the test exercises is not comparable to complexity of actually implementing tests in a real project. The exercises presented to students are commonly designed to be solvable and to demonstrate the beneficial results of testing—for example, reaching a green bar when unit testing or uncovering a hidden bug in a demonstrator system. However, there is little collaboration with other developers. Also, there is little need for regression testing as these isolated exercises are not maintained for a longer period of time. The real complexity of practicing systematic testing is much higher. This is problematic, as it facilitates a "shock of practice" when students are asked to write tests for a real project setting for the first time. Suddenly, students perceive the activity of practicing systematic testing as being highly complex: They need to quickly master its methodologies as well as the technical aspects of the test framework to implement it. This can produce a feeling of being overwhelmed[7]. Such a "shock of practice" can ultimately lead to rejection of the practice of systematic testing.

3.4 The Innovation-Decision Process of Testing

The decision to adopt or reject an innovation is not instantaneous but rather a process consisting of several stages [130]. In this process, an individual tries to reduce *uncertainty* regarding the innovation: It tries to grasp the innovation's impact *in her specific situation* in terms of desirable vs. undesirable, anticipated vs. unanticipated consequences, or direct vs. indirect effects. Rogers proposes a five-stage model for this process ([130], p. 169 and following) and states that each stage may be a point of rejection: Knowledge, Persuasion, Decision, Implementation, and Confirmation.

> **Definition** *The innovation-decision process* is the process through which an individual passes from gaining initial knowledge of an innovation, to forming an attitude toward the innovation, to making a decision to adopt or reject, to implementation of the new idea and to confirmation of this decision. ([130], p. 168)

---

[7]In the empirical student study (cf. chapter 4.1), students *wanted* to learn and apply new testing techniques but were scared off by the high learning curve they perceived. This was especially pronounced with automating GUI tests, for example.

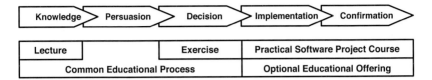

Figure 3.2: Five stages of the decision-innovation process in the educational setting.

This traditional educational setting *Education* (lectures and exercises, cf. section 3.1) only covers the first three stages of the innovation-decision process: Knowledge, Persuasion, and Decision (cf. Fig. 3.2). This first part of the innovation-decision process is shown in more detail in Fig. 3.3. The second part of the innovation-decision process (implementation and confirmation stage) is covered if the educational institution offers a practical software development project, as in the model *Education with Practical Project*. This provides students with necessary project context when implementing the innovation of practicing systematic testing, thus entering the implementation stage. The second part of the innovation-decision process is shown in more detail in Fig. 3.4.

Forced Advancements in the Innovation-Decision Process. The educational setting brings by a special attribute that may change the outcome of the innovation-decision process: Each state may be an exit point at which the individual rejects the innovation for different reasons. In an educational situation, however, a student can be *forced* to advance in this process even though she has already rejected the innovation of systematic testing. For example, by demanding students to participate in exercise lessons and holding back exercise points, which students need to advance their studies. Even though a student may have rejected the innovation of testing at the knowledge stage (she decided to not listen to the lecture), she may be made to enter the trial stage when doing her exercising homework. This particularity is reflected in both Fig. 3.3 and Fig. 3.4 which depict a student's innovation-decision process in more detail. This thesis assumes that a student cannot be forced to think about systematic testing and to ponder it for her own situation (if she does not like it). That is why she cannot be forced to enter the persuasion stage. However, she can be forced to complete exercises, trying systematic testing and thus entering the decision stage. The persuasion stage is also the least distinctive stage. It is hard to tell where it begins and where it ends ([130], p. 198).

3.4.1 Knowledge Stage

The individual is first exposed to the innovation's existence and forms an understanding of how it works. Exposure to a new innovation and the process of gaining knowledge about it can happen actively (individual seeks information) or passively (individual is exposed to information). Rogers notes that individuals consciously or subconsciously influence their exposure to such information *"in accordance with their interests, needs*

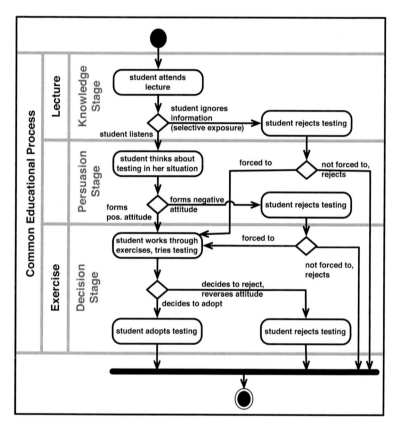

Figure 3.3: Innovation-decision process of a student passing from first knowledge, to forming an attitude, to deciding whether or not to adopt systematic testing.

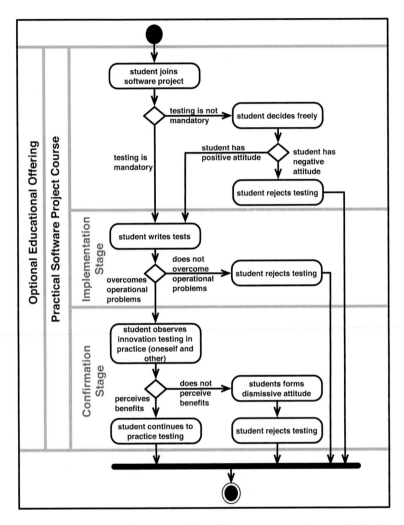

Figure 3.4: Innovation-decision process of a student participating in a practical software project, passing implementation and confirmation stage.

and existing attitudes" [130], p. 171. The more information is consistent with existing attitudes or beliefs, the more attentive an individual is toward it (*selective exposure*).

Applied to the educational situation: This stage occurs when students attend the lecture about systematic testing. They are introduced to this new idea and are informed about how it works. This exposure is *passive*.

In some cases, students may already reject the idea of systematic testing at this early stage: When students first learn about systematic testing, they may not feel a need for this innovation—after all, they have little experience with software development. Combined with a over-assertive self-view, this can lead to *selective exposure* the student does not listen when the lecturer explains systematic testing. This is not the usual case and the opposite may also be true: student feeling a strong need for systematic testing, even though not being able to name it exactly.

3.4.2 Persuasion Stage

The individual forms a favorable or unfavorable attitude[8] toward the innovation. After gaining first knowledge about it in the knowledge stage, the individual now wants to reduce uncertainty pertaining to the innovation's advantages and disadvantages *in her specific situation.* The individual engages in hypothetical thinking and tries to answer the questions *"What if I adopt this innovation?"* and *"What are the innovation's advantages and disadvantages in my situation?"* [130], p. 175. Here, the five attributes of an innovation as perceived by the individual come into play (cf. section 3.2.1). Rogers identifies *relative advantage, compatibility* and *complexity* as most influential when forming an attitude. Also, individuals rely on *social reinforcement* when developing an attitude, for example personal and subjective experiences of near peers.

Applied to the educational situation: This thesis assumes that a student enters the persuasion stage after attending the lectures about systematic testing. Having been informed about the benefits of practicing systematic testing, the students asks herself how and to what extend this practice would influence her situation. However, *environmental attributes* and *attributes of the innovation of practicing systematic testing* may lead the student towards a negative attitude (cf. section 3.3):

It is important to note that the *the current situation* of the student does not specifically demand systematic testing. The student is in an educational situation and quality assurance of the code she produces—if she produces any—is not of particular concern. For example, her income does not depend on it.

As discussed earlier, relative advantage of systematic testing may be perceived as low by students. Systematic testing is a preventive innovation with clear, up-front costs

---

[8]Rogers defines attitude as a *"relatively enduring organization of an individual's beliefs about an object that predisposes his or her actions"* [130], p. 174.

combined with not-guaranteed benefits in the future. Complexity should be perceived as high, as systematic testing is a non-trivial programming discipline.

In an educational setting, positive social reinforcement about systematic testing is be hard to come by. In a group of inexperienced students—of whom none has experienced the benefits of systematic testing yet—the opinion about it is neutral or even skeptical.

3.4.3 Decision Stage

The individual engages in actions that lead to a choice to adopt or reject an innovation as the best course of action in the individual's situation. Prior to deciding for or against an innovation, individuals like to try it on a non-decisive basis. Higher trialability leads to a faster rate of adoption. Innovations that are not easy to try (difficult to setup) or are tied to consequences (e.g. subsequent adoption, getting a tattoo) are rejected more often. Being able to try the innovation in parts or in a small setting supports adoption.

Applied to the educational situation: Practicing systematic testing can be tried without long-term consequences. The fact that a developer has decided to try to write unit tests in one project does mean she has to do it in the next project as well. Systematic testing also provides several degrees of complexity (from automated unit tests, over automated GUI tests, to complex system tests) which can be used for small trial phases.

In the educational setting, students are encouraged to try to write tests. In exercise lessons, they solve exercises of differing degrees of complexity. This high degree of trialability is beneficial to the adoption of systematic testing. After solving the practical exercises, the student decides for herself whether or not she is convinced of its benefits and whether she will practice it in her next software project. This is also the last point at which the student is confronted with the innovation of systematic testing: If the educational institution does not offer any kind of practical software project, students are not likely to experience the innovation of practicing systematic testing in a project context before entering working life. In this case, the next stages, implementation stage and confirmation stage, are not reached within the educational setting.

3.4.4 Implementation Stage

The individual implements the innovation and incorporates it into ongoing practice. In this stage, the individual has to overcome several barriers. At this stage especially, practical problems related to *actually using* the innovation come up. The individual has to figure out how to obtain the innovation and how to implement it. Uncertainties for the individual are *"What operational problems am I likely to encounter, and how can I solve them?"* [130], p. 179. This starts a information seeking process, such as searching for tutorials online. Change agents can supply technical assistance. Especially *how-to knowledge* is needed at this stage and a lack of practical how-to knowledge can pose a high barrier for adoption. When an individual is not able to successfully implement an innovation, rejection is likely to follow.

Applied to the educational situation: The exercise lessons in the educational setting *Education* are not part of the implementation stage but belong to the decision stage: These exercise lessons offer isolated exercises of different testing techniques without any project context. They can account for trialability of these techniques but they do not convey these techniques' problems and benefits in a project: systematic testing as it is being practiced and pictured in lectures. These exercises can provide opportunities to "give the innovation a try" but little opportunities to "implementing it seriously".

Instead, students may enter the implementation stage—if they have not decided against testing in the decision stage yet—in two different ways: either, the educational institution offers a practical software project or she voluntarily engages in an extra-curricular software project in her free time. Here, we will focus on software projects in an educational setting.

Partaking in the practical project, the student enters the implementation stage, which means she begins to write tests. She will encounter *operational problems* regarding how to write tests in a real project context. The situations she encounters are not engineered and need practical solutions. If more sophisticated testing techniques have not been introduced in class (for example, such as GUI automation), the student may even need to gather additional *principles-knowledge*, by searching for tutorials online. If she can overcome these problems, she enters the next stage, confirmation stage. Otherwise, rejection of systematic testing is likely.

3.4.5 Confirmation Stage

The individual seeks confirmation and reinforcement for deciding to adopt or reject the innovation. Even though the adopter has put the innovation into action in the implementation stage and has seemingly concluded the adoption process, there is a follow-up stage. After using the innovation, individuals want to confirm their behavior and may even reverse it if they receive conflicting information about it.

Applied to the educational situation: While and after implementing systematic testing in the practical project, students enter the confirmation stage. The student works together with other students in a team and they exchange their experiences with testing, helping each other and solving problems. This way, they observe how others fare with it and they also observe how the development process is influenced by it, positively and negatively. If, at this point, students perceive their testing efforts to be fruitful and beneficial to the development, adoption of the innovation of practicing systematic testing is likely. This could be the case, if, for example, building up a test suite has enabled regression testing, which has in turn sped up development in later phases or if testing has caught a critical bug. If, however, students did not perceive these benefits, for example, because the test suite only caught minor bugs but was costly in creation, students may reverse their decision to adopt testing and rejection is likely. Being frustrated, this may lead to a dismissive attitude towards testing altogether.

3.5 Change of Perception when Entering the Onboarding Situation

After studying computer science at an educational institution, graduates apply for software engineering positions and take on the role of *newcomers*. They enter an *onboarding process* in order to be integrated into their new development team quickly[9].

For this analysis, it is assumed that the newcomer enters a small team of senior developers with 5 to 10 members. This team works with an agile development process and systematic testing is demanded with written guidelines. One senior developer is assigned as a mentor for the newcomer. Her task is to show the newcomer how to develop at this company and to help with social and technical issues. The mentor has to make sure that newcomer does not commit defects into the production code.

In the onboarding environment, there are many factors pertaining to the perception of systematic testing that change for the newcomer. First, the group of factors that have the smallest effect is described as they help to get an understanding of the newcomer's new situation in general. Second, the most influential factor, the *introduction of a real project context* is analyzed. The, changes in the newcomer's perception of the five innovation attributes of systematic testing are analyzed. Third, the newcomer's further need for support in adopting and implementing systematic testing is explained.

3.5.1 First Group of Factors

Social System and Norms. The *social system* that the newcomer is operating in now is a team of senior developers—instead of a group of inexperienced classmates. The *change agent* is the senior developer assigned to the newcomer. The mentor is motivated and has an interest in helping the newcomer to successfully and quickly onboard. The *mentor's effort* is very high. Regarding the social system's *norms*, the whole situation has changed. The educational institution conveys an understanding of general norms of a software engineer—what is the job of a software engineer and how does she accomplish it? These ideals are put into practice but implementations vary—the newcomer has to learn the team's norms anew. This includes the team's development process and if and how the team practices systematic testing. Here, guidelines and rules can help.

Type of Innovation. The *type of the innovation* of practicing testing becomes either collective or authoritative. Implementing systematic testing may not be an optional decision anymore. It is not uncommon for software development teams to collectively decide to use a development practice, such as systematic testing. Sometimes, quality assurance departments, backed up by management, impose testing as rules. This, however, does not guarantee its vigorous adoption and implementation. In company settings less strict, it may even be up to the developer if she wants to add tests.

---

[9]The onboarding situation and the roles involved are described in more detail in section 5.1.

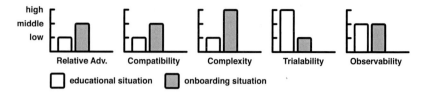

Figure 3.5: Assumed assessment of five attributes of the innovation of systematic testing by newcomers in the onboarding situation, compared to the educational situation (for illustrative purposes only).

Structure of the Social System. For the newcomer, the *nature of the social system* changes. As the size of the development team is small, colleagues communicate with each other more often. The *interconnectedness* between these developers is high. Relatedly, the *nature of the communication channels* changes as well. Communication in small teams is more *person-to-person* than broadcast. This also includes the communication between mentor and mentee. According to Rogers, this kind of communication is able to change strongly held beliefs. This could be beneficial when overcoming a dismissive attitude towards testing. However, this kind of communication is more costly for the mentor as it demands more effort.

3.5.2 Most Influential Factor—Introduction of a Project Context:

Fig. 3.5 shows how the perception the five attributes of testing by newcomers is likely to change in the onboarding situation compared to the prior the educational situation.

The biggest influence to perception of systematic testing is the introduction of a real *project context*. The newcomer is asked to write tests a in a real project. This demands *technical skills* from the newcomer and also changes the *newcomer's involvement* with the project. Now, she works towards a software product that she can relate to. Also, she is now part of a team instead of working alone.

Increased Complexity. Writing tests in a real project and within a real project context is more complicated compared to writing tests for isolated, engineered examples. The newcomer has to overcome technical issues and has to master the test framework that is in use. This raises the perceived *complexity* of systematic testing. With that rise of complexity, *trialability* is reduced. Now, it is not so easy to "test-drive" a new testing technique anymore. Educational exercises were designed for high trialability and encouraged experimentation. In the real world, the newcomer has to setup the development project and has to get the testing technology to work in this context. For example, additional test-related plugins have to be installed first. This decreases trialability. In this context, the newcomer's lack of *how-to-knowledge* becomes very apparent.

In this project context, the newcomer's perceived *relative advantage* of and *compatibility* with testing will increase. However, it is not clear at what pace and how long this realization will take. Essentially, this is due to the change of the newcomer's—former student's—situation and needs: In the onboarding situation, the programs that the newcomer has to write and has to deal with are much more complicated and more complex. This makes *the need* for automated tests more apparent and perceivable. Also, the newcomer is now working with legacy code, which may give her an impression of how tests can help to understand unfamiliar code. In this situation, the *decrease of discomfort* that testing promises becomes more apparent.

Increase of Prestige. Another change is that practicing systematic testing now increases the newcomer's *social prestige*. Prior, the social system of the student did not give prestige to testing efforts as these were focused on isolated exercises. However, testing in the context of a project and a team that is involved, every effort taken for writing tests can be seen as an uniting action to raise the product's quality—which is in the interest of the whole development team, the newcomer's social system. Also, the newcomer is now personally interested in the success of the product (personal involvement) as its success or failure can influence her job situation. Producing and testing code as a member of a team can also have pressure-related cause. The newcomer may feel under pressure to produce code at the given quality level, upholding the team's quality standard. Ultimately, the *need* for systematic testing is stronger within a real project context.

Observability. How *observability* of testing for the newcomer changes is difficult to assess. Developing in a team of senior developers, it is not clear how *visible* the testing efforts and success with practicing testing is to the newcomer. This thesis assumes systematic testing is mentioned in the team's guidelines and testing is also part of the development process. Systematic testing could be automatically demanded by only allowing commits that also include test code. Senior developers may talk to the newcomer about systematic testing and also mention specific successes with their testing efforts—for example, a critical defect that was found just in time by regression testing. This, however, will not be the regular case and observability of the innovation of systematic testing for the newcomer is assessed with a middle level.

Newcomers Kept from Overcoming the KAP-Gap: According to Rogers, the perceived relative advantage is the most influential attribute when deciding whether to reject or adopt an innovation. As the newcomer is put into a real project context, she may understand the benefits and short-comings of testing more clearly and perceive systematic testing in its practical form. In other words, the newcomer begins to understand firsthand why testing is important and in what situations it is needed. This, leads to an increase of perceived relative advantage and compatibility. However, it is not clear how long this process actually takes. Also, it is unclear if the increase in perceived relative advantage and compatibility is strong enough to induce consequent adoption of systematic testing as there are other factors that hinder this adoption: The steep increase of complexity is a strong blocker for the adoption of systematic testing by newcomers. The same is true for the decline of trialability. The newcomer may have changed her mind about testing but now she is not *able* to implement it properly.

Reasons for the occurrence of the KAP-gap in the educational setting have been discussed in detail in the previous section 3.3. Entering the onboarding situation, the "shock-of-practice" may act as a *cue-to-action*, calling for overt behavior change. Newcomers now feel the need for testing and *want* to implement it. At this point, however, the reveal of its true *complexity* and their specific lack of *how-to-knowledge* may prevent them from following through. It falls into the hands of the mentor to resolve this situation, which often demands teaching the newcomer testing from scratch—with additional cost of time and money. Here, the need for a tailored approach to support newcomers and the mentor during onboarding becomes most apparent.

3.6 This Approach & the Diffusion of Innovations

As discussed in earlier sections, different scenarios play out when students are first introduced to systematic testing (cf. section 3.4).

- Students are convinced of the benefits of systematic testing and adopt it.

- Students reject testing from the beginning simply because of a lack of perceived need for it in their educational situation. This results in a dismissive attitude.

- Without a practical project course, graduates leave education with a KAP-gap regarding systematic testing.

- Failing to see the benefits of testing when practicing systematic testing in a practical project course, graduates develop frustration towards it (cf. Fig. 3.4).

Entering the onboarding situation finally confronts these newcomers with a real project context. This acts as a cue-to-action to overcome the testing-related KAP-gap. The steep rise in complexity and a lack of how-to knowledge hinders them in implementing testing. Now, newcomers *want* to write tests but are *not able to*.

In chapters 5 through 8, this thesis presents an approach to help the newcomer adopt systematic testing and support the newcomer in implementing it in the onboarding situation. It is based on the results of the previous DOI theory analysis and its effects on the newcomer can be described using Rogers' terms. The 'goal-configuration' facilitating the desired effect on the newcomer (according to Rogers) is depicted in Fig. 3.6:

- increasing observability of systematic testing to the newcomer,

- reducing complexity of systematic testing for the newcomer, and

- increasing trialability of systematic testing for the newcomer.

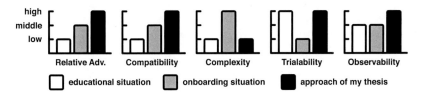

Figure 3.6: The influence of the approach of this thesis on the assessment of five attributes of testing, compared to the educational situation and the original onboarding situation (for illustrative purposes only).

Increasing Observability. The approach targets to increase observability of testing by injecting social transparency traits into the work environment of the newcomer and purposefully revealing other team members' testing activity (Pillar 1, cf. chapter 6). Observability of systematic testing is hard to grasp in both the educational and onboarding situation. In the educational situation, it has only little effect to promote testing—its visibility mainly communicates solving of the exercise but not application of the innovation of testing. In onboarding situation, it is not clear how demonstrative testing is practiced among the senior developers—or if it is done without much display and by each developer in isolation. This approach, however, makes this testing activity *explicitly* visible, quantifiable and relatable for the newcomer. This, in turn, is targeted to also increase relative advantage and compatibility, possibly overcoming any dismissive attitudes towards it. Seeing how others practice systematic testing may nudge the newcomer to re-evaluate her view on testing and her understanding of its benefits.

Reducing Complexity. The approach targets to reduce complexity of systematic testing using multiple strategies: First, by providing *how-to-knowledge* to the newcomer when she needs it. This is achieved by providing the newcomer with runnable test code from the project from which she can quickly and practically learn how to write tests (Pillar 2, cf. chapter 7). As mentioned before, the steep rise in complexity is a main blocker for adoption. The how-to-knowledge within the test code the is *implicit*, that is it is not edited for easy consumption by newcomers. It enables overcoming of technicalities and supports quick implementation.

Second, by providing *principles-knowledge* to the newcomer. This is achieved by providing targeted access to *applicable* learning materials combined with *runnable test examples* taken from the current project (Pillar 3, cf. chapter 8). Being confronted with a testing task that demands overcoming a too high learning curve can turn inexperienced developers away from practicing testing. When newcomers need to gather a deeper understanding of a testing technique, they are in need of *explicit* principles-knowledge, that is knowledge that has been prepared for consumption by them.

Increasing Trialability: Both strategies of Pillar 2 and Pillar 3 emphasize the ability to *execute* the test examples and having access to testing learning materials within the context of the current project. Additionally, all strategies are tailored to be used by newcomers, lowering implementation barriers and provide explanations where needed. These design choices increase the trialability of this approach.

3.7 Chapter Summary

In this chapter, Rogers' Theory of Diffusion of Innovations [130] was introduced, including assessment of innovations and the process of adopting an innovation. Using this theory, it was analyzed how inexperienced developers perceive the practice of systematic testing at three different points in time:

- when they are first introduced to it (educational situation),

- when they first need to actually practice it (onboarding situation), and

- hypothetically, what influence the approach of this thesis has on this perception.

This analysis discusses inexperienced developers often form a dismissive attitude towards systematic testing—despite being informed about its benefits (KAP-gap). It uncovers inherent attributes of testing make its diffusion in education particularly difficult as well as environmental attributes:

- Systematic testing is a preventive innovation with clear-cut upfront costs and not-guaranteed benefits.

- In order to gain an understanding of these benefits and the true complexity of testing, systematic testing requires a real project context.

- The level of how-to-knowledge provided in education is too low. This leads to frustration towards and rejection of systematic testing.

In the following chapters (cf. chapter 5 and following), these insights are used to guide the concrete design of the approach of this thesis. It targets to produce an increase of observability, a decrease of complexity, and an increase of trialability. According to the Theory of Diffusion of Innovations, this supports a higher rate of adoption of the innovation of practicing systematic testing.

4 Motivational Empirical Studies

In this chapter, two empirical studies about the *actual* testing behavior of inexperienced developers are presented. Section 4.1 reports on an empirical study about the testing behavior of students in a practical project just before they leave university. Such a project course requires students to apply their theoretical knowledge and provides them with *project context*. This study explains *how* students perceive the practice of testing and *what* keeps them from practicing it.

Section 4.2 investigates how industry handles the testing behavior and testing skills of newcomers. Practitioners, handling the onboarding process of inexperienced newcomers, report on their experiences, most pressing problems and coping strategies. This study gives *insight into the onboarding situation* for both the newcomer and the practitioner.

These two studies address the *last* university-related phase and the *first* job-related phase, providing a comprehensive view of the testing skills of newcomers. Fig. 4.1 depicts this situation. This gives an empirical view on the testing behavior of inexperienced developers and answers the research questions:

- How do graduates practice systematic testing just before leaving university and are there any problems?

- Which of these problems carry over to the onboarding situation in industry? How do practitioners cope with them?

4.1 Testing Behavior of Students

Findings presented this section have been published in a study titled 'Enablers, Inhibitors, and Perceptions of Testing in Novice Software Teams' [119], conducted by Raphael Pham, Stephan Kiesling, Olga Liskin, Leif Singer, and Kurt Schneider. This research team is subsequently called Pham et al. 2014a. In 2014, Raphael Pham presented it at the 22nd ACM SIGSOFT International Symposium on Foundations of Software Engineering in Hong Kong, China.

4.1.1 Study Design

The Software Project Course. This practical project course is an example of the 'optional educational offering' discussed in the theoretical analysis in chapter 3, cf. section 3.4 and Fig. 3.4. For the successful diffusion of systematic testing, it provides students with a much needed *project context* (cf. section 3.3.2).

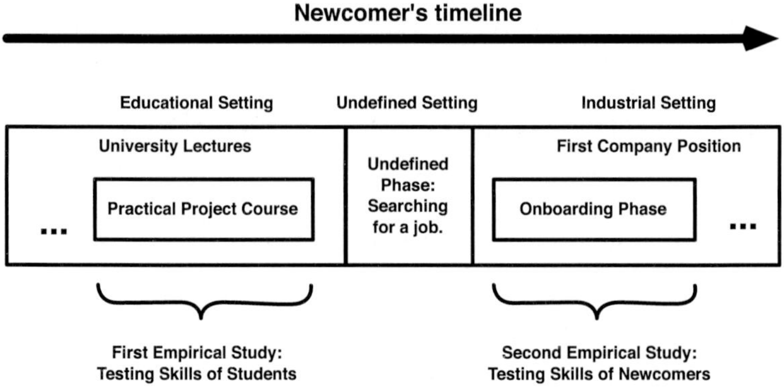

Figure 4.1: Motivational empirical studies spanning undergraduates' last phase at university and first phase entering the software engineering workforce.

In fall 2013, 97 students were divided into 20 teams: 18 teams of five students each, one team of four students, and one team of three students. The project itself lasted 4 months, in which the team needed to elicit requirements, design, implement, and test a software product. Projects followed a waterfall-like process, with each phase ending in a quality gate. Eventually, the customer conducted an acceptance test and either accepted or rejected the product. Customers were members of the Software Engineering research group at Leibniz Universität Hannover, offering projects they were interested in. Students were required to have passed a programming course (Java) as well as basic courses on software engineering, software quality, and version control.

Data Analysis. Pham et al. 2014a interviewed all 97 students at the end of the course and recorded the interviews, each lasting 20 minutes on average. Students were in their 5th or 7th semester, nearing the end of their Bachelor Studies. As suggested by Hoda et al. [77], Pham et al. 2014a used an iterative data analysis approach to extract the Grounded Theory model of the students' testing behavior. An in-depth description of the data analysis phase can be found in the original publication [119].

Research Questions Pham et al. 2014a were interested in supporting factors that helped students to methodically test their product and in inhibiting factors that kept them from doing so. As is often sensible in Grounded Theory, Pham et al. 2014a did not finalize research questions before starting data collection but had topics of interest in mind. After iterative qualitative analysis using open coding, selective coding, axial coding, and writing memos, the researchers arrived at the following research questions:

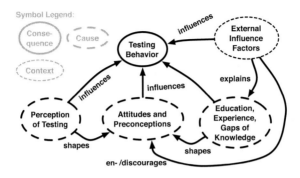

Figure 4.2: Categories forming the GT-model of students' testing behavior.

Testing Strategies
RQ1: How did students test their software products?

Enabling and Inhibiting Factors
RQ2: What factors supported students in testing methodically and what factors hindered them?

Testing Attitude
RQ3: What did students think of testing methodically?

Testing in the SWP process
RQ4: How did students incorporate testing in their engineering process?

4.1.2 Model of Testing Behavior of Graduates

Students' actual **testing behavior** differs from testing practice promoted in lectures and is influenced factors of four categories (c.f. Fig. 4.2).

- **education, experiences, knowledge gaps** form a baseline of technical knowledge.

- This is the origin of the students' **attitudes and preconceptions** towards testing.

- The students' **perception of testing** plays an important role in how they will approach a concrete task.

- Lastly, the students' testing behavior is influenced by **external influence factors**, such as management support or resource constraints.

Core Category: Testing Behavior

The core category describes students' testing strategies, their individual team organization and gives an overview of the timeline of testing activities.

Students' Testing Strategies   Testing took different forms in the project. Pham et al. 2014a distinguished between *automated testing* (denoted this with A) and *manual testing*. Automated testing meant having dedicated test code for the automated execution of some part of the application under test (AUT), excluding the user interface, and some assertion. JUnit tests were the most prominent example. Manual testing was divided into different approaches: when it came to GUI testing, students mostly relied on *smoke testing* (S), even though students did not call it that. Smoke testing was the execution of the AUT to verify the correctness of the currently finished or modified code. Smoke testing was done without documentation and solely served the selective assertion of freshly made changes. *Manual GUI testing* (MG) differed from smoke testing in that it encompassed several steps for asserting a whole use case in the GUI and not just one step. Sometimes, these manual GUI tests were conducted in a more systematic manner using a protocol or a checklist (MG*). Lastly, some teams automated their GUI tests (AG) through a framework such as Selenium or Android's Robotium.

Test Preparation and Organization   Out of 20 teams, only four teams discussed their testing strategy in the first phase of the development process. Another five teams planned their testing strategy in the implementation phase and only two of those in the beginning of that phase. 11 teams did not plan testing in advance (cf. Table 4.1).

When it came to team-internal organization of testing efforts, 18 teams implicitly decided to let every author test their own code. In two cases (teams I and L), the quality agent of the team took the role of testing mentor. He managed the test process and provided the team with example tests to work on.

13 teams felt pressured by the project deadline into ceasing testing efforts:

> *"[We had] by far too little time to be able to write extensive tests. Then we could have tested the GUI with Selenium ... Yes, it was mainly the time. [Other member:] Yes, I also felt time pressure."* — team T

The testing activity that was omitted the most frequently was the automation of GUI tests. GUI tests implied a learning time that some teams were not able or willing to invest. Only 3 teams conducted automated GUI tests (teams I, K, and P, cf. Table 4.1).

Timeline of Testing Activities   Table 4.1 shows all 20 teams' testing efforts in context of the development process. All teams started testing in the last phase of the project—even though some had talked about it earlier. Starting testing efforts that late differs strongly from how testing practice has been pictured in lectures. In lectures, students are explicitly informed that software quality cannot be infused into a finished software product afterwards but quality assurance efforts should be part of the whole development

Table 4.1: Test timetable of 20 teams (B: beginning, M: middle, E: end). Legend: (T) talk, (A) automated testing, (S) smoke testing, (MG) manual GUI testing, (MG*) manual GUI testing with protocol, (AG) automated GUI testing.

Phase	Requ.			Design			Implementation			
Team↓	B	M	E	B	M	E	Begin.	Middle	End	
E									S, MG*	no test autom.
F							S, MG	S, MG	S, MG	
R							S	S	S, MG*	
C							S, MG*	S, MG*	S, MG*	
D									T, A	very late test automation
H									T, A	
L									A	
N									A	
Q							S	S	A	
B							MG	MG	MG, A	
J							A		S, MG*	early, contin. test autom. GUI autom. even (x3)
M							T, A	A	S, MG	
O							A	A	A	
A							A	A	A	
G	T			T	T	T	MG, A	MG, A	MG, A	
T							MG, A	MG, A	MG, A	
K							MG*, A	MG*, A	MG*, A	
S		T					A		S, MG*, AG	
I	T						A, AG	T, A, AG	A, AG	
P		T					S, A, AG	S, A, AG	S, A, AG	

process. Practicing systematic testing as an afterthought is strongly discouraged. 10 teams managed to automate tests earlier than at the end of the implementation phase. The rest opted for manual testing and automation at the end of the project. Underestimating the effort required for implementation, testing became a secondary concern.

> "I have been caught on the implementation until the end. [Other student:] Me too. I have been working on everything and then thought, testing is admittedly nice, but it's of secondary importance. First, something must be up." — team J

Most of the teams that prepared testing beforehand and talked about it early managed to automate their tests *during* implementation and even produce automated GUI tests (teams I, P, and S). Team G specifically decided against automated GUI tests, as they were confident to have tested their GUI sufficiently in manual runs with protocols.

Reasons for late Writing of Tests Why do students push testing to the end of the project even though they have been advised differently? First of all, they are already overwhelmed with programming, and testing becomes a secondary concern. At project start, the AUT is still fuzzy and students explore the problem's solution space. Automated testing seems hindering at this stage:

> *"Especially in the beginning, I always find it difficult to grasp automated test cases. In the beginning, [everything] is still vague. One thinks, 'Yeah, right now I'd like to just see how it works and just start implementing.' Yeah, it's this uncertainty again."* — team S

Second, students prefer to start writing tests when the AUT is nearly finished. Students have the feeling that an AUT in an unfinished state is not ready to be tested automatically—even though they have been lectured about methodologies such as test-first[1]. They perceive the added test code as a burden, which introduces additional test maintenance. Students misinterpret the added test maintenance as technical debt—accumulating technical debt in form of untested production code in the process. This feeling was especially strong regarding the user interface of the application. The GUI of an application changes a lot during implementation and thus introduces high maintenance costs for automated GUI tests. Students rob themselves of the advantages of having automated test suites *during* implementation and not only at the end.

> *"[I] thought, testing is admittedly nice, but it's of secondary importance. First, something must be there. Particularly if I start right now—while our work is pretty unstable and we are permanently reconstructing things—I'm finding it relatively pointless to write a test, which one also would have to change every time. Because the things that we were testing were changing heavily. Because everything was still far too dynamic. At the end, there was no time left. That's why we never tested."* — team J

Third, students avoid automation and opt for manual testing instead. By manually smoke testing the application repeatedly during implementation, students uncover a lot of defects—by hand. This is repetitive, time-costly, and monotone. In addition to this manual effort, students still introduced automated tests at the end of development—as the development process guidelines required an automated test suite. Students are then disappointed by the low defect detection rate: As most defects have been uncovered by manual labor before, the newly added test suite does not perform as hoped. At this point, students clearly recognize the cost of automation but perceive only little benefits, which is problematic.

However, students did present a general understanding of the relation between upfront-costs of writing tests and its benefits. At the project's end, six teams agreed that testing earlier in the development process would have been beneficiary. One student pinpointed that testing *does* have a cost—a cost one will have to pay anyway. The earlier one invests in these tests, the more benefit can be gained from them. However, being aware of this, one still has to conquer one's weaker self.

---

[1]The test first methodology advocates writing of test code before any production code

"One thinks that the actual logic that one writes is the major thing, and not the test cases. But that's this contradictory thing. When one writes automated tests, that's a constant effort, but it also brings infinitely many benefits - especially the earlier you write them. But you have to conquer your weaker self to write tests earlier." — team S

Students' Testing Behavior in Context of the Theoretical Analysis Students had considerable problems finding the best moment to start to engage in systematic test efforts. This is a symptom of little real-world experience with practicing systematic testing and a sign of a lack of practical experience, which can be associated with a lack of *how-to-knowledge*: Students *do* know how practicing systematic testing works (*principles-knowledge*), but do not know how—or when—to actually implement it. This lack of practical principles-knowledge is a consequence of the *isolation of test exercises* and the *lack of project context*: While practicing a certain testing technique can be covered in an exercise, the context and timeline of a real project is difficult to emulate.

Students were reluctant to implement systematic testing and opted for manual testing efforts instead. When they ultimately engaged in test writing at the end of the project, they were disappointed by the defect detection rate. Testing is a *preventive innovation* and is difficult to convey others to adopt it. For the upfront effort of writing test code, systematic testing promises to help in detecting defects. In this case, students failed to implement the innovation of systematic testing properly, which made the upfront costs even more visible in relation to its benefits. They implemented it too late—for the sake of process requirements—and diminished their returns. Such a behavior can potentially lead to students misjudging the effectivity of systematic testing in general.

While mostly rejecting systematic testing and not engaging in test writing, students were aware of its benefits. Those who engaged in systematic testing experienced its benefits first hand. Still, students felt an inner barrier to invest into testing efforts. In context of Rogers' DOI-Theory, this notion of "having to conquer one's weaker self in order to practice systematic testing" is an indicator for the existence of a *Knowledge-Attitude-Practice Gap*, often found in association with *preventive innovations*, cf. section 3.3. Through lectures and exercises, students are informed that they should be practicing testing and how to do it, albeit in a basic manner only (Knowledge). Regarding their attitude (Attitude), students appear torn between mixed signals: Lectures promote the of practicing systematic testing while students recognize associated costs. Eventually, they are aware of better practice but do not apply it (missing Practice).

This is in line with the interviewers' experiences with nearly all interviewed student teams. Every interview started with the introductory question "Did you test your software product?" which was met with a wholehearted "Yes, we did test.". In the following discussion, students quickly weakened their statement with comments like "We tested, but not in the [systematic, automatic] way that we should have, you know?". Students are aware that they *should* practice systematic testing and understand that their failure to do so is indeed not good engineering practice. Still, their understanding of and prior experience with the practice of testing lead to too little application of it.

Category: Education, Experiences, and Gaps in Knowledge

The category **Education, Experiences and Gaps of Knowledge** summarizes how the students' education and experiences shaped their testing behavior.

Education. In this study, students' educational situation follows the *Education with Practice* Projects model (cf. section 3.1): Students attend broadcast-like lectures in which the topic of systematic testing is presented. In exercise groups, students solve pre-engineered exercises about these testing topics. As an additional offering, students participate in a software engineering project.

The university lectures provide students with a lot of practice-relevant testing knowledge. For example, students were introduced to the testing technique test first. The use of JUnit was practiced in class. Different test design strategies, such as partition testing, white box testing, black box testing were explained in lectures and practiced in exercise groups. However, students complained that the importance of testing is not conveyed strongly enough in these courses. The satisfying feeling of uncovering an actual defect is never experienced and students do not feel accomplished. This, ultimately, hinders them in developing a habit of practicing systematic testing.

> *"You don't realize what a good feeling it is when you run a test. [Other student:] I think in the practical part many things are missing, too. The software quality course was very theoretical."* — team S

Experiences. Similar to the assumptions made in the theoretical analysis of chapter 3, in this study students had little practical experience with systematic testing outside of university. Out of 20 teams, only two teams (S, I) had team members with prior experience in testing. Eight teams claimed to have no prior experience in methodical testing and test automation—except for knowledge from lectures and exercises. This heightened the barrier of getting started with testing.

Also, most teams did not know any other testing tool besides JUnit, which had been introduced in a course. Some students self-directed their learning and used books and internet tutorials as resources. However, some topics were harder to find than others, such as GUI automation with Eclipse.

Gaps of Knowledge. Several gaps of testing-related knowledge became apparent. Students struggled with GUI automation, debugging methods and test coverage measurements. Six teams admitted to have no idea how to automate and test a GUI, which is why they resorted to repeated manual executions. This ranged from automating actions on the GUI as well as automatically checking correctness of visual shapes and layout.

> *"I was responsible for the visualization and mostly, I just tested by executing [the program]. I constantly changed something and then looked at it, because I didn't have any ideas at all on how to test that."* — team D

Students encountered problems with debugging. Five student teams constantly put print statements all over their code to output variables for debugging. This method required a constant clean-up of debugging code and when an error reappeared, the statements were reintroduced.

> *"When you're using* `System.out.println`*, you also have to remove it when you're done. And suddenly you notice that it doesn't work again, and you have to add all the statements all over again."* — *team* R

Four teams tried to gain insights into their applications' inner workings and states by excessively making use of Java's `Logger` class. This indicates that the population was not familiar with proper debugging mechanisms. Another relevant topic is the use of *measurement tools* to keep track of a project's testing efforts. Twelve teams admitted that they had never used any coverage tools when testing. Even though they did engage in automated testing, measuring their progress did not seem important to them. According to one team, testing was finished when "all possible errors" were detected. That same team later complained to have no feeling when to stop testing, as they could not cover all possible inputs.

Education, Experiences and Knowledge in Context of the Theoretical Analysis

Gaining a feeling of accomplishment and raising appreciation for testing is an effect of introducing a *project context*. As reported by students, testing exercises alone were not able to convey this. Such a raise of attitude can influence a student's *value system*, thereby increasing the perceived *compatibility*. Without access to software projects, students leave university with a lower perceived compatibility towards systematic testing.

Lecturers operate on a limited time frame. This can lead to different testing topics (such as automation of GUI test) not being explored in full detail, leaving students with little *principles-knowledge* on that matter. A lack of principles-knowledge can lead to wrongful application of an innovation and a lack of *how-to-knowledge* can ultimately prevents its adoption. Students had *awareness-knowledge* but limited *principles-knowledge* and little to no *how-to-knowledge* of automated GUI testing. They knew that automation of GUI tests existed, understood its mechanics on an abstract level but did not know how to implement it. This lead to rejection of automated GUI testing. A similar situation is given for systematic debugging, however, in this case, it lead to a very basic, if not wrongful, application (debugging with `system.out.println`).

Lectures are well-suited to establish awareness-knowledge and basic principles-knowledge. How-to-knowledge is mostly covered in exercises. As reported above, students are still left with major gaps in how-to-knowledge. This leaves them wanting to apply a testing technique, but not being able to, possibly frustrating them in the process. Additionally, this promotes the emergence of the KAP-gap regarding systematic testing.

Category: Attitudes and Preconceptions

Students' testing behavior was influenced by their general attitude towards it and different factors that they did not further explain and which they regarded as common knowledge. The influence of these factors on a project's need is challengeable and Pham et al. 2014a categorize these factors as preconceptions.

Attitude towards Systematic Testing. Students generally saw testing as being a part of software engineering and not as being a separate discipline. However, they were not particularly fond of test automation. Students value implementing over testing. A functional product is more important than automation of tests and many teams resort to manual testing efforts.

> *"I am not really fond of it. I like to implement, but eventually these [tests] are fair and help a lot if there is a defect, so that one can really fast uncover that."* — team S

Different factors induce this attitude towards systematic testing: First, students are eager to finding a solution to the proposed problem and are eager to begin writing code. Writing test code instead of source code does not feel as accomplishing as creating new functionality. Worse, compared to producing new functionality, writing test code feels unproductive to students. Second, some students displayed an anxious attitude towards testing. Testing uncovered defects in their work, and this entailed more work, which students did not like.

> *"Well, it feels unproductive if you write tests at the beginning and actually you are thinking 'no, I'd rather start with implementation straightaway; quickly building a website, have a look how this will come out."'* — team S

Lastly, students recognized the maintenance cost of a test suite and felt demotivated by it. New written tests meant higher test maintenance when the AUT changed again. To them, introducing tests into development felt like increasing the technical debt to them—instead of lowering it in the long run.

> *"personally, I found this GUI test even more impracticable. I mean, me writing GUI tests incidentally all the time and because our GUI changes all the time dynamically... I thought that to be too much effort and I did not like that one bit."* — team S

Student Preconceptions towards Systematic Testing. In their decision whether or not to adopt systematic testing, the project size was an important factor for students. According to them, smaller projects would not need to be tested. At which point a project would become large enough to justify systematic testing did not become clear.

The criticality of a project was also important to students. They felt that systematic testing would be justified by the potential damage that could be done by software defects. Games, for example, would not necessarily need the same quality assurance as software for ATMs. As some of the proposed software projects were indeed games, this attitude may have influenced the teams testing behavior negatively. Additionally, the educational nature of the software project influenced some students' testing decision negatively. Out of 20 teams, four teams explained to test less because of the educational status of the project. One student explained that his testing effort was reduced as this project would end with the course and would not be developed further.

Lastly, students adjusted their testing effort according to the perceived complexity of the code or their project's requirements. However, at which point source code or a proposed problem became complex enough to warrant the practice of systematic testing was highly subjective and inconclusive. For example, one student explained that "a small number" of conditional statements would generally not need to be tested.

> *"The program is not complex enough for some error to come up. If it was a complex program, then there could be a hidden defect that one could uncover with a test. But these programs are mostly if-statements or something like that, and you check that it should work—except when you make a mistake. But even your unit test can be faulty."* — team A

Another common preconception was that the unit testing framework JUnit is best suited to test mathematical functions. Five teams saw the greatest value of JUnit in checking internal calculations only. One team member of a Web application project with little calculations explained their lack of JUnit tests with the absence of calculations and the use of third-party libraries—which were already tested and would therefore require no more testing efforts at all. The misconception that JUnit is best suited for mathematical comparisons may be founded in the way JUnit is often presented in a mathematical context when introduced in software engineering courses.

Students' Attitudes and Preconceptions in Context of the Theoretical Analysis. Students value implementing source code over writing test code and assign testing a secondary role. With writing source code, the perceived *relative advantage* is higher and easier to grasp than the perceived *relative advantage* of writing test code: If done correctly, new functionality will be added and will be accessible to the development team. New tests have the potential to find defects—this outcome is not guaranteed, though. Further lowering the perceived relative advantage of writing tests is the lack of *immediacy of reward*. Producing test code now may be beneficial down the road, however, writing new source code will immediately advance development progress.

All preconceptions that students expressed can be traced back to a lack of *how-to knowledge* of testing, assessing in on the basis of their current knowledge and understanding of previous idea. Even though they have participated in exercises, they have not gathered enough practical experience with the innovation of systematic testing to alleviate them of misconceptions about it. Practitioners know that even small projects can encompass a high complexity and warrant extensive testing. Misjudging the complexity of if-statements is problematic and this is one situation in which vigorous systematic testing could be beneficial. JUnit's potential lies far beyond mathematic-related use cases, but requires easy access to an object's attributes. Lack of exposure to testing in a *project context* combined with little *how-to-knowledge* has lead to several misconceptions.

Category: A Student's Perceptions of Testing Tasks

From the point of view of a student, the practice of systematic testing encompasses a number of advantages and disadvantages. The students who implemented test code experienced the benefits of regression testing with an automatic test suite. Being able to quickly uncover newly introduced erroneous changes to the AUT heightened their confidence in the code and their confidence to apply changes to it. Students found this to support collaboration with other team members, as one would not break other people's code unknowingly. Writing test code had another positive side-effect: thinking about test design helped them find important edge cases to test.

> *"Having tests was useful, especially if one thought about them and saw the reason for them. Writing tests makes you think what kind of translation could trigger what kind of failure. Special cases like that you can write tests for and then you can always be sure that if someone changes the code and executes your tests, that in 99% of cases the program will work as expected."* — team S

However, students are also aware of the costs of practicing systematic testing. Writing automated tests takes cognitive and manual effort. In this project, students were under time pressure already and did not have time to read up on testing techniques. Additionally, they could not easily find adequate tutorials for their specific situation online. The cognitive load and a high learning curve did not seem to warrant the effort of writing test code. Some students expressed this amount of efforts in number of lines of test and source code. From the perspective of a student, the amount of lines of test code needed to be much smaller than the corresponding source code.

> *"No, I will not go through the effort of writing 20 tests and think them all through, just to cover one line of code or so."* — team T

Instead of investing in writing tests, most students decided to manually test. Students perceived a faster execution time with faster feedback and found it to be cognitively less taxing. However, students also experienced the downsides of manual GUI testing: These kinds of tests have to be repeated after every change to the AUT, which can be tiring. If the AUT needs to be in a specific state to start testing, this setup state needs to be established manually *every time.* One team wanted to test the behavior of a later stage of a card game and had to play through all preceding stages for each manual test. Also, testers tend to forget steps or make mistakes. One advantage of manual GUI tests over automated GUI tests is that humans are more robust against changes in the test script.

> *"These were tests on the GUI of the application, I did not know how to automate these. Anyways, I was quicker, when we just clicked through it myself and checked whether it worked or not. [...] Perceived, this automation would be more effort than to just do it manually."* — team B

GUI testing is perceived as something very difficult and ominous by the students. 6 of 20 teams regarded GUI testing as generally difficult. Defining the target value for a GUI test is challenging. One reason might be that the purpose of "GUI testing" can be interpreted in different ways, posing different challenges. Some students reduced GUI tests to asserting that some GUI element is placed correctly—instead of asserting correct interaction with these elements. Students rightfully wanted to assert certain geometrical attributes of elements in an editor—but did not know how to do so. This team could not find any technical solution to their problem and opted for visual checks.

> "I find it difficult to check if some pixels are displayed correctly. How could one formulate this correctly? If it is about two lines being perpendicular, I find it easier to execute it and visually check for myself." — team D

Students' Perception of Testing in Context of the Theoretical Analysis. A perceived high learning curve for testing is an indicator of the high complexity of practicing systematic testing and writing tests. According to Rogers' DOI-Theory, a perceived *high complexity* lowers the rate of adoption of an innovation. Additionally, the activity of writing tests in this practical project does not encompass a *trialability* as high as in the lecture exercises. In this project, the situations in which to write tests have not been pre-engineered and focused towards conveying one certain testing topic. Students had to setup testing environments on their own. In Rogers' terms, this lowered the perceived *trialability* of practicing systematic testing.

Category: External Influencing Factors

Since the course's team members were undergraduate students, other courses may have influenced their working behavior by limiting their available time and consequently influencing the time they may have spent on their projects.

Organizational Advice. Some coaches of student teams partially discouraged their teams from testing their products. One coach advised her team to give up unit testing. Another coach recommended writing tests after coding only because he regarded test first as being too hard to applied by novice teams. One team had been completely excused from automated testing because of time pressure. Many coaches excused their teams from automatic GUI altogether. In the case of Eclipse applications or Java-based games, GUI automation was regarded as too difficult for undergraduate teams. Even though one team had already begun to automate their GUI tests, one advice form above sufficed and the team stopped all efforts in that regard.

At the same time, teams complained about missing organizational guidelines about required tests as well as missing specifications for testing processes. Imprecise guidelines influenced the teams' testing behavior. Guidelines did not specify a high number of tests, thus students did not feel obliged to deliver many tests.

> "We really did not know how much we were supposed to test in order to pass this Quality Gate. It just did not say and that was frustrating!" — team C

No Time to Learn. Although testing is taught in courses, students have no practical experiences in testing and even so, students may have forgotten how to do it correctly. In this case, teams have to learn how to test. Because of the time pressure mentioned above, time is short in their project, which leads to having no time to learn testing. Especially GUI testing is time-consuming while learning how to test or becoming acquainted with frameworks, which led to missing GUI tests.

4.1.3 Limitations and Threats to Validity

Even though 97 students participated in this study, it does not claim statistical significance. As this study was conducted within a student project, some limitations apply. Participants said that they did not take the project too seriously, as it was a course for learning and no critical software was developed. Students were also busy with other courses at the same time, which probably intensified the time pressure they felt. Yet, time pressure applies in commercial projects as well.

The study population was self-selected, as students were free to decline the interview without any consequences. Yet, none made use of this option; the student population was the complete set of one semester's software project course participants.

The interviews took part when all students had already successfully passed the project. Students were encouraged to talk freely and interviewers found them to be very candid, e.g., some openly admitted that they only tested their project because at least some testing was mandatory in the course. The research group has no reason to believe that the study participants might have given them an inaccurate picture of events.

The findings of this study cannot be generalized to other populations. This is a known limitation of Grounded Theory studies. More studies are needed to find out which of these phenomena appear in other contexts. These findings might still hold for many other novices that have just completed their university degrees in computer science.

Teams comprised only of novice developers are unlikely to be the norm. However, the relatively extreme manifestation in this population leads Pham et al. 2014a to assume that these phenomena might be present in weaker forms in many individuals or teams.

4.1.4 Summary: Testing Behavior of Students

In this study, Pham et al. 2014a have found empirical data to support the findings of the analysis of chapter 3 (KAP-Gap, missing project context):

- too late engagement in systematic testing, manual testing prevailing (systematic testing as an afterthought)

- students' dismissive attitude towards testing

- students' lack of how-to knowledge,

- a hindering lack of applicable learning materials

Problem 4.1.1: Systematic testing as an afterthought. Students demonstrated very little planning ahead regarding their testing efforts—which indicates that testing does not appear important to them. Only one quarter of the student population had talked about testing during the early phases of their project and over one half did not plan their testing effort at all. Student teams underestimated the testing effort and started systematic testing very late in the process. Students were not able to decide when to start testing an application that was still in development and undergoing change and pushed systematic testing activities to the very end of the project. Beginning systematic testing this late resulted in students not perceiving the advantage of a written test suite during development and a seemingly small error detection suite (as major errors had been uncovered in tedious manual testing beforehand). In this case, students perceived the costs of systematic testing clearly but saw very little benefit in it.

Problem 4.1.2: Students' attitude towards testing. Overall, writing tests felt unproductive to students. It appeared as a secondary concern to them and they valued implementing over systematic testing. It was more important to add another untested functionality to the software than to write tests for existing ones. This made any systematic testing effort feel unproductive to students.

Through lectures, students were aware of the benefits that early and systematic testing could bring. However, in engineered exercises, they have not felt a motivating sense of accomplishment when writing tests and finding bugs. When encountering a project context for the first time, the benefits of systematic testing became more clear to them.

Problem 4.1.3: Lack of practical how-to knowledge. University focus on conveying principles-knowledge first and provide how-to-knowledge second. This leaves students with very little how-to-knowledge of systematic testing in a real-world situation. Students felt overwhelmed by *actually* writing tests in a real project and were limited to JUnit-Test assertions and unit testing in general. Students wanted to engage in GUI automation, but could not. GUI automation appeared very difficult to them and its purpose is misunderstood. Higher forms of testing, such as system's tests or integration tests were difficult for them and mostly left out. Students perceived a high learning curve of systematic testing, which lead to opt for unsystematic, manual testing without any testing protocol. Only half of the student population engaged in some form of automated testing throughout the implementation phase, while the other half either wrote tests *at the very last* or not at all.

Problem 4.1.4: High Learning Curve. When students decided to engage in systematic testing, even if that meant overcoming a lack of how-to-knowledge, their efforts were often cut short. Students had problems finding suitable and applicable tutorials for their specific situation that would help them to start writing tests. They perceived a high learning curve for applying tutorials that they found online. This perceived high complexity stopped their systematic testing efforts.

4.2 Testing Behavior of New Hires in Industry

The findings presented in section 4.2 are currently under review for publication by the Software Quality Journal. The title of the original study is 'Onboarding Inexperienced Developers: Struggles and Perceptions Regarding Automated Testing' [120]. The original study was conducted by Raphael Pham, Stephan Kiesling, Leif Singer, and Kurt Schneider in 2014. This research team is called Pham et al. 2014b.

Pham et al. 2014b conducted a qualitative study in which they surveyed 170 and interviewed 22 practitioners about their experiences with recent graduates, focusing on software testing skills. Practitioners do recognize a skill gap between university graduates and industry expectations. This perception is engrained deeply enough to influence hiring practices. Practitioners use different and at times costly strategies to alleviate this skill gap, such as training and mentoring efforts. The core findings were validated in a survey with 698 professional software developers.

4.2.1 Research Questions

This study explores the views and concerns of practitioners who handle the onboarding phase of newly hired software engineers, with a focus on inexperienced newcomers such as recent university graduates. Pham et al. 2014b had no prior knowledge about this population's views and employed a Grounded Theory approach [65]. The researchers formulated their initial field of interest as the first two research questions. During the study, the researchers focused more in *how* practitioners manage a lack of testing skills and added the last two research questions. An in-depth description on the research procedure, questionnaire design, and data collection can be found in the appendix (p. 174). Reading these, however, is not mandatory for understanding this work. All three questionnaires and the coding system of the GT study are also provided in the appendix.

RQ 1: Do software companies see problems with the testing skills of new hires?

RQ 2: What are these problems, exactly?

RQ 3: How are companies coping with these problems?

RQ 4: What is the impact of new hires' lack of testing skills?

Population Description. This study's focus were real-world experiences with onboarding newcomers and the target population was software developers currently working at a software company. The questionnaires were sent to a random set of practitioners who in turn answered on a self-selected basis. This resulted in a diverse population.

Participants were asked to provide some background information of their companies and the testing process they used. The first questionnaire was exploratory and was not analyzed further for the final Grounded Theory model. This section describes the population of the second questionnaire (with 170 usable data sets).

Participants were located all over the world, with most of the developers coming from the USA (52 participants, 31%), followed by Brazil (13 / 8%), France (9 / 5%),

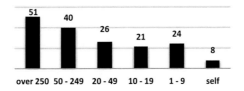

Figure 4.3: Number of respondents, split by company sizes (in number of employees).

Germany, and the Netherlands (both 7 / 4%). All in all, developers from 41 countries participated. These practitioners worked at software companies of different sizes. About half of the population worked at a *very large* (over 250 employees) or *large* company (50–249 employees, cf. Fig. 4.3). While focusing on employed developers, two unemployed respondents were included as well. They shared experiences from former jobs.

Participants were asked to classify their product in terms of criticality. Most of the participants (117 / 69%) worked on products that caused monetary damage if they failed. 39 (23%) participants classified product failure as *non-critical* ('it is not the end of the world'), and 14 practitioners worked on *safety-related software*. The respondents' level of sophistication regarding their testing process was inquired. A large number of practitioners (109 / 64%) used *systematic* and *automated* approaches to software testing. All other combinations remained equally at 12% (about 20 respondents each).

Most of the respondents (106 / 62%) hired newcomers that came directly from some kind of educational institution, such as recent university graduates. 64 respondents focused on hiring newcomers from other sources, such as modern development job offer platforms (e.g. `odesk.com`), headhunters, through engagement in open source development, or through personal connections.

Analysis of Questionnaire Data. The second questionnaire posed the question: *"Are you satisfied with the testing skills of new hires?"* This section presents numerical data and describes the satisfaction among practitioners from different points of view. The population is self-selected and this data provides little in terms of statistical significance and is presented for illustrative purposes only.

Overall, more than half of the practitioners of this study (95 / 55%) are dissatisfied with the testing skills of new hires.

Splitting by *company size* (cf. Fig. 4.4a), dissatisfaction surpasses the rate of satisfaction in most cases. From large companies (50–249 employees) to very small (1–9 employees) companies, practitioners are discontent with the testing skills of new hires. Only for very large companies (more than 250 employees), the majority is satisfied.

Splitting the data by the origin of the new hire (*"Where do your new hires come from, mostly?"*, cf. Fig. 4.4c), it becomes clear that *very large* (over 250 employees) and *large companies* take in quite a high number of new hires straight from educational institutions (e.g. universities). This is not as obvious for *mid-sized* or *small* companies: The ratio

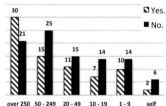

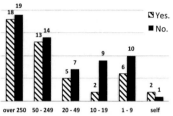

(a) General satisfaction with testing skills of new hires.

(b) Satisfaction with fresh graduates' testing skills.

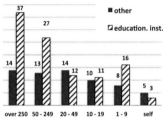

(c) Educational origin of new hires per company size.

Figure 4.4: Split by company sizes: ratio of satisfaction with testing skills (a) and (b), and origin of new hire (c).

between fresh graduates and new hires from the job market is nearly 1:1. Interestingly, the rate of graduate hiring spikes again with *very small companies* (1–9 employees).

Regarding testing skills of graduates only (cf. Fig. 4.4b), dissatisfaction seems prevailing and is most prominent in *mid-sized* (20–49 employees) to *very small* companies (1–9 employees). *Very large* and *large* companies seem equally content as discontent with graduates' testing skills.

All in all, practitioners in this study are dissatisfied with the testing skills of new hires. Especially mid-sized to very small companies seem to struggle with recent graduates (cf. Fig. 4.4b). Here, dissatisfaction rates were equal to or surpassed satisfaction rates. Larger companies seem to fare better than smaller ones.

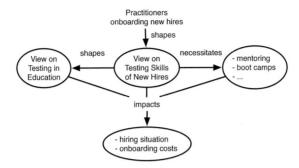

Figure 4.5: Overview of the interplay between practitioners' experience with new hires' testing skills and its impacts.

4.2.2 Model of Testing Skills of Newcomers

Practitioners' **experiences** in handling newcomers has led to certain **views on newcomers' testing skills** and certain **views on education** which in turn spawned different **coping strategies** (cf. Fig. 4.5). Ultimately, these phenomena influence the **hiring process** for both the practitioner and the newcomer.

Practitioners' Views on Testing Skills

Many of the insights gathered in the study about the actual testing behavior of students are reflected in the experiences that practitioners make with newcomers. This underlines the fact that these problems (cf. section 4.1.4 for a short summary) presented in the first empirical study (section 4.1) do carry over to the industrial situation of onboarding and eventually need to be taken care of by practitioners.

Practitioners find that interest in development generally surpasses testing efforts and testing engagement in new hires. Newcomers have difficulties putting their theoretical testing knowledge to work and implement actual tests. Fundamentally, new hires display **gaps in testing knowledge** and a **lack of hands-on experience** and training. This impression has already solidified in the minds of practitioners, so that it negatively influences the expectations they have regarding the testing skills of new hires when those apply for a position. Ultimately, practitioners **blame the educational system** for this lack of practically relevant testing skills.

General Views and Expectations. New hires applying for a software engineering position do have experience implementing and building software. For example, pre-graduate students sometimes work voluntarily on open source projects or small personal projects. However, testing skills are usually low in comparison and unsystematic manual testing is the prevailing method for quality assurance. Practitioners rarely find good test automation skills in new hires.

> *"They generally have been building for the Web or small personal projects and their concept of testing is 'try it and see if it works."'* — KG

Worse yet, there are practitioners who assume that recent graduates will have no testing skills at all. They are under the strong impression that newcomers usually have no knowledge about basic testing techniques and test automation. They have come to expect no testing skills in new hires.

Test knowledge and automation skills are regarded as skills that new hires will only learn 'on the job', not in university. This notion is usually given with discontent and in a bitter manner: These practitioners would prefer university graduates to have more testing skills but are being disappointed again and again.

> *"New hires never have sufficient experience with the test workflows in the development process. [...] These sorts of skills are acquired on the job in industry and not at university."* — TR

Lack of Experience. One reoccurring complaint from practitioners is that new hires have no real-world experience in systematic testing. This is a more global complaint that can be split into two concrete situations: experience in *actually writing tests* and experience with following an *overall test process*.

Regarding *actually writing* test code, practitioners find that new hires seldom have had hands-on experience and assume that they have never implemented tests before.

> *"Automated testing is an entirely new concept to most new hires. High-level test suite design and real-world experience is universally lacking."* — CH

New hires often do not know *what* to test and *how* to do it. They *do* have a general idea of testing, but have problems putting their knowledge into action. Their test code does not quite hit the target and usually under- or over-asserts. Practitioners then deem their test code impractical and inefficient.

The study participants also noticed that newcomers display weaknesses in fundamental test knowledge, such as *test-related definitions* and their purposes. Their educational knowledge of systematic testing appears to be limited to unit testing and does not cover other, more sophisticated test types. For example, they cannot distinguish between integration tests and system tests. Practitioners need newcomers to break free from such a limited point of view and advance to behavior-driven testing—for example, in order to automatically test complete user interactions.

Regarding new hires' *understanding of test processes*, participants drew a similar picture. Inexperienced new hires—and especially new graduates—have had no experience with real-world projects and their testing processes. They have no understanding of the role and importance of a well-defined testing process in commercial software development.

"They know what testing is but often don't understand how important it is in big projects. They are not used to big scale testing processes." — AL

From the newcomer's point of view, systematic automatic testing is not *intertwined* with the main software development process.

This is similar to the findings of the first empirical study (cf. section 4.1). Students treated systematic testing as an extra activity that they took care of rather reluctantly. Instead of making it an ongoing effort, it was done—if at all—at the end of development. This kept students from experiencing the benefits of automatic testing during development, such as tests catching regressions or the influence of testing on architecture.

Some practitioners, however, have ambivalent feelings towards the lack of real-world experience of new hires. After all, these are recent graduates and not senior developers. Often, these practitioners pointed out that the new hires they had been working with were fast learners and easy to teach.

"University students have not had much experience writing tests for information systems. Limited experience, but they learn quickly." — FE

Attitudes Towards Testing. Underpinning the lack of hands-on experience of newcomers, practitioners have observed a problematic attitude towards testing in general. Testing is regarded as unimportant additional work and as fundamentally not really needed. Often, newcomers prefer a leisured approach to bug discovery altogether and do not take testing seriously. This touches upon a more fundamental problem: For newcomers, the role of testing as a discipline and as an integral part of software engineering remains unclear. Again, this skewed view on systematic testing relates to findings of the first empirical study (cf. section 4.1): Students preferred to implement new features and regarded automated tests as technical debt. Testing did not seem as important as implementing new features.

"A large majority of new hires [...] do not have any concept of testing as a discipline. It is not so much that they are unaware of a particular testing methodology; it is that they have never conceived of testing as something that would even have methodologies." — RE

Practitioners hypothesize that the reason for such a dismissive view is that these young developers have not had a chance to recognize the benefits of an automated test suite yet, due to their lack of first-hand experience. For example, they have not yet dealt with things like regression bugs.

Another issue adding to this situation is the perceived reward of test efforts. When new hires *do* write tests, they have the impression that they do not benefit from them. As reported in the first empirical study (cf. section 4.1), misunderstanding of the benefits of systematic testing may even occur during university studies: Adding a test suite late left student developers disappointed by the low failure detection rate. All bugs had already been found by trial & error during development.

"They do not think they benefit from testing. [...] they actually write tests, but they don't get any benefit from it. What I called benefit is preventing failures in production, preventing bugs." — AS

Practitioners' Views on Education

Some of the study participants said they were disappointed by the low level of testing skills in new hires and blame educational institutions. A subset of them had gained the impression that software testing is not taught at universities at all.

> *"We don't study testing and we don't know anything about testing in the university, so junior developers have nothing at all about testing. They don't know there is something in the development process named testing, actually."* — AB

Practitioners see several problems with education in software testing. They feel that it is outdated and not adequate for their industrial needs and today's pragmatic standards.

In line with the lack of hands-on experience, software testing education in university is perceived as too theoretical: Pre-engineered examples used in testing lectures do not cover the range of skills needed for testing in the real world and are too simplified. Students develop a general idea about testing, but they cannot apply it while real world testing demands a whole new set of technical skills (use of test libraries and frameworks).

> *"Real human interaction, say ticking on a web page or tapping on a mobile device, [...] connecting to databases, mocking web connections [...]. They're the real sort of 'juicy bits' which are very difficult and they've had very little exposure to."* — LS

Practitioners feel that testing lectures in university are not given the importance they deserve. They criticize that taking a course in software testing is only optional when studying software engineering. As per their experiences, students can skip those and avoid learning something about testing in their studies altogether.

Coping Strategies

Pham et al. 2014b found different coping strategies that companies employ to overcome this experience gap. Their general goal is to help the inexperienced developer learn how to work in the company as effectively and efficiently as possible. Different approaches gradually push the load of engagement from the new hire to the practitioner—with varying advantages and effects.

In the worst cases, **no onboarding** was offered at all and the new hire was left to overcome problems by herself. Other strategies encompassed **teaching the new hire** how to systematically test from scratch. The researchers divided these strategies into two types: *semi-active* and *active strategies*, depending on the level of support that the practitioner had to provide to the newcomer.

Semi-active strategies provide the newcomer with support from a senior developer, but only in an ad-hoc manner: the newcomer has to ask questions herself and learn proactively (e.g. in mentoring). Active strategies require the practitioner to actively teach the new hire. Here, the effort lies on the practitioner's side. As the level of support on the practitioner's side grows, the learning effect may grow as well. However, so would the effort and induced costs.

Besides coping strategies to remedy the lack in testing skills of new hires, Pham et al. 2014b also found that practitioners had **worked around it altogether**: Inexperienced new hires were not required to be able to automatically test their software but were specifically expected to do only manual testing during their onboarding phase. This would give them time to learn about systematic testing and allow them to advance to automatic testing later. This strategy, however, demands that the company's test process and quality assurance system can handle and accept *only manually tested* software written by newcomers. For example, the source code handed in by a recent hire may need to be tested by a senior developer afterwards.

Environmental Properties. Practitioners find a test-intensive workplace to be effective in diffusing testing practices: New hires adopt testing faster if they are put into teams that already practice automated testing. In such an environment, new hires can observe and study how to test, provided team dynamics and commit mechanisms permit them. Left to their own devices, new hires with low testing skills do not adopt testing well.

Pham et al. 2014b have seen a similar effect in another empirical study on testing behavior on GitHub [122] (cf. chapter 11): the site has a high degree of social transparency and makes other users' actions visible, including how they write tests. Seeing that other users engaged in testing efforts, being able to analyze their test code, and use it as a basis for their own tests often had contributors engage in test efforts themselves. The researchers believe that making the test culture in a team visible and actionable lowers the barriers newcomers to adopt it.

> *"They are quick to adapt into doing auto testing if they work in teams that does so already. But if they are put alone in a new project it does not come naturally to do any testing at all."* — SW

Another important aspect is the documentation of the testing process. Short and textual how-tos describing tools and how to operate them allow newcomers to orient themselves and help in answering basic questions. This in turn can lower communication load during the onboarding phase. However, good documentation is worthless if the new hire has no access to it or cannot find it by herself. Especially unguided onboarding is dependent on strategic placement of guidelines, documentation, and communication thereof. Another challenge is to organize these guides in an accessible manner. Here, practitioners preferred short and pragmatic texts. If the barrier for using documentation is too high, a newcomer may not benefit from it.

> *"There were documents on how to test, how to write tests that fit into our automated framework. [...] The problem with the wiki was that it wasn't well organized and there was an awful lot of pages."* — KG

Semi-Active Onboarding Strategies. During onboarding, specific questions arise that documents cannot answer. In this case, one semi-active strategy that the study participants mentioned was to assign a senior developer to the new hire as a mentor. The *mentor's* task is to get the new hire up to speed, explain company-specific processes, and help the new hire with technical questions. The new hire is expected to ask questions when something is unclear, which can be a problem: Being a mentor is an additional role for a senior team member and as such, this can impact this team member's productivity. New hires are aware that they are occupying the senior's time and they do not want to impose too much. This makes asking questions for a new hire difficult and stressful. They do not want to keep the senior developer from completing their work.

> *"You need to understand everything very, very fast. You will almost not get a chance to ask this really deeply. So you need to prepare your questions before, just not to take too much time and ask everything you need at one talk."* — IO

Active Onboarding Strategies. Strategies for onboarding that involve active teaching efforts on the company side ranged from seminars to carefully curated sample projects. Every project endeavor with the new hire used the company's development process and was designed to make the newcomer become acquainted with it.

One teaching technique used was the *bootcamp*. New hires are categorized by proficiency and strategically grouped to facilitate knowledge transfer between participants. Then, they are sent off to a quick hands-on crash course. They implement a small but valuable project for the company including testing efforts. Often, courses are located in-house and newcomers are supervised by senior developers, providing a good starting experience: Newcomers create a viable product and feel proud of their accomplishments.

Hosting and managing such a specifically curated course in programming, testing, and the company's processes was said to be effective and to help the new hires overcome testing skill gaps. However, the associated efforts and costs were said to be relatively high. Companies of small size may not be able to conduct such an event.

> *"A lot of the new hires are proud of that and they like to present what they have build and more important, more of them present what they have learned."* — RS

If no bootcamp is available, small and manageable projects are used as a playground for improving the newcomer's skills. These projects are non-critical and sometimes not related to the company's product at all. Practitioners are aware that newcomers are not able to perform on commercial products straightaway. They do not want to overwhelm the newcomer and try to provide a *low pressure but real* environment where newcomers can train their programming and testing skills.

> *"[being thrown in] is a little bit of dancing for developers as well, especially if you come straight out of university ... to be put on client work and to be expected to deliver a level, which you're probably not able to deliver at."* — LS

Some companies still decide to let the new hire work on real-world commercial software from the start. In these cases, she was assigned a small and self-contained task that was not critical to the success of the commercial product, such as maintenance or bug fixing activities. This way, the new hire contributes something valuable to the code base and gets to know it in the process.

Another approach that practitioners reported is putting the newcomer on a new project with a fresh code base, with a senior developer taking the lead and reviewing their work. The newcomer is not taking full responsibility and can safely experience the company's development process.

When it comes to diffusion of culture and team knowledge, pair programming seemed popular among practitioners. Practitioners said they were able to show how things work in detail, while at the same time seeing how the new hire approaches problems. Dubbed *cross pollination*, senior developers not up-to-date with recent technologies and practices in systematic testing were paired with a newcomer to refresh both their testing skills.

Impact of Low Testing Skills

The gap between what is provided by university education and industry's needs has different impacts on the onboarding phase. First, teaching practical testing is **time-consuming and overall costly**. Onboarding an inexperienced developer can negatively influence a team's productivity. Second, a perceived low level of practical testing skills in graduates has given practitioners a **negative impression** of testing education. Third, not all companies decide or can afford to take on the effort of onboarding an inexperienced developer. In some cases, the hiring process had changed and the **hiring bar had been raised**, excluding inexperienced developers altogether.

Costs of Teaching. Practitioners care for code quality but do not find appropriate testing skills in new hires. However, specific lecture courses, bootcamps, or mentorships are costly in terms of both time and money. Generally, these endeavors are more effective if the new hire is capable and willing to learn. In line with what Singer et al. [137] have found about how recruiters assess software developers, practitioners often look for 'quick learners' and try to filter for 'quick learning' abilities when interviewing. Yet, teaching testing from scratch remains effortful, even with quick learners. Also, not every capable graduate computer science student may pass as such a quick learner instantly.

> *"Fresh graduates almost never have any testing skill or experience. We make a point of recruiting quick learners, so they pick up automated testing fast, but it takes up quite a bit of energy."* — SH

Mentoring is costly: often a senior developer is appointed as a mentor. This additional role can impact productivity, which can especially hurt small teams.

> *"We have three guys and when we hire another one, we stop one of the three guys to basically teach this new hire from the scratch. So in a team that have three guys we have one off for a bunch of time. It will suddenly impact the speed of all."* — FR

Such real-world onboarding strategy could point to a deeper organizational problem masked as an onboarding issue: for smaller development teams, it could be more beneficial to evenly distribute the effort of mentoring to all team members. This, however, is an insight that these companies need to be made aware off, before they can take action.

Raising the Hiring Bar. Onboarding efforts and associated costs influence hiring strategies. For some practitioners, it is no longer sensible to hire inexperienced developers. They increase their hiring bar in the hope of reducing training efforts and costs. Testing questions are included in interviews and testing exercises are demanded. Finding candidates with both acceptable engineering and testing skills proves difficult.

> " there just didn't seem to be so many candidates who had both experience in engineering and had experience in any sort of meaningful testing." — JC

The opposite approach is to exclude recent graduates altogether. Several of study participants said they were content with paying more for more experienced developers rather than having to onboard newcomers. This makes it hard for recently graduated university students when applying for a position at one of these companies. They have little practical experience when finishing their studies, their potential employer however demands such experience. Larger companies with more resources offer training courses and bootcamps, but smaller companies often cannot, instead raising the hiring bar.

> " after you graduate you just cannot find a work because at work no one wants to teach you from the beginning and what you are learning at university [...] if you don't know how to code simple things, then who will hire you?" — IO

4.2.3 Validation of Core Findings

In order to validate the Grounded Theory model, Pham et al. 2014b designed a final third questionnaire. Core findings were translated into 14 statements and questionnaire respondents were asked to rate them on a five-item Likert-type scale ranging from "strongly disagree" to "strongly agree." In July 2015, this final questionnaire was sent out to 10,000 GitHub users who had set an organization in their profile. The researchers received 941 answers. After sorting out hobbyists, practitioners not in contact with new hires, and only manually testing participants, 698 usable responses remained.

As with the second questionnaire, participants were located all over the world, with most of the developers again from the USA (217 / 31%), followed by Germany (43 / 6%), Brazil (37 / 5%), UK (36 / 5%), and India (30 / 4%). All in all, developers from 75 countries participated.

The of this questionnaire results are shown in Fig. 4.6 and Fig. 4.7. Agreement and disagreement are represented by shaded bars, percentages, and absolute numbers. Neutral answers are not shown explicitly, but can be derived from the white space in a chart. The researchers chose this representation to emphasize agreement and disagreement.

Statements 2, 10, and 16 are not included[2]. Statement 2 is left out because statement 5 (cf. Fig. **??**) is a more testing-focused version. Statements 10 and 16 were control questions. The numbering of the statements indicates the ordering of the statements in the questionnaire. They are grouped by topic for a more cohesive presentation.

Participants of the final questionnaire were largely dissatisfied with the testing skills of new hires (*"Are you satisfied with the testing skills of new hires?"*: 359 / 51% dissatisfied vs. 293 / 42% satisfied, 46 no answers).

Working with newcomers. Practitioners' experiences with writing tests with newcomers largely align with the main findings (cf. Fig. 4.6a, statements 4, 6, 7) of the Grounded Theory model. When it comes to *actually* writing test code, new hires appear to be limited to unit testing to a degree, lacking knowledge and experience to write tests in a real world situation.

Attitude towards testing. Regarding new hires' higher level understanding of industry test processes, practitioners' opinions diverged a little from the main findings (cf. Fig. 4.6b, statements 12, 13). There is no decisive majority to either agreement or disagreement regarding statements 12 and 13, although a very slight skew towards agreement can be observed. Practitioners appear to encounter both new hires *with* and *without* a proper understanding of high-level testing processes in a nearly equal manner. In the interviews, interviewees complained about a lack of general understanding of industry testing processes and their importance. Relatedly, this phenomena is similar to the findings of the first empirical study (cf. section 4.1) about students' test behavior. For more decisive conclusions, further research is needed.

Strategies. The participants agree that being put in a team that already practices systematic testing facilitates the adoption of testing (cf. Fig. 4.6a, statement 14).

Impact. The lack of testing skills in newcomers has impacted the hiring situation. Most participants of the questionnaire struggle to find newcomers that meet their testing needs (cf. Fig. 4.6b, statement 5).

Rectifying a lack of testing skills is costly as mentoring or training endeavors cost either productivity, time, or money. The previous questionnaire results (cf. section 4.2.1) and interview data suggested that the extent of this struggle differs depending on company size. To this end, Pham et al. 2014b designed this final questionnaire to validate the hypothesis: *Smaller companies struggle more with onboarding new hires without testing skills than bigger companies.* The researchers asked participants about the size of their company in number of employees and assigned size ranges into five different categories: 'working alone (self)', '1-9', '10-19', '20-99','100 or more'. The researchers included two opposite statements of the hypothesis (cf. Fig 4.7, statements 9, 15) and analyzed results with respect to the participants' company sizes.

Did participants from smaller companies answer differently than those from larger companies? Fig. 4.7 shows the overall population's answer on top and split by company size below. Pham et al. 2014b did find a weak correlation between the participants'

---

[2]The statements not depicted are:

(2) In hiring, we're having trouble finding software developers that meet our needs.

(10) Testing is an integral part of software engineering.

(16) Testing is something that is separate from actual software development.

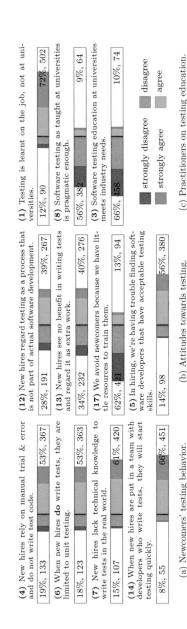

(a) Newcomers' testing behavior.

(b) Attitudes towards testing.

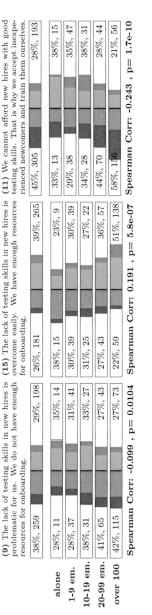

(c) Practitioners on testing education.

Figure 4.6: Practitioners' views on testing skills of newcomers.

Figure 4.7: Practitioners' struggle with the lack of testing skills, split by company sizes in number of employees.

answers and their company size. Participants from the two smallest company size categories appear to struggle with the lack of testing skills. Participants of the next company size tier appear to struggle less with resources for onboarding. Larger companies (20-99 and over 100 employees) fare well, reporting to overcome the lack of testing skills easily.

The Spearman Rho Rank Correlations is given below each diagram and indicates a statistically significant correlation between responses and company size ($p < 0.05$). In this population, Pham et al. 2014b may have been able to validate the hypothesis: smaller companies perceive the lack of testing skills and its demand for resources differently. However, the researchers expected the results to show a greater effect. While they assumed larger companies to fare better, Pham et al. 2014b expected a greater and more distinct need for onboarding resources from smaller companies as suggested in the interview and previous questionnaire data.

Regardless of company size, the population mostly disagreed on rejecting newcomers to avoid training expenses (cf. Fig. 4.6b, statement 17). One reason for practitioners to take in untrained newcomers even though are dissatisfied with their testing skills (instead of focungsing on trained alternative candidates) could be: practitioners have trouble finding new hires with acceptable testing skills (cf. Fig. 4.6b, statement 5)—and demanding better testing skills makes hiring more expensive.

Fig. 4.7 (statement 11) shows that smaller companies more often opt to take in new hires and train them, simply for a lack of budget for better trained alternatives. Meanwhile bigger companies appear free of this notion, which is in line with the previous finding: the lack of resources for onboarding and training is not a big obstacle for larger companies, while practitioners from smaller companies perceive it as challenging.

View on Testing Education. Lastly, practitioners who were in contact with recent university or college graduates strongly felt that testing is only learnt on the job (cf. Fig. 4.6c, statement 1). They deemed current testing education not pragmatic enough and said that their needs are not met (cf. Fig. 4.6c, statements 8 and 3).

4.2.4 Limitations and Threats

This study is a first exploratory investigation into the views of practitioners. As a result, an approach based on Grounded Theory was chosen. While saturation was achieved in the interviews and questionnaire responses, it is likely that Pham et al. 2014b did not uncover all possible perspectives. The population was chosen semi-randomly and the final interview participants and questionnaire respondents were all self-selected volunteers.

As with most Grounded Theory studies, the results are not generalizable and would need to be verified in other populations. This study provides a view of testing skills as seen by a certain self-selected population. The results of the third and final questionnaire can only serve to heighten the confidence in the findings but cannot provide certainty.

Location. Participants of this study are located all over the world. This presents the threat of local and cultural differences. Among a lot of other things, educational institutions and study programs, work values, or industry requirements may differ from country to country. Although clusters can be observed—for example, the majority of respondents coming from the USA—the threat of local influences remains. In this regard, results of this study can only be seen as a first overview. Further research is needed to understand problems of practitioners with a focus on their respective local industry.

Focus on Dissatisfied Practitioners. This study focuses on practitioners' problems and concerns with new hires. Opportunities and advantages that give practitioners a positive opinion about new hires are rarely reflected. This is due to field of interest that the researchers based this study on. The numerical analysis (cf. section 4.2.1) reflects both positive and negative attitudes towards new hires' testing skills alike. As the negative trend dominates the results, Pham et al. 2014b decided to dig deeper into the concerns and struggles of practitioners. The resulting Grounded Theory model is thusly focused on the negative impression. Further research is needed to analyze the positive aspects of new hires' testing skills.

Varying Bucket Sizes. The results of the third questionnaire is split by different company sizes (cf. Fig. 4.7). Due to the voluntary nature of this questionnaire, the researchers had no control over the number of participants for each size category, resulting in possibly over- or underrepresented categories. This, in turn, could heighten the influence of outliers on the results.

4.2.5 Summary: Testing Behavior of Newcomers in Industry

In this Grounded Theory study, Pham et al. 2014b investigated what practitioners think of the testing skills of newcomers. The researchers interviewed 22 professional software practitioners and received 170 answers from online questionnaires. The core findings were validated in a final questionnaire with 698 practitioners.

Practitioners assess the testing skills of newcomers as low. They report several areas of concern about the testing behavior of these inexperienced developers. Interestingly, these areas of concern are similar to the areas of concern describing the testing behavior of the student population in the first empirical study in section 4.1.

Regarding the software testing education, practitioners deem that it does not meet industry's needs. They are dissatisfied with the testing skills of newcomers to the extent that they exclaim "Testing is learnt on the job, not at university". Some practitioners think that testing is not taught in universities at all and if so, it is taught too theoretically. They criticize that systematic testing does not get the importance it needs.

Practitioners have developed different coping strategies to bridge the skill gap in newcomers and industry's expectations. The most common teaching strategy was mentoring, representing a middle path between bootcamps and doing nothing. Many practitioners reported that their companies opted to teach newcomers how to test from scratch. Most notably, practitioners reported that newcomers were quicker to adopt systematic testing when they were put into testing-intensive environments.

Onboarding efforts such as mentoring or boot camps are costly. Especially smaller companies struggle with onboarding newcomers without testing skills, while larger companies embrace them. Pham et al. 2014b suspect larger companies to have more and better resources for overcoming the testing skill gap than smaller companies, and found a weak correlation between perceived lack of onboarding resources and company size.

Problem 4.2.1: Little Hands-on Experience. Practitioners find that newcomers exhibit very little hands-on experience with writing tests and practicing systematic testing. Newcomers do have a general idea of how systematic testing works, but do not seem to be able to implement or automate it. Practitioners have difficulties finding newcomers with acceptable skills in test automation. Mostly, newcomers perform tests manually and if they do write tests, they appear limited to using JUnit. Relatedly, newcomers exhibit gaps in basic testing knowledge and definitions.

Problem 4.2.2: Role of Systematic Testing is unclear. Practitioners report that newcomers seldom understand how the activity of systematic testing fits into the software engineering process. Newcomers have little experience with the overall test process and the importance of systematic testing.

Problem 4.2.3: Testing is Regarded as Secondary. According to practitioners, newcomers appear more interested in programming than systematic testing. Some even sport a dismissive attitude towards it and would rather neglect it altogether, if possible. In the newcomer's eye, systematic testing lacks importance and provides little benefit. Practitioners assume that newcomers have not come to appreciate systematic testing yet as they have not been involved with complex project situations yet.

Problem 4.2.4: Learning Materials need to be Suitable for Newcomers. During onboarding, documentation of the testing process is an important source of information for newcomers. However, guidelines, wikis and other learning materials need to be designed with newcomers in mind, kept up-to-date and accessible to newcomers at the right time. Otherwise, the barrier for a newcomer to use it is too high.

4.3 Chapter Summary

In this chapter, the *actual* testing behavior of inexperienced developers is described—at two points in time: shortly before these developers leave the educational setting and just when they enter their first onboarding phase. This comprehensive view facilitates different perspectives:

- newcomers testing skills and lack thereof

- newcomers' motivations and inhibitors for and against systematic testing

- how newcomers' testing behavior impacts performance in industry

- how industry copes with a lack of testing skills

Common Problems with Newcomers' Testing Behavior

Both empirical studies provide an in-depth and qualitative understanding of the testing behavior of inexperienced developers. Each study concludes with a list of most prominent testing problems (cf. summaries in sections 4.1.4 and 4.2.5). Comparing these problems, common *problems areas* emerge: more general topics that students as well as newcomers struggle with. In both empirical studies, these topics have been touched upon in different concrete situations. Table 4.2 gathers these concrete situations from both empirical studies and links them to their respective, more abstract problem area. The rows of the first two columns do not describe identical problems but problems pertaining to the same problem area. This problem area is given in the most right column. These problem areas describe problematic topics regarding testing behavior of inexperienced developers and mark a good starting point for support:

Problem Area 1: Following a Test Process   Inexperienced developers have little understanding of a general test process. They struggle to implement testing as a continuous effort and not as an afterthought.

Problem Area 2: Lack of How-To-Knowledge   Inexperienced developers have much too little hands-on experience with systematic testing and test automation. This hinders them in implementing their ideas about testing.

Problem Area 3: Dismissive Testing Attitude   Inexperienced developers perceive little benefit from systematic testing and exhibit little appreciation for it. They have little understanding of its role in commercial software engineering.

Problem Area 4: High Learning Curve   Even though inexperienced developers want to learn about testing techniques, they cannot find suitable learning materials that are applicable for their real-world situation. This barrier is enough to stop testing engagement. Inexperienced developers need learning materials that take their actual real-world situation into account.

Connecting both Empirical Studies

Both empirical studies in section 4.1 and section 4.2 used the Grounded Theory approach and are only valid for their respective population. Due to the strong focus on its population that GT studies exercise, they can claim little generalizability only.

The first study analyzed students' testing behavior in a university setting. While its findings are inline with the theoretical analysis in chapter 3, they only apply for this one population. At most, they can serve as indicators for the validity of the analysis.

The second study analyzed the testing behavior of newcomers in industry. In contrast to the first empirical student study, its main findings were validated with a larger set of practitioners worldwide. The newcomers' testing behavior is largely similar to the testing behavior of students. This similarity is an indicator for the following two hypotheses:

Table 4.2: Common Testing Skill Problems found in empirical studies.

Students' Testing Behavior (First Study)	Practitioners' Experience with Newcomers (Second Study)	Common Problem Area
Problem 4.1.1: Systematic Testing as an Afterthought. Students do not plan testing efforts ahead and write test too late in the development process.	**Problem 4.2.2: Importance of Testing Unclear.** Newcomers have little understanding of the role of systematic testing in a commercial development process.	**Problem Area 1: Following a Test Process**
Problem 4.1.3: Lack of How-To-Knowledge from University. Students opt to manually and unsystematically execute the AUT instead of engaging in test code writing. They have difficulties implementing test cases in real-world situations and appear limited to the JUnit test framework.	**Problem 4.2.1: Little Hands-On Experience with Writing Tests.** Very few newcomers have acceptable test automation skills. Newcomers have a general idea of systematic testing but cannot implement it.	**Problem Area 2: Lack of How-To-Knowledge**
Problem 4.1.2: Implementation Over Testing. Students perceive testing as unproductive work and prefer to implement production code instead of test code. Lectures do not convey a feeling of accomplishment when testing.	**Problem 4.2.3: Testing is regarded as secondary.** Newcomers are more engaged in writing new source code than test code. Often, testing appears negligible to them and unnecessary.	**Problem Area 3: Dismissive Testing Attitude**
Problem 4.1.4: High Learning Curve. Students who want to learn a testing technique have trouble finding suitable learning materials. The learning curve to apply tutorials found online is too high.	**Problem 4.2.4: Documentation and Guidelines must be kept Accessible for Newcomers.** Newcomers are in need of specific learning material that they can easily access and understand. Wikis and other platforms deprecate and can be hard to understand.	**Problem Area 4: High Learning Curve**

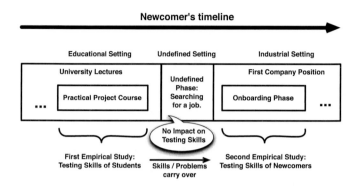

Figure 4.8: Skills and problems found in students at university carry over to industry and need to be taken care of there.

- There is little change in students' testing behavior between university and the first job position. The testing behavior students exhibit at the end of their Bachelor studies is largely the testing behavior practitioners have to work with during onboarding. The problems found in student testing behavior *do* carry over to the industrial onboarding situation (cf. Fig. 4.8, extending Fig. 4.1).

- A lacking testing behavior is not confined to the student population of the first empirical study in section 4.1. Practitioners around the world agree on similar problems with newcomers' testing behavior. This suggests that students from other universities and educational institutions around the world share a similar testing behavior when finishing their studies.

Empirical Support for the Theoretical Analysis. While the theoretical analysis is modeled after a software engineering course at Leibniz Universität Hannover, it retains a broader applicability to other universities: The concepts used (*lecture* or *exercise*) are kept general and can be found at other educational institutions around the world, making the analysis is valid for educational settings that employ similar concepts.

Another indicator for the validity and broader applicability of this analysis is given by the two extensive empirical studies: The findings of the two Grounded Theory studies are largely inline with suggestions of the theoretical analysis of chapter 3. Most notably, the second empirical study has been validated with a larger set of nearly 700 active practitioners from around the world. This indicates a more general problem with the way that inexperienced developers are introduced to systematic testing when using the aforementioned concepts, independent from university or country.

5 Three-Part Approach

In this chapter, the main goal of the approach, its connection to newcomers' real-world problems and the interplay between the different parts are described.

5.1 Stakeholders

First, each stakeholder is introduced, including his or her context. Then, each stakeholders' goals are defined. Lastly, a stakeholder's requirements regarding the onboarding process are described. At the end of this section, assumptions are discussed and related to other relevant options found in software engineering practice.

Newcomer: She has applied for her first position as a software engineer. She has had educational training of the model setting *Education with Practical Project* in Computer Science, having been educated in both programming and testing.

Goals: She wants to be successful as a software engineer. She does not have much experience with writing code in a real-world situation. Up until now, she has only written code in a classroom setting.

Requirements: As her experiences with a commercial development environment are limited, she needs specific and tailored support. She cannot be expected to be have a senior developer's expertise or confidence. Her technical knowledge is limited (e.g. *how-to-knowledge*). The onboarding situation stressful for her and she needs support in completing her new tasks. She has to understand the company's working values and development processes and has to collaborate with a new team.

Practitioner mentoring the newcomer and handling the onboarding: This senior developer's tasks are to make the newcomer acquainted with the development process, to support the her in getting started and to help her with social or technical issues. Besides that, the senior developer has to work on her usual development tasks. When the newcomer has produced new code, it is her job to check if this new code can be committed to the production code. Also, she has to either provide systematic tests for this code or make sure that the newcomer provides it.

Goals: She wants to help the newcomer, while having to take care of her own tasks. The more she has help the newcomer, the harder it is for her to complete her tasks. Introducing the newcomer to systematic testing is time-intensive for her.

Requirements: She does not want the mentoring process to become more complicated. On the contrary, she would embrace a less-effortful onboarding.

Onboarding Phase and Onboarding Process. The onboarding phase starts after the decision to hire the newcomer has been made. It describes the time span between the point in time when the inexperienced developer joins the team and the point time when this newcomer becomes a fully functional member of the team. During the onboarding phase, the newcomer is subjected to an onboarding process, which is designed to help her become acquainted with the team and the team's working culture. During the onboarding process, a senior developer is assigned the role of the mentor for this newcomer. Common first steps of this process include introduction to the team, setup of work environment (setup of computer, logins into company-services,...), explanation to development process, and introduction to guidelines and documentation. Whenever the newcomer needs help, she asks the mentor and together they solve the problem. It is the mentor's task to get the newcomer to adhere to the team's development process.

Development team: A development team is a group of senior software developers collaborating to produce a software product. The team is co-located. The team develops software according to a development process.

Goals: The team wants to efficiently produce a high quality software product. They care for quality of code and do not want erroneous code introduced into the production code. Every failure of the product requires additional attention from them for debugging.

Requirements: The team has an interest in the newcomer becoming a productive member of the team as soon as possible. The team also wants the newcomer to follow to development process, including the test process. Generally, the team wants every member to finish their tasks in time. In case of the mentor, the team decided to relieve her from some tasks and accepts an overall reduced team productivity. The team has an interest in the onboarding process being as little effort as possible—while still onboarding the newcomer effectively. Changes need to be easily implementable and of low effort.

Management: The management has the economical interests of the software company in mind and controls cash flow of the company. It decides on hiring new developers.

Goals: The management has an interest in reducing the costs of running the company and increasing profit. It has an interest in reducing the expenses of the onboarding process. Any changes to the current onboarding process have to be economically justifiable: changes to the onboarding process need to make it less expensive.

Requirements: Management would prefer to hire experienced developers from the start. However, developers with enough software engineering experiences are either hard to find or too expensive. Hiring newcomers is less expensive. Management has an interest in the newcomer reaching full productivity as soon as possible.

Development Process. The team uses a pragmatic, agile development process. User stories are broken down into development tasks for easier and more self-contained implementation. Even though TDD is demanded, tests are written after writing code. A company guideline demands that test code for each commit, however, there is no mechanism enforcing this. The development team a version control system.

5.1.1 Discussion of Assumptions

The Newcomer. There are different types of newcomers applying for software engineering positions everyday. In this case, it is based on a fresh graduate in Computer Science from the Leibniz Universität Hannover (LUH), Germany. This model is inline with the description of newcomers by practitioners in the second empirical study (cf. section 4.2). Vastly differing types of newcomers are out of the scope of this thesis.

Development Team: This approach focuses on co-located teams and remote working settings are out of scope. Onboarding to a remote working team or onboarding as a remote newcomer can be seen as a special case of the onboarding process. Not being co-located to the new team changes the onboarding process and presents different problems. The team's working culture is not easily observable as the newcomer is not present to observe it. Salient, verbal and non-written information is lost to the newcomer. The remote newcomer is dependent on information given in written guidelines and information explicitly mentioned to her—she cannot simply observe or overhear her team members in order to deduce or request new information.

The Onboarding Process. Current onboarding processes range from 'doing nothing' to full-blown lectures and programming crash-courses. They are discussed in more detail in chapter 4.2. A middle ground between those extremes is the approach of mentoring. However, this approach is not exclusive to onboarding processes that use mentoring. It can also be applied to a newcomer's onboarding phase after she has returned from 'programming boot camp' or other measures have taken place. This approach exercises its best effect on the phase when the newcomer settles in and needs to understand how to perform like a senior developer. Regarding the mentoring approach, this coincides with the whole mentoring phase. Regarding 'boot camp' strategy, this coincides with the phase *after*.

5.2 Constraints

After analyzing all involved stakeholders, several requirements for any changes to the onboarding process arise. As the depicted development environment and its roles represent only a model and not an actual software company, these 'requirements' are not clear-cut nor concrete. They are more abstract in nature, which is not an attribute of high-quality requirements. That is why they are 'constraints'.

Onboarding is a part of day-to-day business, which is stressful. All stakeholders involved with onboarding want changes to onboarding to not increase its effort. The newcomer is busy completing the onboarding process effectively, the mentor wants to complete her development tasks and the team wants to maintain productivity.

> **Constraint 1:** *The approach must not make the onboarding process more effortful for the mentor or the development team.*

For example, increasing the effort for the onboarding process could mean: increasing number of steps the mentor has to do to start off the onboarding process or the number of tasks the mentor has to complete to onboard the newcomer successfully.

Constraint 2: *The approach must not make the onboarding process more effortful for the newcomer than necessary.*

The goal of this thesis is to support the newcomer in adopting prevailing testing practices quickly. The onboarding process itself is a phase that is already stressful for the newcomer. Any change or action that does not support this thesis' goal is deemed *unnecessary* effort.[1]: When this approach is applied to the onboarding process, the newcomer will be supported in engaging in testing efforts—in that sense, the amount of effort the newcomer has to provide increases (she now writes more tests). However, this particular increase in effort is accepted, as it serves the goal of this approach. If, for example, the newcomer is made dive into other, not directly testing-related disciplines (like 'providing customer-support'), this would be regarded as unnecessary effort from the viewpoint of this approach.

Constraint 3: *The technical barrier for implementing the approach must be low for newcomer, the mentor and the development team.*

If it is too complicated to implement the proposed changes to the onboarding process, practitioners will refrain from doing so. For example, the effort to install new software or software plugins for a better onboarding should be minimal.

The inexperienced status of the newcomer makes a specific tailoring of the approach necessary. If the newcomer is not able to work with the new approach, for example because it has not been designed with the newcomer's needs in mind, it would miss its target audience. This would endanger reaching the goal of this approach.

Constraint 4: *The approach targets to improve the testing issues of the newcomer.*

The Testing skills of graduate students have attributes that make a specialized approach necessary (cf. chapter 4.1), for example a negative perception of testing efforts leading to a dismissive attitude towards test automation efforts.

Constraint 5: *The approach is tailored to the experience level of a newcomer.*

Similar to the specific testing behavior of newcomers, their experience level has to be taken into account. In accordance to the model of a newcomer presented in the previous section, a low level of experience is expected. In this case: mostly experience with pre-engineered lecture exercises and little to no experience in real-world development such as open source or industry projects. It is very important to tailor the approach towards this experience level. Otherwise, the approach is in danger of being too difficult for the newcomer and not supporting her. For example, it is not adequate nor practical to give the newcomer *unguided* access to the testing server, as in 'let her figure it out herself'. In regard to their low testing experience, this may have negative effects, such as making the discipline of testing seem more overwhelming.

---

[1]This view may clash with other improvement endeavors pursuing other goals for the onboarding process—however, this is outside of this thesis' scope.

Constraint 6: *The approach should provide technical support whenever possible.*

Taking the experience level into account, the newcomer can benefit from technical support. Technical support could—for example—automate manual steps that are necessary when engaging in test writing (e.g. 'creating and opening a testing class'). When the approach can be implemented either with automated or manual support, the automated version should be preferred. Freeing the newcomer from tedious manual steps where possible can help her in concentrating on actually producing and writing tests.

Company management has the economical reasonability in mind.

Constraint 7: *The approach must decrease the costs of onboarding. Alternatively, the approach must bring benefits that warrant the increased costs.*

For example, decreasing the costs of the onboarding process could be achieved by making it quicker (while maintaining or increasing effectivity). The company's management has an interest in making the onboarding process quicker as it means that the newcomer reaches full productivity earlier.

5.3 Overview of the Three-Part Approach

Getting newcomers to engage in testing is not trivial. On the one hand, the approach must be tailored to the requirements, skills and shortcomings of a newcomer, otherwise it risks alienating its target audience. On the other hand, the approach also needs to take into account practitioners' requirements for onboarding newcomers. Otherwise, it risks losing practical applicability and ultimately relevance for the real world development.

Problem Areas & Main Goal. In chapter 4, four problem areas have been uncovered (cf. summary of chapter 4, section 4.3) that inexperienced developers struggle with the most:

Problem Area 1: Following a Test Process.

Problem Area 2: Lack of How-To-Knowledge.

Problem Area 3: Dismissive Testing Attitude.

Problem Area 4: High Learning Curve.

Each of the problem area describes a complex and *non-trivial* problem situation: Problem area 1 describes that inexperienced developers do not plan their testing efforts ahead and end up writing test code much too late for various reasons. Additionally, problem area 1 describes that inexperienced developers have little understanding of a professional testing process when they join the working life. In-depth descriptions of these problem areas can be found in chapter 4.

The approach presented in this thesis is specifically tailored to improve on these areas. Its main goal is the following:

Table 5.1: Three pillars of the Approach improving different problem areas. ✗ marks first-order effects and (✗) marks second-order effects.

	Pillar 1: Establish Awareness	Pillar 2: Enable Practice	Pillar 3: Provide Knowledge in Context
Problem Area 1: Following A Test Process	(✗)	(✗)	
Problem Area 2: Lack of How-To-Knowledge		✗	(✗)
Problem Area 3: Dismissive Testing Attitude	✗		
Problem Area 4: High Learning Curve			✗

Main Goal: *Support the newcomer in adopting a team's testing culture and increase the newcomer's test writing activity.*

Pillars & Sub-Goals. In order to tackle the multi-facetted and complex situations posed by the problem areas, the approach of this thesis employs the divide-and-conquer paradigm on its highest level: It separates concerns and tackles the main goal from three different perspectives. Therefore, it is divided into three parts that are called *pillars* and that have separate (sub-) goals. Table 5.1 states the problem areas that each pillar focuses on. Each pillar has a primary focus to achieve a positive effect on this problem area, enacting a *first-order effect*. It is also expected that each pillar will have a positive *second-order* effect on another problem area.

Pillar 1: Establish Awareness.

Pillar 2: Enable Practice.

Pillar 3: Provide Knowledge in Context.

Interplay of Pillars. Figure 5.1 depicts the interplay of the three pillars with the problem areas, emphasizing their connection with empirical results presented in the previous chapters. Each pillar is rooted in two problem areas of the model of newcomers' testing skills and spans two problem areas. It supports newcomers in overcoming problems related to that problem area (e.g. problems related to a dismissive testing attitude, problems related to a lack of how-to-knowledge, ...). Together, they improve the newcomer's onboarding experience from different perspectives as stated by the problem areas.

The model of the newcomers' testing skills is based on the two empirical studies presented in chapter 4. The theoretical analysis of chapter 3 suggests that the educational

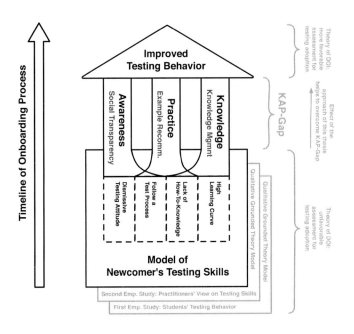

Figure 5.1: The 3-pillar approach of this thesis. Each pillar is tailored to specific problem areas of newcomer's testing skills, supported by empirical studies.

situation facilitates an emergence of a KAP-Gap and both empirical studies support this claim. According to Rogers' theory of Diffusion of Innovations, the innovation of systematic testing is assessed poorly by inexperienced developers at first. This situation can be found at the rectangle base below the pillars (also depicting the model of newcomers' testing skills). By applying the tripartite approach, this assessment of systematic testing improves, resulting in a situation where testing appears more attractive to inexperienced developers (triangle on top). Between the rectangle (starting situation) and the triangle (resulting situation) lies the KAP-Gap, which the tripartite approach supports newcomers in overcoming.

The chronological order of the onboarding process is depicted on the left: time flows from bottom to top. It represents the newcomer entering the onboarding process with their specific skills (and lack thereof) and application of each of the pillars. This ultimately results in an improved testing behavior of the newcomer.

Each pillar uses a certain strategy to improve the newcomer's testing behavior regarding their corresponding problem areas. Each such strategy is rooted in real-world

Table 5.2: The goals, strategies and implementations of the three pillars of this approach.

	Pillar 1: Establish Awareness	Pillar 2: Enable Practice	Pillar 3: Provide Knowledge in Context
Goal	overcome attitude-related barriers	overcome skill-related barriers	overcome knowledge gaps
Strategy	make team's testing culture visible, raise awareness	provide how-to-knowledge (implicit) at the right time	provide principles- and how-to-knowledge (explicit) at the right time
Implementation	increase social transparency, raise observability of testing activities	automatically recommend the right test code at the right time	operate knowledge base tied to running test code examples

experience from commercial practitioners who onboard newcomers and successful testing strategies found in open source development. These strategies are named in gray under the name of each pillar. Here, they are described only in a very high-level. They are explained more in-depth in their respective chapters 6, 7, and 8.

Even though these pillars separate concerns, they work in tandem and should be applied together. This delivers the best support to the newcomer regarding their testing skills. Application of one pillar alone may have a positive effect on one or two problem areas. However, not applying the other parts of this approach may leave the other problem areas without any improvement.

5.3.1 Interplay of Pillars

Each pillar stems from problem areas of newcomers' testing behavior. An overview of goals, strategies and implementations is given in Tab. 5.2.

Pillar 1: Establish Awareness. Inexperienced developers are prone to being deterred from systematic testing by having a dismissive attitude towards it (problem area 3) and have difficulties understanding the role of systematic testing in context of a commercial software engineering process (problem area 1). The goal of pillar 1 is to help newcomers in overcoming **attitude-related barriers** that hinder them in practicing systematic testing. The strategy of pillar 1 is to **make the team's testing culture prominently visible to the newcomer** by strategically **employing traits of social transparency**. A team's test interaction has several facets and different aspects of the team's testing culture are displayed. As a second-order effect this establishes an understanding of testing in commercial development.

Pillar 2: Enable Practice. Even if inexperienced developers sport a positive attitude towards practicing systematic testing, they often are not able to engage in it. Stemming from a lack of how-to-knowledge and hands-on experience, they struggle to produce test code in a commercial setting (problem area 2). The goal of pillar 2 is to support newcomers in overcoming such **skill-related barriers** to practicing systematic testing. The strategy of pillar 2 is to **provide the newcomer with concrete how-to-knowledge found in existing test code**. This lowers the barrier for implementing test code in a real-world setting for the newcomer and enables her to write her own test code. Pillar 2 implements this strategy by **automatically recommending the right test code to the newcomer at the right time**. The knowledge in test code is *implicit* as it has not been prepared for consumption by an inexperienced developer. However, it is suited to help newcomers in learning technicalities related to testing in a real-world setting.

Pillar 3: Provide Knowledge in Context. Awareness- and principles-knowledge conveyed in education is on a conceptual level and is not tailored to the specific situation that the newcomer meets at her first job. Inexperienced developers struggle to find learning material that is easily applicable to their situation (problem area 4). They are in need of further learning material that is *contextually relevant* and *applicable*. The goal of pillar 3 is to support the newcomer in **overcoming gaps in knowledge** that hinder her in engaging in test efforts. This enables the newcomer to solve testing issues herself and advance her testing skills in a self-directed manner, which makes her more independent of the mentor. The strategy of pillar 3 is to **provide the newcomer with actionable principles- and how-to-knowledge** when she needs it even though she may not be able to correctly formulate her need. Pillar 3 implements this strategy by **operating a contextually-sensitive knowledge base with runnable code examples**. It is tailored to the needs of an inexperienced developer and makes use of executable test code examples. The knowledge in this knowledge base is *explicit* as it is prepared for consumption by an inexperienced developer.

Overall Support Process. All three pillars are designed to enact their support of the newcomer in sequence (cf. Fig. 5.2). From pillar 1 to 3, they provide increasing clues and level of support and ideally the newcomer is enabled to write test code as early as possible. Pillar 1 ensures awareness for the testing culture and demand for systematic testing. For some newcomers, this is enough to increase testing activity. Other newcomers request help in actually writing test code and pillar 2 delivers concrete how-to knowledge in form of test code. Finally, pillar 3 helps to fill in deeper gaps in testing knowledge by providing both principles- and how-to-knowledge in form of test tutorials. This sequence of support is designed to handle most testing-related help requests by newcomers. Thereby, the mentor is relieved of certain mentoring duties. If all three strategies fail, however, the newcomer can still request help from the mentor.

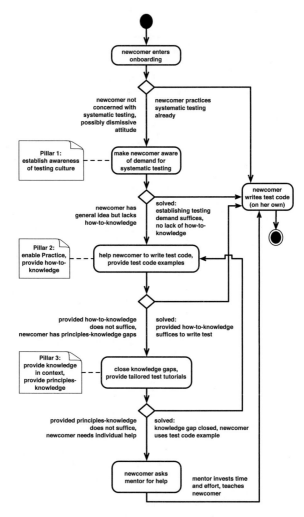

Figure 5.2: Sequence of support provided by the approach of this thesis.

6 Establish Awareness (Pillar 1)

The first part of the tripartite approach (pillar 1) is concerned with overcoming inhibiting problems related to a newcomer's attitude towards systematic testing.

Novices Have a Dismissive Testing Attitude. Following the analysis of chapter 3, the testing appears unattractive to novices when they are first introduced to it due to a heavy focus on principles-knowledge, little how-to-knowledge, and no project context. Even if a positive attitude is kept, the lack of how-to-knowledge and high complexity can frustrate inexperienced developers and turn their attitude negative.

Chapter 4 provides empirical data supporting this theoretical analysis: Generally, the willingness to write tests is low (both student and practitioner studies). Writing new and untested source code is awarded more importance than writing test code to maintain quality (both studies). Inexperienced developers would even like to neglect altogether, if possible (practitioner study). Occupying oneself with writing test code instead of new source code is perceived as being unproductive (student study). Already struggling to implement test code correctly (both studies), inexperienced developers cannot see the immediate benefits of testing (both) and are disappointed with the immediate failure-finding rate of test suites (student study). They perceive a high learning curve with testing methods and cannot find suitable learning materials (student study) which is discouraging and adds to a dismissive attitude. Ultimately, in education and engineered class-room exercises, inexperienced developers do not feel a motivating sense of accomplishment when writing tests and finding bugs (student study).

Consequences. A dismissive attitude hinders newcomers in engaging in test writing and leads to ignoring the practice of testing. Students and newcomers during onboarding alike tend to rely on unsystematic and manual testing and refrain from writing tests (both studies). This facilitates source code of low-quality, prolongs the onboarding process and increases the effort on the mentor: the mentor has to show the newcomer the benefits and costs of systematic and automatic testing.

6.1 Proposed Solution - Make Testing Culture Visible

Making the team's testing culture explicitly visible to her can influence the newcomers' testing attitude and engage her in more test writing. Pham et al.13 found supporting empirical evidence for this claim on a social coding site:

> **Finding:** When voluntary code contributors perceived the project's testing culture clearly, they were more inclined to engage in test writing (cf. chapter 11).

A social coding site has a high degree of social transparency, which makes team member's test actions visible to other users. This increases these users' willingness to write tests[1]. The strategy of pillar 1 is to *systematically leverage this effect and to transfer* it onto the onboarding situation for newcomers. Therefore, pillar 1 makes the team's testing culture explicitly and prominently visible to newcomers.

Strategy 1: Make the team's testing culture visible to the newcomer.

> **Tactic 1.1:** Convey *when* and *how often* other team members are engaging in testing efforts.

> **Tactic 1.2:** Convey *how much* other team members are engaging in test efforts.

The term 'testing culture' is broad and encompasses many different aspects. Making the team's testing culture visible should focus on conveying specific aspects of it. Therefore, strategy 1 is divided into two tactics. Each tactic focuses on raising the newcomer's awareness of one aspect of testing culture (*when and how often*, and *how much*).

Rationale for Strategy 1

The general idea of strategy 1 is to make the newcomer aware of the testing culture, overcome her negative attitude and trigger her to engage in test writing herself. Both theoretical arguments and empirical indicators support the underlying hypothesis:

> **Hypothesis 1:** *If the newcomer perceives the team's testing culture, she will more likely overcome her negative testing attitude and engage in test writing herself.*

Theoretical Argument. The effect seen on the social coding site (github.com) can be explained using DOI theory. By sporting a high degree of social transparency, every users' action is visible to other users, creating a *heightened observability* of testing efforts of team members. In the case of githum.com, this increase in observability of testing efforts is enough to raise github users' testing adoption.

Pillar 1 systematically raises the observability of testing for the newcomer: As discussed in chapter 3, systematic testing usually does not have high degree observability. Rogers associates a high degree of observability of an innovation with a higher adoption rate—employing strategy 1 will increases testing adoption by newcomers. The newcomer is reminded of the existence of systematic testing and made aware of the testing culture. She can observe her peers engaging in testing and being successful in doing it. This can influence the newcomer's attitude towards testing: making the newcomer more open towards systematic testing.

A social factor relating to making the testing culture visible is *normative behavior*. By making the testing culture visible, the newcomer can understand it as the normative

---

[1]This phenomenon is explained in more detail in section 6.2 below.

behavior of the team. This will make the newcomer try to adapt to this behavior: humans are social beings and generally have a need to adapt and act like the human beings around them in order to meet social norms [7]. This is also true for inexperienced newcomers joining a team of senior developers. The newcomer's goal is to quickly integrate into the team and to become a full member of the team.

Regarding software engineering, Singer proposes a process for improving the adoption of software engineering practices by developers [136]. For preventive innovations like testing, Singer introduces a pattern named *normative behavior*. This pattern suggests to make the social norm visible in order to appeal to the human need for acting according to a social norm. Even though the idea of strategy 1 was conceived independently of Singer's pattern, strategy 1 can be interpreted as a specialization of it. Singer's work supports the validity of hypothesis 1: Being made aware of the testing culture, developers tried to fit the normative behavior and improved their testing efforts. Strategy 1 is a systematic operationalization of this effect in the onboarding situation.

Empirical Indicator. In chapter 4.2, another empirical indicator for the validity of hypothesis 1 is presented.

> **Phenomenon:** Exposing the newcomer to a test-intensive environment greatly facilitates the adoption of test writing by the newcomer.

A newcomer who is introduced to a team that practices test writing will start to do so as well[2]. However, a newcomer introduced to a non-testing environment will not start to write tests on her own. Assuming that the newcomer must be able to *observe* the team's testing culture *somehow* for this effect to take place, the degree of *observability* becomes an important and supporting factor of test adoption by newcomers. In commercial software engineering, however, it is not clear *if* or *to what degree* observability of testing activity is given, especially from the viewpoint of an inexperienced newcomer. How can the newcomer perceive the testing efforts of other team members and get an understanding of the team's testing culture? Does it suffice to simply inform the newcomer of testing guidelines and rules or does she need to shadow senior developers writing test code? Furthermore, the development process, tooling (for example, the commit mechanism) and team interactions need to support it. As reported by practitioners in chapter 4.2, guidelines and wikis have a limited effect on newcomers, are difficult to maintain and outdate quickly. They grow too complex and difficult for newcomers quickly. Strategy 1 helps to achieve the aforementioned phenomenon in a more controlled manner.

Rationale for Tactic 1.1 and Tactic 1.2

Tactic 1.1 and 1.2 specify *how* the testing culture of a development team should be made visible to the newcomer. Both are rooted in problem areas 3 and 1, which are covered by pillar 1 (cf. Fig. 5.1 and Tab. 5.1).

---

[2]In an online questionnaire, active practitioners agreed or disagreed with the statement "When new hires are put in a team with developers who write tests, they will start testing quickly.". The majority (451 / 67%) of 676 participants agreed with the statement (cf. chapter 4.2).

Frequency. Tactic 1.1 focuses on making the point in time (e.g. in the development process) and frequency of testing activities observable to the newcomer: *when* and *how often* senior developers engage in testing. Problem area 1 states that newcomers have difficulties with following a commercial test process and that they struggle to find the best moment to start engaging in systematic testing. The application under tests perpetually appears 'too fuzzy' (unfinished) to begin testing while newcomers want to avoid test maintenance. They do not keep systematic testing in mind when they are busy developing and only think of testing as an afterthought. Tactic 1.1 supports the newcomer in overcoming problems of problem area 1. Showing the newcomer when others are beginning to write tests can help her in deciding to write tests earlier. Observing the frequency with which other team members engage in writing tests can help the newcomer in adopting a similar testing frequency. This way, the newcomer is supported in following the seniors' test behavior and the team's test process.

Quantity. Tactic 1.2 focuses on making other team members' test effort quantifiable: *how much* other developers engage in testing. Problem area 3 states that newcomers often sport a dismissive testing attitude, which is a barrier to adoption of systematic testing. Newcomers are seldom convinced of the benefits of systematic testing. Testing is seen as of secondary importance to implementing and systematic testing appears unproductive to them. Tactic 1.2 supports the newcomer in overcoming problems of problem area 3. Showing newcomers how much effort can convince the newcomer of the importance of systematic testing and its role in commercial software engineering. For example, effort could be measured in working time spent on writing and executing tests vs. time spent on writing actual new source code.

6.2 Effects of Social Transparency on Testing Behavior

In chapter 11, an empirical study about the testing behavior on a social coding site is presented. This study influenced the design of the approach of this thesis and its most influential finding is presented here.

> **Finding:** A highly visible testing culture has positive effects on testing behavior on the social coding site.

On the social coding site github.com, users can collaborate on software projects on a voluntary basis. Project owners create software repositories and other users can offer them changes to these projects, becoming so-called contributors. Github.com calls itself a *social coding site* and mixes many traits of social media sites and offers a high degree of social transparency: A user's actions and artifacts, such as discussions, commits, code snippets, are highly visible to other users. This has an influence on users' test behavior.

As a project owner, a common strategy of getting contributors to write tests was to make it more obvious that systematic testing was a customary in a project. The ways of making the contributor aware of this ranged from active demands (e.g. setting up rules and guidelines) to passive but implying signals. Such passive signals could be artifacts produced when testing or information about testing activities in the project. For example, contributors were more inclined to write tests if they saw that there were already written tests in the project's test suite.[3]

Other such signals of testing culture were more implicit: Just seeing a badge declaring the use of a CI-Service on the project's profile site made contributors aware of the project's testing culture—and subsequently made them write more tests.[4]

The effect of communicating a demand for tests became clear if it was omitted altogether: If there was no clear demand for tests, no guideline or no sign for testing activities given in the project, contributors would simply not engage in testing. They would simply assume a non-existent testing culture.

6.3 Possible Solutions

There are easy-to-install and low-effort strategies that are aimed at supporting newcomer in overcoming a negative testing attitude and adopt the team's testing culture. However, practitioners remain dissatisfied with the current situation (cf. chapter 4.2). The approach of this thesis is designed to support the existing strategies and complement them—not to replace them completely.

One strategy is to make written tests mandatory for each commit, rejecting commits without tests. After several failed attempts to commit test-less production code, this would certainly give the newcomer the understanding that commits need to be accompanied with tests. However, it is not clear if this approach actually helps the newcomer to consider systematic testing *during* development of source code. Giving early regard to later test efforts can positively influence software architectural decisions and improve testability of components. Being reminded about missing tests *after* implementing, the newcomer misses out on these benefits. Furthermore, this strategy does not improve on the feeling of test writing being unproductive work (problem area 3). Here, strategy 1 acts as a reminder about systematic testing *while* developing. Also, strategy 1 has the potential to make the important role of systematic testing in a commercial development process clearer to the newcomer.

Another common strategy is to make the demand for written tests clear by setting up rules and guidelines and documentation about it. Providing access to test documentation and guidelines for testing is an important first step in communicating a team's testing culture. In open source development, guidelines and documentation on testing reduce a contributor's uncertainty on whether or not and how to provide tests with new contributions (cf. chapter 11). Similarly, practitioners report that test documentation and guidelines help newcomers to better orientate themselves and helped them understand the test process better (cf. chapter 4.2). However, practitioners also

---

[3]Surveying the statement 'When I see that there are tests in a project, I will also include tests in my pull request.', the majority of 499 active users agreed or strongly agreed.

[4]In an online questionnaire, we asked active github users to agree or disagree with the statement "When I see that there are tests in a project, I will also include test in my pull request". The vast majority of 499 users agreed with it (cf. chapter 11).

point out problems with test documentation and guidelines during onboarding: The newcomer needs to be told about the documentation and gain access to it. In the buzz of day-to-day business, this can be forgotten, leaving the newcomer without crucial information. Furthermore, documentation needs to be written with newcomers in mind and needs to be easily understandable. Practitioners report on problematic documentation that simply was overwhelming, its information not easily retrievable. Also, such testing documentation needs to be kept up-to-date regularly. It is not clear whether reading test documentation and guidelines can alleviate the newcomer's demotivation to test, rooted in never having felt accomplished when testing or being frustrated with it (problem area 3).

7 Enable Technical Adoption (Pillar 2)

While strategy 1 overcomes attitude-related causes, adoption and implementation of the team's testing culture are further hindered by *skill-related* causes: to a newcomer, the technical barrier for writing test code is high. Even though newcomers are knowledgeable about testing in theory, they often have problems actually implementing and applying this knowledge in a real-world situation.

Writing test code is difficult and demands concrete how-to-knowledge. Besides knowing *what* to test (designing the test case, using principles-knowledge), the developer needs to know *how* to automate it (problem area 2). In practice, this encompasses:

- awareness-knowledge of the existence of features of the test framework (for example, JUnit's assert-function or the headless-browser feature),

- principles-knowledge on applying test techniques in a real-world situation.

- how-to-knowledge on how to use these features correctly (e.g. how to invoke and control a headless browser),

For newcomers, the last point is especially hard: testing techniques learnt in an educational environment may not be transferrable to a real-world development environment without effort. Newcomers have a theoretical understanding of test techniques but lack how-to-knowledge and contextual information for implementing them[1]. They have only written tests in a class-room setting with engineered class-room examples. However, actually writing tests in a commercial software development demands practical and technical skills that the newcomer has not come in touch with yet.

Newcomers lack Technical Testing Ability. When newcomers join the workforce, they exhibit a testing behavior that suggests that they are hitting a technical barrier (problem area 2). When they *do* write tests, their test writing skills appear to be limited to more simple and contained test techniques (students and practitioner studies). Newcomers often are only able to write unit tests, omitting more complex test types, such as system or integration tests (practitioner study)[2]. According to practitioners, most newcomers have trouble applying their theoretical testing knowledge to write test code for a commercial project. They do have a general idea about testing, but do

---

[1]For example, correctly implementing clean test setups or tear downs demands how-to-knowledge. Then, finding and providing test-data to a new test case demands contextual information such as knowledge of how to connect to the test-server of the company.

[2]Surveying the statement 'When new hires *do* write tests, they are limited to unit testing', 363 (53%) of 681 practitioners agreed or agreed strongly.

not know *what* and *how* to test it in a real-world setting (both studies). Students feel overwhelmed by *actually* writing tests in a real project (student study).

Consequences. If the newcomer is not supported in writing test code during onboarding, several short- and long-term effects arise.

- Short-term effect: Her testing skills (limited usage of test framework's features, mocking, etc) will limit the power and scope of the test code she writes. This could lead to degrading the quality of the test suite with low-quality test code.

- Short-term effect: Having to overcome the technical barrier of writing test code in a real-world setting by herself will slow down her progress during onboarding. This will prolong the onboarding process.

- Long-term effect: not being able to overcome the technical barrier, she may refrain from writing test code. This can lead to not adopting the team's testing culture and hinder her progress in becoming a proficient software developer.

7.1 Proposed Solution - Provide Existing Test Code

For overcoming the lack of how-to-knowledge, pillar 2 provides the newcomer with *existing* test code in a *contextually-sensitive* way.

Strategy 2: Provide existing test code to the newcomer.

    Tactic 2.1: Provide test code that is *executable* (runnable) in the newcomer's situation.

    Tactic 2.2: Provide test code that is *suited* to be used as a basis for adaption.

Rationale for Strategy 2

Newcomers suffer from a lack of exposure to real-world testing (how-to-knowledge) and during onboarding they have to catch up quickly. Exposing them to test code written by other developers can help them in writing their own test code:

Hypothesis 2: Providing existing test code to the newcomer will help the newcomer to write test code and increase her test code writing activity.

Empirical Indicator. Studying the testing behavior on a social coding site (cf. chapter 11), empirical data displaying the positive effects of existing test code and supporting hypothesis 2 emerged: Similar to onboarding newcomers, volunteering contributors joining a new open source project also face a technical barrier when writing test code: new contributors have to grasp the prevailing testing culture quickly in order to have their contribution accepted by the project owner. Access to existing test code immensely helps these new contributors in overcoming the technical barrier of writing test code: Project owners report a steep increase in number of delivered tests when they provided accessible test code in their projects[3]. This increase suggests that the existing tests play a role in supporting the contributors in writing tests of their own. Contributors report to use existing test code as a source for education—they actively seek written tests and learn from it. Surveying the statement 'Existing tests help me in understanding how to test in a specific project.', the majority of 499 active users agreed or strongly agreed (cf. chapter 11). Similarly, project owners report that the existence of written tests lowers the number of support requests—indicating that contributors learn from existing test code on their own[4]. Ultimately, contributors *rely* on these existing tests to write their own tests: they copy & paste a similar test and adapt it to their own needs[5]. Copying and adapting considerably lowers the barrier to write tests.

Rationale for Tactic 2.1   Inexperienced developers are easily be sidetracked by high a transfer-effort regarding the application of tutorials. When they are looking for tutorials for solving technical issues, having to transfer these technical implementations to their own situation makes application of that tutorial more difficult. The effort of having to technically change the suggestions of the tutorial to fit one's own demands can add to the feeling of being overwhelmed. Providing the newcomer with educational material that is *directly applicable and executable without changes* may increase the newcomer's confidence and make its application easier. The underlying hypothesis is:

> **Hypothesis 2.1:** *Providing the newcomer with examples that are* directly executable *supports the newcomer in writing their own tests.*

If the example provided to the newcomer is directly executable, the newcomer does not have to go through the additional step of transferring the technicalities of that solution to her own situation (applying a solution written in C to a test code written in Java). The less technical transfer effort such an educational material demands from a newcomer, the easier it is for her to apply it to her individual coding situation. Being provided with runnable test examples, the newcomer can quickly execute these examples and observe their results. Additionally, the newcomer can begin to make changes to these examples straightaway and observe the effects of these changes. This should make adapting these examples for her own test easier. This is not immediately possible with educational material that is not directly executable for the newcomer.

Rationale for Tactic 2.2   Inexperienced developers feel overwhelmed when confronted with actually writing tests. Having to scout a whole test suite for a suitable test to use as an example can be daunting and overtaxing to a newcomer. The newcomer usually

---

[3]The majority of 452 users agreed or strongly agreed to 'As a consequence of providing tests in my project, more pull requests include tests.'.

[4]The majority of 457 users agreed or strongly agreed to 'When I have tests in my project, contributors need less help in writing tests.'.

[5]Surveying the statement 'I use existing tests as a basis for my own tests: I copy and paste them and adjust them accordingly.', the majority of 496 users agreed or strongly agreed.

does not know what kind of test to look for. Helping the newcomer in finding the best suited test code for her coding situation supports her in writing tests of her own. Here, the hypothesis is:

Hypothesis 2.2: *Pre-selecting the example according to the newcomer's specific coding situation supports the her in writing tests.*

Pre-selecting test code removes a barrier for the newcomer: she does not have to search the best test code example on her own, making the process of starting to write a test less effortful. In the case of github.com, contributors often had to find suitable examples of test code themselves. However, project owners specifically helped contributors in finding best suited test codes by pointing them out in the test suite (cf. chapter 11).

7.2 Possible Solutions

Practitioners have devised different coping strategies to help a newcomer learn how to write tests quickly. Active strategies and high-effort strategies such as actively teaching the newcomer are discussed in section 4.2.2. This section focuses on low-effort strategies. The strategy proposed in this section is not meant to replace the existing strategies but is meant to complement them as an alternative.

Providing the newcomer with learning material on how to test in the company helps the newcomer. However, providing such documentation has benefits and disadvantages. It becomes outdated quickly, needs to be written in such a manner that the newcomer can understand it and it needs to be well-organized. Even if this documentation fulfills these requirements, it can still add to the newcomer's feeling of being overwhelmed.

Another educational source on how to write tests in the new team is the existing test code itself. Written test code is an artifact of very practical testing knowledge and it can act as a source for education. It disseminates the team's testing culture and is a practical example of 'how the team writes tests'. Studying the *right* test code at the *right* time helps to facilitate the following changes in the newcomer:

- she can learn about test framework features that she did not know about and she can learn how to use them.

- she can learn how testing techniques are applied in a real-world setting.

- she can observe how senior developers approach test design and test automation.

For a newcomer, *undirected* to a big test suite access is problematic: As she is inexperienced in handling test code and may have a hard time defining what she is looking for, ending up with non-applicable test code. Test suites can grow to considerable sizes, having to search through a big amount of test code is an additional barrier and can be daunting for a newcomer. This can add to the feeling of being overwhelmed. In this sense, just granting the newcomer access to a test-suite is less beneficial than to provide guided access (e.g. the right test code at the right time).

8 Provide Knowledge in Context (Pillar 3)

Strategy 1 of the tripartite approach focuses on *attitude-related barriers* to test adoption, establishing an awareness for the development team's testing culture (pillar 1). Strategy 2 provides the newcomer with very practical how-to-knowledge through test code recommendation and supports her in overcoming *skill-related barriers* to test adoption (pillar 2). The third and last part focuses on *overcoming gaps in testing knowledge* that keep the newcomer from engaging in systematic testing (problem area 4). Its goal is to provide missing awareness- and principles-knowledge to the newcomer when she needs it—even though she may not be able to correctly formulate her need. Problem area 4 states that inexperienced developers struggle to find learning materials that is easily applicable to their situation. They are in need of learning material that is *contextually relevant* and *applicable*.

Theoretical Claims. Chapter 3 presents a theoretical explanation for the emergence of problem area 4:

- focus on awareness- and principles-knowledge first and on how-to-knowledge second, and

- lecturers have limited time at their hands to convey a multitude of software engineering topics.

Not every testing-related topic is covered in-depth in lectures, but rather a selection of basic techniques. This way, for example, simpler techniques, such as Java's JUnit-assertion framework is covered while its Robot-GUI-automation framework is not. This leaves students with gaps in testing-related awareness- and principles-knowledge. Awareness- and principles-knowledge conveyed in education is on a conceptual level and is not tailored to the concrete situation that the newcomer meets at her first job. Gaps in knowledge form naturally over time and students do not memorize every topic in class perfectly.

Empirical Indicators. Both students and newcomers display gaps in testing knowledge (both student and practitioner study). They appear to be limited to using the unit testing (e.g. JUnit-framework) while higher testing forms are left out, such as system or integration tests (both studies). They are in need of further information on these testing topics when being asked to engage in testing in a real-world situation (both studies). However, students have problems finding suitable and applicable tutorials for their specific situation that helps them to start writing tests (student study). They perceive a high learning curve for applying tutorials found online (students study). This perceived high complexity is enough to stop their efforts in systematic testing altogether. They give up on test automation and proceed to test it manually (student study). Automated GUI testing is an example of a testing technique that students regard as ominous and hard and cannot find suitable tutorials online.

Consequences. The consequences of these gaps in knowledge and the unresolved need for applicable educational material are manifold. Newcomers stop their engagement in test automation, giving up on it and reverting to laborious and monotone manual testing. A short term effect of this is that development of the current application is slowed down. Ultimately, this hinders the newcomer's progress to become a high-quality engineer. In other instances, the newcomer has to ask the mentor for support and explanation of a particular testing technique and how to apply it in the specific project situation and configuration. This puts more load on the mentor and prolongs the onboarding process. However, as stated in the second empirical study in chapter 4.2, newcomers are sometimes intimated to take up the mentor's time.

The goal of pillar 3 is to support the newcomer in overcoming gaps in knowledge that hinder her in engaging in test efforts. This enables the newcomer to solve testing issues herself and advance her testing skills in a self-directed manner. This makes her more independent of the mentor and lessens the onboarding effort for the mentor.

8.1 Proposed Solution - Provide Applicable Learning Materials

Strategy 3 provides the newcomer with *actionable principles-* and *how-to-knowledge* when she needs it—even though she may not be able to correctly formulate her need.

> ***Strategy 3: Provide the newcomer with principles- and how-to-knowledge of testing techniques when she needs it.***
>
> **Tactic 3.1:** Provide tutorials on testing topics to the newcomer that are understandable and applicable by newcomers.
>
> **Tactic 3.2:** Make these tutorials easily accessible and contextually-sensitive recommend them to the newcomer automatically.
>
> **Tactic 3.3:** Connect these tutorials with runnable test code examples and vice versa.

Rationale for Strategy 3 and its Tactics

Strategy 3 is directly influenced by the problems described by problem area 4 and the empirical findings underpinning it (cf. introduction to this chapter). Students and newcomers have gaps in testing knowledge and are in need of further educational material. Strategy 3 tries to provide said material and close these gaps.

These tutorials need to be designed with newcomers in mind (tactic 3.1): Inexperienced developers are easily deterred by a perceived high complexity. If they feel that the testing topic is too complicated, they will abandon it.

Tactic 3.2 proposes a recommendation system for tutorials on testing topics: inexperienced developers have difficulties finding educational material on their own (for example, tutorials on GUI testing online). They may even struggle to word their need correctly as they lack awareness-knowledge of a certain testing technique: for example, if they have never heard of automated GUI testing before, it is harder to look for such tutorials. When the newcomer changes or adds code that warrants a certain test automation, the system recommends the associated testing tutorial automatically. For example, when the newcomer changes GUI code, the system can push a tutorial on GUI automation to the newcomer. This way, the inexperienced developer is informed about a testing technique independently of the state of her testing knowledge.

Lastly, tactic 3.3 demands the use and inclusion of runnable test code in the tutorial material. As argued in the rationale for strategy 2 (cf. chapter 4), access to runnable test code supports engagement in test writing. In this case, newcomers can directly run the tutorial test code and use it as a basis for their own test code. Also, they can start to modify it and observe associated effects easily. This will lower the perceived complexity of the testing tutorial, provide concrete how-to-knowledge and newcomers can start quickly.

8.2 Possible Solutions

The strategy of Pillar 3 proposes to operate a contextually-sensitive and newcomer-tailored knowledge base that employs runnable code examples and uses an automatic recommendation system. In practice, there are already strategies and methods in use that thrive to provide the newcomer with testing knowledge, such as wikis and in-house tutorial databases. Strategy 3 does not mean to disrupt these strategies but rather to complement them as they have certain shortcomings.

In practice, practitioners often use information wikis for knowledge transfer and point the newcomer to it. However, it is unclear whether or not these wikis are written with newcomers in mind, providing enough principles- and how-to-knowledge to facilitate understanding while not being overwhelmingly complex. Wikis and other platforms deprecate and can be hard to understand if they are written too technical. Then, the barrier for a newcomer to use it is too high. Additionally, these wikis are usually passive systems that do not prompt the user to do anything. For example, the newcomer must be pointed to it (gain access) and it will not recommend itself to the newcomer. If this first access step fails, the newcomer is without support. Here, strategy 3 proposes a self-acting recommendation system that "nudges" the newcomer to access it (contextually sensitive automatic recommendation).

At first glance, it may seem that pillar 2 and pillar 3 of the approach of this thesis both provide 'educational material' that the newcomer can learn or copy from. Pillar 2 and pillar 3, however, satisfy different needs: Pillar 2 provides access to very practical how-to-knowledge, which is very *implicit* and technical. It is embedded in the real-world test code recommendations and it is not curated for consumption by the newcomer on a general principles level. It is rather designed to help the newcomer in overcoming hindering technicalities when writing test code. Pillar 3, on the other hand, specializes in gaps of principles-knowledge. This is useful when the provided how-to-knowledge delivered by pillar 2 is not sufficient to engage the newcomer writing test code. For example, seeing real-world test code, the newcomer may still have questions about the underlying principles of the test technique used in these test code recommendations and how to apply it to her situation. In these cases, the newcomer can use the tutorial recommendation proposed by strategy 3 and gain explicit principles-knowledge. Similar to pillar 2, the strategy of pillar 3 uses runnable, real-world test code in order to provide technical how-to-knowledge. This lowers the barrier for applying the new technique for the newcomer.

8.3 Implementation Proposal

In contrast to pillar 1 and pillar 2, the strategy of pillar 3 is not implemented in a tool in the scope of this thesis due to time constraints. Instead, this section offers a concrete proposal on how to realize pillar 3 and emphasizes the interplay of pillar 2 and pillar 3: pillar 2 supports the newcomer with test code first and pillar 3 takes over with more in-depth test tutorials when these test code examples fail to help the newcomer in writing test code. This section details the setup and usage process of the so-called *test tutorial base* which implements strategy 3.

8.3.1 Setup of the Test Tutorial Base

In commercial development, a *test suite* is a collection of automated tests. Usually, these automated tests are implemented as test code (for example, Java methods with the attribute `@test`) in specific test classes. The approach of this thesis primarily deals with these test codes (test methods) and not with the encompassing test classes.

Strategy 3 demands the introduction of a *test tutorial base* which collects all *test tutorials*. A test tutorial presents and explains one test technique and is similar to a wiki page. Fig. 8.1 shows a mockup of a test tutorial. However, strategy 3 and its tactics demand the certain differences to a usual wiki page. The relationship between all following constructs are documented in the class diagram shown in Fig. 8.2.

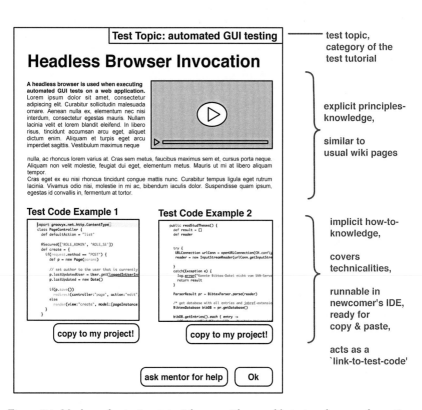

Figure 8.1: Mockup of a testing tutorial page with runnable test code examples acting as a "link-to-test-code".

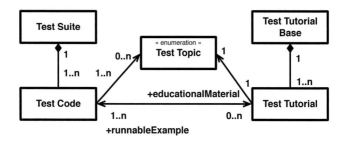

Figure 8.2: Class diagram for the proposed test tutorial base.

Test Tutorials for Newcomers. *Test tutorials* are written for newcomers and with newcomers in mind and are adapted to their skill- and knowledge-level (tactic 3.1). It is important that test tutorials are applicable to the newcomer's project setting: the test techniques described in the test tutorials are actually applied in the newcomer's project and the test code provided in the test tutorial is actually runnable in the newcomer's project—without changes to the test code example. This ensures a low barrier for application of the presented test technique for the newcomer ("click, copy, and apply"). Test tutorials may be written specifically for the newcomer's project setting—if this project's test setting similar across the company's projects, they may be used company wide.

Runnable Test Code Examples. Each test tutorial has at least one example of the presented test technique as *runnable test code* (tactic 3.3).

Link From Test Codes to Test Tutorials and Vice Versa. There is a link between test codes and test tutorials (tactic 3.3). Test codes are categorized by *test topic*. A test topic is a very short description of a test technique. If a test code is associated with a test topic, it means that this test code is suitable to be used as an example for the associated test topic (e.g. the test technique). One test code can be associated with more than one test topic.

Not every test code must be associated with a test topic. For example, when the approach of this thesis is applied to legacy systems, the categorization of test codes into test topic categories can be laborious and may not be fully completed. However, a high ratio of categorized test codes vs. uncategorized test codes supports the effectiveness of supporting the newcomer as the newcomer has more opportunities to gain more in-depth principles-knowledge about a certain test code. What categorization ratio is necessary to for this test tutorial base to gain enough traction needs to be evaluated in future research. As a starting point, a ratio of 50% is recommended. This way, when the strategy 2 recommends a test code to the newcomer, the newcomer is enabled to jump to a more in-depth explanation of this test code (which only provides implicit knowledge) and gain

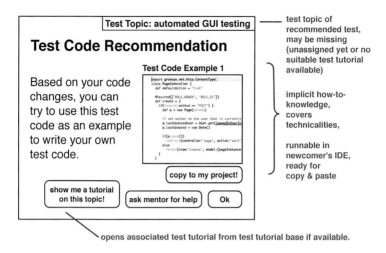

Figure 8.3: Mockup of the test code recommendation window with a test topic and button to request a test tutorial. Pressing the button "show me a tutorial on this topic!" opens up the window shown in Fig. 8.1.

explicit principles-knowledge. Also, as each test tutorial has runnable code examples, there is a "back-link" from principles-knowledge to concrete how-to-knowledge.

For example, the test code example in Fig. 8.3 is a runnable example of how to invoke a headless browser for GUI automation in web application development. In the newcomer's project, the testing technique of automated GUI testing is realized through browser automation, therefore this test code is associated with the test topic "automated GUI testing". Additionally, it depicts how to do a proper test setup and test tear down and is associated with the test topic "test setup and tear down". However, this second test topic association is not pictured in Fig. 8.3 in order to keep the figure focused.

Relying on Pillar 2 to Realize Contextually-Sensitive Test Tutorial Recommendations. Tactic 3.2 demands that the test tutorial is recommended to the newcomer in a *contextually-sensitive* manner. This means that the newcomer is recommended just the *right* test tutorial at the *right time*. Assuming that the test code (and associated in-depth test tutorial) needed in a certain situation is dependent on the changes made to the source code, this requires knowledge of the code changes that the newcomer has made in order to infer the best suited test topic and test tutorial. Strategy 2 of pillar 2 already demands something similar (contextually-sensitive recommendation of test code): Newcomers are inexperienced and have trouble formulating their needs correctly, therefore contextually-sensitive recommendation seems suitable. When implementing strategy 3, the test tutorial base can "piggyback" on the implementation of strategy 2^1. Whenever the newcomer is recommended a test code (sensitive to the changes she made to the source code), the system can additionally recommend an associated test tutorial—or at least provide means to access it easily. This reflects how pillar 2 and pillar 3 are intertwined: pillar 2 provides implicit knowledge and pillar 3 provides further explicit in-depth knowledge. Pillar 3 takes over when pillar 2 does not suffice: When the newcomer studies the recommended test code but still has questions regarding the underlying principle of the respective test technique before applying it to her situation, she can request the corresponding test tutorial. Fig. 5.2, p. 82, depicts this interplay between pillar 2 and pillar 3, including pillar 1.

8.3.2 Usage Process for the Tutorial Base

This section describes how the test tutorial base should be used in the onboarding phase and what its setup process and maintenance process look like.

Using the Test Tutorial Base During Onboarding Phase. The process of using the test tutorial base is depicted in Fig. 8.4. 8.2. As the implementation of strategy 3 relies on the use of test code recommendation (pillar 2), the process step of test code recommendation is included in this process. However, if the test code recommendation is successful in supporting the newcomer in writing new test code, the use of the test tutorial base is mostly skipped: the new test code is categorized with a test topic from the list of available test topics and thusly connected to a test tutorial in the test tutorial base^2.

If, however, the recommended test code and the implicit how-to-knowledge within is not sufficient for the newcomer to write new test code, a need for further information arises in the newcomer and she begins to look for help. At this point, the test tutorial system can recommend a test tutorial based on the test code recommendation: the newcomer can jump from the recommended test code to a more in-depth test tutorial with the click of a button in the test recommendation window (button: "show me a test tutorial on this topic"). Fig. 8.3 shows a mockup of a test code recommendation window with a test topic in the upper right and button to request a test tutorial at the lower left.

This test tutorial explains underlying principles (provides principles-knowledge) and demonstrates how to implement them using the concrete test code example (which provides how-to-knowledge). The newcomer studies this tutorial and uses the test code example within to write her own test. Lastly, this new test code is attributed with a test topic and thusly connected with a test tutorial.

---

[1]An example of the implementation of strategy 2 and how the *right* test code is recommended at the *right* time is given in chapter 10.

[2]Not modeled in Fig. 8.4: The lack of a suitable test topic in the list of test topics indicates that the test topic of the new test code has not been covered by a test tutorial yet. In this case, the respective test tutorial needs to be written by the mentor first and attributed with said test topic second.

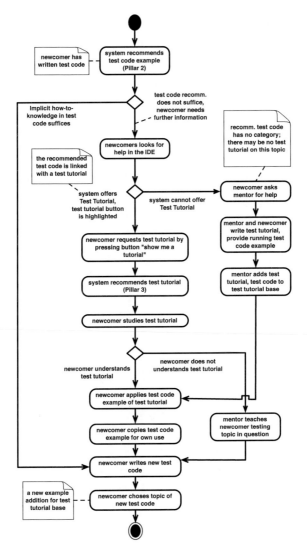

Figure 8.4: Process of using Test Tutorials, strategy 3 of pillar 3.

If the system is not able to provide a test tutorial for a given test code example, the newcomer will have to ask the mentor for help. This situation may arise for two reasons:

- The recommended test code is not attributed with a test topic, however, there is a suitable test tutorial in the test tutorial base. The mentor will attribute the recommended test code with said test topic and advise the newcomer to study said test tutorial. This is not modeled in Fig. 8.4 due to space limitations and distraction from the main scenario.

- The recommended test code is not attributed with a test topic and there is no suitable test tutorial in the test tutorial base. The mentor will write a suitable test tutorial together with the newcomer.

Setup and Maintenance of the Test Tutorial Base. The test tutorial base relies on a link between test codes in the test suite and test tutorials. This link is realized by categorizing the test codes into test topics. Together with actually producing (writing) the test tutorials, this categorization is a manual task[3]. These two tasks dominate the setup and maintenance process for running the test tutorial base. Fig. 8.5 shows the setup and maintenance process in an activity diagram.

Setup. Existing test codes need to be categorized into test topics. This is a manual task which can be done by the mentor of the newcomer or any other team member. Outsourcing of this task is also possible. Not all of the existing test codes need to be categorized, however, the more test codes are categorized, the more effective the test tutorial recommendation system can help the newcomer.

Setup. For each used test topic, one test tutorial must be written. Again, this is a manual task which can be done by the mentor or any other team member.

Normal use. The newcomer enters the onboarding process, begins to write source code and requires test code examples (pillar 2). When she is recommended a test code example which has a test topic, she can request the corresponding test tutorial and (hopefully) use it to write her own test code.

Maintenance. If the newcomer is not able to write her own test code after studying the recommended test code example and the associated test tutorial, she will ask the mentor for help. This is a signal that the test tutorial is in a state unsuited for supporting newcomers during onboarding[4]. The mentor revisits the test tutorial and updates it accordingly. This way, test tutorials are maintained every time a newcomer is not able to write her own test code—with the help of a test tutorial.

---

[3]Automation of these tasks may be possible. This, however, is outside of the scope of this thesis.

[4]This state may be reached two different ways: The test tutorial was not suited for newcomers' needs to begin with. Or it may have grown deprecated, for example because of a change of technologies in the company. One scenario could be: the company switched from headless browser GUI testing to a capture-replay-technology which demands visible GUI elements.

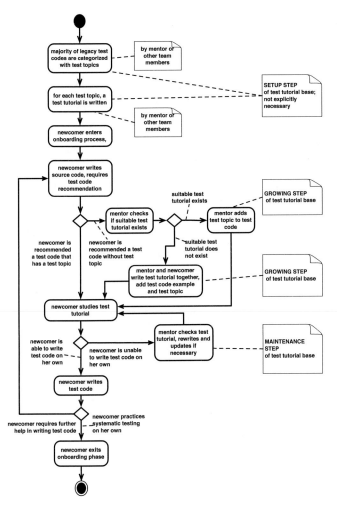

Figure 8.5: The setup, normal use and maintenance process of the test tutorial base.

Growing the test tutorial base. If the newcomer is recommended a test code example, which is uncategorized (no test topic attributed), the newcomer will ask the mentor for help. The mentor will then check if the test tutorial base contains a suitable test tutorial for this particular test code example—and if so, categorize it accordingly. This situation may arise because the setup stage does not require every test code to be categorized. Adding this link, the test tutorial base grows in recommendation power: the next time this test code example is recommended to a newcomer, she will not have to bother the mentor with it.

If the mentor cannot find a suitable test tutorial, she and the newcomer will write a new test tutorial. This test topic has not been covered in the test tutorial and succeeding newcomers may come to develop similar questions. Adding a test tutorial at this point can help to reduce mentoring effort in the future. This way, the test tutorial base grows every time the newcomer asks the mentor for help.

The usage and maintenance process of the test tutorial base is designed to grow and maintain test tutorials on every "question-event" triggered by the newcomer. This assures that the most used test tutorials are kept accessible and understandable by the current and succeeding newcomers. This is desirable as a high barrier for understanding and applying test-related tutorials (as found online) keeps inexperienced developers from engaging in systematic testing (cf. student study in chapter 4.1). Additionally, this update mechanism entails that the tutorial base could (theoretically) be used without any explicit setup steps. In this case, every test code recommendation (which would be without test topic and without test tutorial) could trigger a "question-event" and test topics would be written in a more ad-hoc manner *during* this onboarding process. This, however, carries the danger of slowing down this newcomer's onboarding process.

9 Implementation and Evaluation of Pillar 1

The findings presented in this chapter have been published in a study titled 'Communicating Software Testing Culture through Visualizing Testing Activity' [121]. In this thesis, these findings are presented in a more concise manner. The original study was conducted by Raphael Pham, Jonas Mörschbach, and Kurt Schneider. This research team is subsequently called Pham et al. 2015a. In 2015, Raphael Pham presented the original study at the 7th International Workshop on Social Software Engineering (SSE) in Bergamo, Italy. This original study was based on the Master's thesis of Jonas Mörschbach [111], which Raphael Pham proposed and supervised.

This study is a concrete implementation the strategy proposed in chapter 6 (strategy 1, p. 84). Pham et al. 2015a make the team's testing culture visible by strategically employing traits of social transparency: They introduce six dashboard-like monitors for other team members' testing activity into the novice's IDE and prominently display how senior developers are testing. These monitors are called *testing displays*.

9.1 Testing Displays Approach

Strategy 1 of pillar 1 suggests to make team's testing culture visible to the newcomer in order to engage her in test writing (cf. p. 84). Pham et al. 2015a tentatively define a visible cue of testing activity in a project as *testing signal*.

> **Definition** *A testing signal* is a visible cue that communicates the prevailing testing culture of the development team and that is perceivable for an inexperienced developer in her working environment.

Testing signals can be artifacts that are directly produced when practicing systematic testing, such as a test suite. However, other, more indirectly produced artifacts can also act as a testing signal. For example, on github.com the aforementioned CI-badge is not a directly necessary artifact of engaging in continuous integration with systematic testing—still it communicates that the concerned project practices systematic testing (cf. sec 6.2). Pham et al. 2015a strategically employ social transparency to realize strategy 1 of pillar 1 (making the team's testing culture visible). Their goal is to achieve similar test-related effects.

> **Goal:** Making the newcomer aware of the testing activities around her and increasing her own test activity by increasing the visibility of testing efforts through strategically placing testing signals.

9.1.1 Research Process

Pham et al. 2015a conducted a three phase research process for engineering testing signals. The first two rounds were concerned with analyzing and finding current testing signals in open source environments and in commercial IDEs. Equipped with knowledge of the current state of testing signals, the researchers used these insights as a basis to engineer testing signals suitable for controlled and commercial use, called *testing displays*. The last phase included evaluation rounds for these testing displays.

Phase 1: Analyzing Testing Signals in Open Source. As a first step, Pham et al. 2015a sought to get a better understanding of the nature of testing signals. To this end, they re-analyzed the data from the study[1] that first uncovered testing signals and the effect of a heightened social transparency [122]. Their research question was: "What perceivable displays influenced the testing behavior of voluntary contributors?". Additionally, they studied 15 new popular github projects. The researchers looked for signs and artifacts of testing activities that were already present on github's project interface per default. As such, they were easily visible to contributors and inexperienced developers. The researchers curated a preliminary list of testing signals that could be perceived by an novice developer and that could potentially lead to more test writing. The list includes a CI-Badge, a test-folder and test-files in the project tree, and documentation about the project's test process.

Phase 2: Analyzing Testing Signals in Commercial IDEs. As a second step, Pham et al. 2015a sought to get an understanding of the visibility of testing signals in modern IDEs (Eclipse, IntelliJ, MS Visual Studio). The researchers analyzed what testing signals were already present and easily visible per default. They took the point of view of an inexperienced software developer. All IDEs provide specific views for systematic testing. These views are separate from the main development workflow. In fact, all IDEs allow an inexperienced user to implement a software project without touching these test views at all. These views are designed to be accessed *when the developer has already decided* on writing automated tests. This, however, is problematic when an inexperienced developer does not want to practice systematic testing or ignores it.

Phase 3: Engineering Testing Signals for Controlled Use: Testing Displays. Pham et al. 2015a use the insights from the first two phases as a starting point to engineer testing signals. However, the engineered testing signals differ from common testing displays in that they are *specifically designed* to achieve a positive effect on testing activities while common testing signals are not. Common testing signals can achieve this effect, but are not guaranteed to do so. For example, a test suite with only one single test code file *can* communicate to the inexperienced developer to start testing—but it can also communicate that testing is neglected in this project. A testing display showing the same thing will emphasize on the first message. This leads to the specialization:

---

[1]This study is presented in chapter 11.

Definition *A testing display* is a monitor designed to display the prevailing testing culture and to encourage inexperienced developers in practicing more systematic testing. (By definition, a testing display is also a testing signal.)

In order to make testing displays available for the current software engineering community and in order to preserve practical relevance, the researchers constrained themselves in the design process: they used only information regarding the team's testing activities that is available in a modern software development collaboration environment. This is for example, information on source code files gained from versioning systems. Testing-related information that cannot be extracted from a usual software development environment was not regarded.

Again, the researchers took the point of view of an inexperienced developer and employed a GQM approach [11]. The GQM approach helped the researchers to break their general goal down to metrics and devise actions from that—all while keeping a traceable rationale for their design decisions. The GQM research question was:

RQ: How can the visibility of the team's testing activities be improved, from the point of view of a newcomer?

Pham et al. 2015a used goal trees to break down their goals and get a more finegrained, concrete understanding of them. Abstraction sheets [10] [151] pushed them to concretize their reasoning behind a new testing display and allowed them to back-check their reasoning regularly[2]. Originally, the researchers produced eight potential displays. After first evaluations with the target audience regarding *understandability* of these displays (cf. section 9.5), six displays remained. These six testing displays conveyed the strongest call to test more and were understood best by our population. They are presented in section 9.2 (one testing display) and 9.3 (remaining five).

9.2 Testing Display Reference Model

This section presents a reference model for testing displays In this case, these are varying forms of visualizing testing activities with the goal to facilitate more testing activities. This model describes more abstract similarities across the proposed testing displays so far. Not all testing displays fully feature every aspect of this model. However, Pham et al. 2015a take a pragmatic view on that matter and regard this model as a first iteration. It can help researchers in extending and refining the testing display approach in a standardized manner. This reference model is explained while introducing the first testing display 'Latest Test Code Commits' as an example (see Fig. 9.1).

Strategy of a Testing Display. The general goal of testing displays is to facilitate more testing effort in the perceiver of the display, the newcomer. However, the number of artifacts or the multitude actions of team members that *could* be visualized and can *potentially* have this effect is large. When designing a testing display, the engineer needs

---

[2]These abstraction sheets and the GQM-process can be found in more detail in Jonas Mörschbach's Master thesis [111].

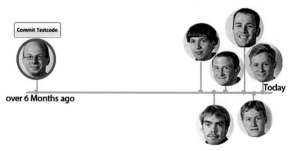

Latest Testcode Commits

Commit Testcode

over 6 Months ago

Today

Figure 9.1: Visualization of the testing display 'Latest Test Code Commits', showing the newcomer on the left of the team's timeline of test code committing.

to reason about the expected and concrete effect of this display: *why should this specific perspective (on testing culture) be visualized as a testing display and what effect do I expect this to have on the newcomer?* Pham et al. 2015a propose a *"If the newcomer sees that ..., then she will ..."* notation to structure these strategies. For example, applied to the testing display in Fig. 9.1: If the novice sees that all other team members have committed test code lately, she will commit test code herself.

Mode of a Testing Display. Visualizing specific aspects of a team's testing activities can have positive effects that encourage the novice to write more tests. However, it can also have negative effects that keep the novice from testing. Regarding Fig. 9.1, seeing vivid committing of tests (all other team members on the right side) can encourage to write tests on her own (positive effect). However, if most of the team has not committed tests lately (all team members remain on the left side, including the newcomer), this could communicate to the novice that testing is not important (negative effect). The *mode of a testing display* describes whether or not the display can have only positive or both positive and negative effects as well. There are two different modes[3]: *encouraging* and *both.* The latter means: this testing display can act both encouraging as well as discouraging (in certain circumstances, see next attribute 'range of a testing display'). The testing display in Fig. 9.1 is of mode *both.*

Range of a Testing Display. When designing a testing display, the engineer needs to consider all the possible states it can assume, depending on the state of the team's testing culture. This is an important step, as different states of the testing display can have different effects on the novice (different modes of the testing display). They can take many different forms, such as a limited or unlimited number of discrete states, or a

---

[3]The introduction of a third option, *discouraging*, is left out, as by definition of a testing display, encouragement for testing is targeted, not discouragement.

continuous value (for example, the percentage value of tested lines of code vs. untested lines of code). However, not *all* possible states are relevant—subsets can have a similar effects on the novice. Similar to partition testing, Pham et al. 2015a define the set of groups of states that a testing display can assume and that have the same effect on the novice as the *range of a testing display*. In the case of 'Latest Test Code Commits', there are different states to consider: In Fig. 9.1, the novice can be isolated to the left (encouraging), he can join the herd on the right (encouraging), he can be isolated to the right (encouraging), or he can be joined by the majority of the team on the left (discouraging), or team members are distributed all over the timeline (discouraging).

Threshold of a Testing Display. Distinguishing between positive and negative (mode) in the set of different states of a visualization (range), the threshold of a testing display describes the tipping point between the set of positive states and the set of negative states. This threshold depends on the goal of the visualization and is set by the engineer of the testing display. For example, if the engineer wants to encourage the novice to test, she should present her with a high testing activity around her—and not with a barely existent testing culture. Regarding the display in Fig. 9.1, the threshold is set to "majority of the team is on the right side".

Remedy Strategy of a Testing Display. Displaying a novice's negative testing performance can be discouraging for the novice. In order to facilitate quick and positive actions by the newcomer, such a testing display needs to be bundled with a fast and low barrier way to remedy the situation. This 'way out' is defined as the *remedy strategy of the testing display*. However, the actual tools to implement these strategies are beyond the scope of this thesis and are potential ideas for further research. In Fig. 9.1, there is a prominent button marked "Commit Test Code". When the novice sees that her test commit quota is low compared to her team members, she can use the this button to begin the process of committing more test code. The IDE could jump to a generated test class stub to help the novice commit a new test (outside of the scope of this thesis).

9.3 Six Testing Displays

This section presents the remaining five testing displays relates them to the reference model. Fig. 9.2 shows all testing displays integrated into Eclipse.

Testing Display 'Test Code Ratio'. In the study with soon-to-be graduates, one of the inhibiting factors for automated testing was that students felt unproductive when writing tests (cf. chapter 4.1). They would rather implement more functions and the time they spent on writing test code seemed lost to them. In professional software development, systematic software testing takes up a lot of time and resources—often as much as developing the production code itself. The testing display 'Test Code Ratio' is designed to give the novice a sense of how much test code a senior developer writes and what a normal test code vs. production code ratio looks like (see Fig. 9.3a).

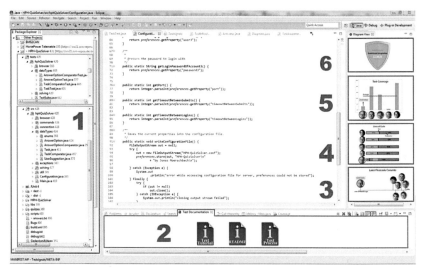

Figure 9.2: All six testing displays integrated in Eclipse: 'Test Code Explorer' (1)', 'Test Code Documentation' (2), 'Latest Test Code Commits' (3), 'Test Code Ratio' (4), 'Test Code Coverage' (5) and 'Using Test Services' (6)

The strategy of this testing display is: *'If the novice sees that other team members are writing a substantial amount of test code (and not only source code), too, writing tests code will seem less unproductive to her and she will write more test code'.*

Testing display 'Test Code Coverage'. Similar to the testing display 'Test Code Ratio' (Fig. 9.3a), the testing display 'Test code Coverage' compares the novice's testing performance to the performance of the team (Fig. 9.3b). This time, the focus lies less on a healthy ratio but rather on testing performance as measured in test code coverage. This testing display is more of competitive nature and less focused on conveying the normative behavior of the team. Code coverage—as a value—is measured by a percentage number, with 100% being the highest. Such a measure is easy to grasp. The strategy for this testing display is *'If the novice sees that her test coverage is below average, she will try to increase her test coverage by writing more tests'.*

Testing Display 'Test Code Explorer'. Often, test files are hidden away in the project tree in a rather easy-to-overlook folder named 'test'. The testing display Test Code Explorer' places a stronger focus on the test suite and gives the test suite its own prominent placing in the IDE (see Fig. 9.4a). Such a prominent placement lowers the barrier for accessing and adding to the test suite. They underlying strategy of this testing display is *'If the novice sees test files, she will be reminded to test herself and*

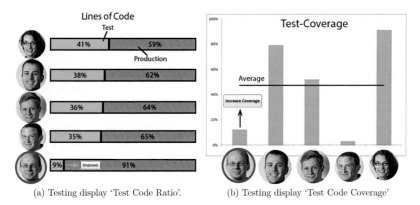

(a) Testing display 'Test Code Ratio'.   (b) Testing display 'Test Code Coverage'

Figure 9.3: Two testing displays showing off different aspects of testing culture, both featuring a remedy strategy button.

write more tests'. Similarly, just seeing test classes around the open projects nudged contributors on github.com to write their own tests (cf. chapter 11).

Testing display 'Using Test Services'. Clear displays of test activities and testing tools encouraged code contributors on GitHub.com to add tests to their contributions (cf. chapter 11). In this case, a badge symbol for a continuous integration service on the project's profile side conveyed the team's testing activities. Pham et al. 2015a want to use a similar effect and integrate a stylized shield into the IDE (see Fig. 9.4b). It symbolizes protection and refers to the use of CI in a project. However, novice developers may not be familiar with CI. As a remedy strategy, the testing display offers a link to a definition and tutorials on how to use it and set it up.

Testing display 'Test Code Documentation'. A well-defined process and tutorial documentation can be of great help when a developer tries to learn a new technology. However, these documents are not always easy to find. Finding suitable tutorials is a general problems for inexperienced developers (cf. problem area 4) For example, in the standard view of the popular IDE Eclipse, document files are not featured any more prominently than other files in the project explorer. The testing display 'Test Code Documentation' gives instructional documentation files a more prominent placement.

9.4 Discussion of Implementation

Privacy Concerns. Making team member's progress visible to other team members can invoke privacy concerns. In this case, only the newcomer can see the progress of

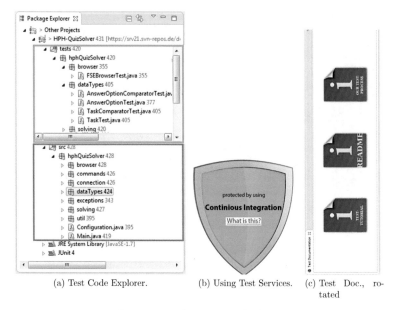

(a) Test Code Explorer.   (b) Using Test Services.   (c) Test Doc., rotated

Figure 9.4: Three testing displays.

senior developers—and assuming a healthy testing culture, seniors should fare well in the testing displays visualizations. Pham et al. 2015a propose to make senior participation an opt-in process and recognize that privacy concerns require further research.

Requiring an Active Testing Culture.   The approach of testing displays requires an *active to very active* testing culture in order to *encourage* newcomers to test more—and for example, not to discourage. If no one on the team is systematically testing, all testing displays will have a negative mode and be discouraging. For example, testing display 'Latest Test Code Commit' (see Fig. 9.1) will show all developers on the right side.

However, if an active testing culture is already enacted in the development team, one could argue that the newcomer will pick up testing by herself quickly. This line of thought is actually supported by a phenomenon[4] observed in the second empirical study with practitioners (cf. chapter 4.2):

> *Phenomenon:* Exposing the newcomer to a test-intensive environment greatly facilitates the adoption of test writing by the newcomer.

Pham et al. 2015a agree that a good testing culture is beneficial for overcoming the testing skill gap in inexperienced developers. However, the researchers argue that in

---

[4]This phenomenon is discussed in more detail in section 4.2.3, p. 65, and section 6.1, p. 85

order to be able to pick up the testing culture on her own, the inexperienced developer must be able to *observe* it first. It is not clear what mechanisms support the newcomer in observing the prevailing testing culture in the current work environments of software engineering companies. In this sense, the approach of testing displays is an continuation and operationalization of the phenomenon above: Testing displays target to make the phenomenon above achievable in a *systematic manner*.

Social Translucency & Transparency. At its core, the testing display approach builds upon the concepts of visibility and awareness of actions of other team members (cf. section ??, p. 9). Testing displays are essentially dashboards of other team members' testing efforts and performance—they make the team's testing culture *visible*. This makes the novice *aware* of the testing efforts around her. By making the newbie aware of *how* and *how hard* senior developers around her test, Testing Displays induce a change of attitude towards testing in the newcomer as well as an understanding of testing activities as a team norm.

Currently, the element of *accountability* is not explicitly included in the approach: Newcomer and senior developers are both informed that the testing stats are only seen by the newcomer. Sharing these testing displays with senior developers could create a performance pressuring situation for the newcomer. The approach does not hold the newcomer accountable for poor testing performance—however, the newcomer can develop such a feeling herself: Seeing her performance displayed against other's performance can make her feel accountable. In the preliminary evaluations, Pham et al. 2015a have seen a related effect (bad conscious, slight feeling of uneasiness, cf. section 9.5).

The testing display approach and is inspired by positive effects of social transparency on testing behavior on social coding sites (cf. chapter 11). Testing displays use real profile pictures of colleagues. This form of *identity transparency* creates a closer connection for the newcomer and gives the visualizations a bigger impact. Informing the newcomer about how many tests a team member has written or when a team member has written them, brings by a form of *content transparency* for the test suite: The newcomer can maintain a mental model of changes to the test suite and understand its evolvement better. Much activity on the test suite enables the newcomer to infer its importance. Seeing who committed tests can help the newbie in identifying expert testers for further questions.

Evaluations with Students, Statistical Significance. Even though the sum of participants of the evaluations is relatively large (76 students), statistical significance cannot be claimed. This is due to the different focus of the evaluations (exploratory, qualitative, quantitative). The statistically evaluable results come from only 22 students (quantitative evaluations 2, 3, and 4). An evaluation showing the statistical significance of the effect of testing displays is still missing.

Evaluations for testing displays were done with students only, which could challenge its applicability with newcomers. However, students just before their graduation are a suitable evaluation population for this target population (graduates that have just entered the job market). As discussed in section 4.3, p. 70, this thesis assumes that the experience level in graduates between university and onboarding does not differ.

Although evaluations were promising, a confirming final evaluation, showing a measurable advantage of the testing display approach in a *real-world* setting (an actual onboarding) is missing. This final evaluation was not achievable in the time frame of this thesis. It can, however, serve as future work.

Smart Display Strategy. Displaying all six testing displays at once can seem overwhelming or intimidating, even. The effects of different combinations of testing displays or disabling certain displays have not been researched yet—during evaluations, participants saw all six final testing displays at once. Less influencing or displays with similar message could be strategically disabled for a less cluttered work environment.

Additionally, not all testing displays show a positive messages at the same time. Testing displays react differently depending on the extent of testing activity. For example, regarding the testing display 'Test Code Commits' (see Fig. 9.1): Having committed one little, simple test, will bring the novice to the right, joining the crowd—this may have an uplifting effect, but actually does not imply a heightened and meaningful testing activity. In this case, other testing displays like 'Test Code Coverage' (see Fig. 9.3b) would still display a negative novice performance—test code coverage would not be increased by much. One approach to remedy this, is to implement a *smart display* strategy that strategically enables and disables testing displays to increase positive impact on the novice. In the scope of this thesis, this could not be researched.

9.5 Evaluation: Testing Displays

Testing displays have been evaluated in five different rounds *during* their design phase and *after* their implementation. Two evaluation rounds (evaluation 1 and 2) during the engineering process of testing displays fundamentally influenced their final design and also decided on the research directions. These evaluations answered the following questions regarding the *understandability* and the *ranking of impact* of testing displays:

- What effect do testing displays have on inexperienced developers and do they understand them? (understandability)

- Which testing displays have the highest or lowest effect? (ranking of impact)

Testing displays that were deemed too complex by the population were no longer pursued, other testing displays were improved according to the qualitative feedback[5]. These first evaluation rounds used paper printouts of early designs of testing displays.

The next three evaluations employed working implementations of the final six testing displays in an Eclipse IDE. Two of these evaluations are quantitative and one is qualitative. They answer the following research questions:

---

[5]An in-depth comparison between old and final versions of testing displays can be found in Jonas Mörschbach's Master's thesis [111]. In this thesis, only the final versions are presented.

- Do inexperienced developers write more test code when exposed to testing displays? (two quantitative evaluations with different-skilled populations)

- What impact do testing displays have on inexperienced developers? (qualitative evaluation)

All in all, five evaluations have been conducted, using different configurations:

Evaluation 1: understandability of testing displays, paper prototype, qualitative, 18 Bachelor students.

Evaluation 2: ranking of impact, quantitative, paper prototype, 6 Bachelor students.

Evaluation 3: measurable impact on test writing, working implementation, quantitative, 10 Bachelor students.

Evaluation 4: measurable impact on test writing, working implementation, quantitative, 6 Master students.

Evaluation 5: qualitative impact on students, working implementation, qualitative, 36 Bachelor students.

9.5.1 Evaluation 1: Understandability

The goal of the first evaluation was to evaluate how inexperienced developers understood testing displays and what kind of reactions they provoked. This evaluation was done during the design phase of the testing displays using paper prototypes. Results influenced the final design of the testing displays.

18 computer science undergraduates (5th Bachelor semester or up) at Leibniz Universität Hannover, Germany, participated. These undergraduates were nearly finished with their Bachelor studies and were about to enter the job market. All of them attended the lectures 'Software Engineering' and 15 additionally attended the lecture on 'Software Quality'. It was explained to each participant that she was the newest addition to a team of senior software developers. The other team members were introduced with photographs (as used in the testing displays, cf. Fig. 9.1).

For each testing display, we interviewed three students independently for about 20 minutes. Each interviewee was presented with a printout of a standard Java Eclipse IDE and included one testing display as a pen&paper prototype. This setup was similar to Fig. 9.2, however, sporting only one testing display at a time. The participant was asked to describe the visualization, its message and her emotions when viewing it. The researchers inquired what her next action would be after seeing this visualization. Finally, each participant was invited to give feedback for improving the visualization.

Evaluation 1: Results

Conveyed Message and Impacts on Students. Nearly all testing displays conveyed the message, which they were designed to convey. Participants understood that their testing activity was rated as low and—in comparison to their team members'—needed to improve. *"My testing activity is too low. I need to do more."*

Our participants felt motivated to improve themselves. They reported that being ranked to colleagues so visibly gave them an extra nudge to improve and sparked competition. *"I need to write more tests to get a higher rank."*

Using social transparency to make testing behavior explicitly visible—and thus, comparable—can evoke different feelings in novices. Seeing their own test performance made participants a little bit uneasy: They reported to have a slightly bad conscience for not testing. Most participants did not feel offended—however, three participant's first reaction was indeed to 'click away' the testing display. They simply did not want to be confronted with their own misbehavior. There is a fine line between rejection and adoption when it comes to personal mistakes or shortcomings. Care needs to be taken when presenting these insights to people and more research is needed to fully understand these effects. Four students noted that the feeling of uneasiness and the reaction depend on their relationship to the other team members and the working atmosphere.

Improving the Visualizations. Participants contributed valuable feedback to all visualizations. Feedback mostly consisted of minor improvements like adjusting colors (not red, but more green and blue) or using clickable buttons instead of hyperlinks (displaying the remedy strategy). Figures 9.1 - 9.4c show all final visualizations.

Two students had a noteworthy request for the testing display 'Test Code Explorer' (see Fig. 9.4a), proposing to place the window containing the productive code above the test code. Their explanation emphasizes one aspect of the problem that the researchers wanted to address: *"Productive code is still more important, isn't it?"* One inhibitor to systematic testing in student projects is that students attribute testing little importance and value source code and new function more than quality assurance efforts (cf. chapter 4.1 and problem area 3, section 4.3). Thus, researchers left the testing display untouched with the test classes above the source code classes.

Effects of the Remedy Button. Two third of the students wanted to click on the remedy button—simply *'to see what happens'*. Using labeled buttons combined with arrows successfully conveyed the offer of help. Students correctly assumed that they would get help on how to improve their testing performance, when clicking these buttons. Generally, students wanted to improve—especially regarding in rankings that explicitly compared them to others (testing displays 'Test Code Coverage' or 'Tests Code Commits'). The remedy button served as an easy way to start.

Table 9.1: Testing displays ranked, sorted by median, accumulated placements per rank.

Testing display	1st	2nd	3rd	4th	5th	6th	Median
Test Code Coverage	3	2	1				1.5
Test Code Ratio		3	2		1		2.5
Test Code Commits		3	1	1	1		2.5
Test Code Explorer		1	1	2		2	4
Test Code Doc.			2		3	1	5
Using Test Services			1	1	1	3	5.5

9.5.2 Evaluation 2: Ranking of Impact

The second evaluation served to determine the testing displays' impact on inexperienced developers. The researchers wanted to understand how to rank the different testing displays regarding their encouragement to test. They interviewed six computer science undergraduates (5th Bachelor semester and up) of which all had completed the course on software engineering and 4 had completed the course on software quality. Each participant was presented with all six testing displays (as seen in Fig. 9.2). As a sanity check, the researchers required each participant to describe all visualizations briefly. This way, they verified that participants had understood the message of the testing displays. The researchers asked them to rank the testing displays according to the perceived influence to start writing tests, from high to low. Further, they inquired why participants had ordered the testing displays this way.

Results. Researchers suspected that different testing displays had varying impacts on the novice developer: some testing displays conveyed the need for testing activity more explicitly while others were designed to be implicit in nature. They inquired whether our students felt influenced to test more by the testing displays and asked them to rank them from highest to lowest perceived influence. Table 9.1 shows how often a testing display was placed at which rank. For example, 'Test Code Coverage' was placed three times in first rank, two times in second rank and once in third rank.

An interesting tendency emerged: Testing displays that used more social transparency features—such as pictures from team members or their activity—were attributed a higher influence by students, being placed in ranks one to three more often. More 'passive', less prompting displays ('Using Testing Services', 'Test Code Documentation') were located at the other end of the ranking. 'Test Code Explorer' stayed in middle ground.

Reasoning about the students' ranking, three arguments stood out: First, better knowledge of and higher familiarity with the metric used by the testing display lead to better ranking. Students were more familiar with the commonly known metrics of 'Test Code Coverage' and 'Test Code Ratio' (number of lines of code), accepting these better as performance indicators. *"Test Coverage says most about [my testing activities]."* Second, the profile pictures created a very close connection and facilitated a competitive feeling between colleagues: *"The direct comparison to colleagues has a strong influence on me."* Third, the other testing displays did not prompt the student for more tests as

Figure 9.5: Altered Eclipse IDE, six working and live adapting testing displays.

strongly. The researchers assume that this is due to their passive and more informative character. They provide information if clicked or viewed but do not nudge the new hire to do something. *"[The Test Code Explorer] does not prompt me to do anything."*

9.5.3 Evaluation 3: Impact on Test Writing.

This evaluation used working implementations of the final six testing displays. Its goal was to measure if inexperienced developers would write more tests when exposed to testing displays. 9 computer science undergraduates and one computer engineering undergraduate participated (between 4th Bachelor semester and 1st Master semester). All participants had completed a course on software engineering, 7 participants had additionally completed a course in software quality. No participant had more than 5 years of programming experience and most participants had less than one year experience in writing tests, representing the population of inexperienced developers well.

It was explained to participants that they were the newest addition to a team of developers and they were shown photos of their team members. Every participant was given a laptop running an Eclipse IDE to work on a project with the team. The current project was a simple calculator with a GUI written in Java and participants had access to the whole repository (source code and test code). Participants were divided into two groups (6 students and 4 students). Participants of the first group were asked to implement the faculty function using a standard Eclipse IDE view. After that their Eclipse IDE was interchanged to a version showing testing displays and they were asked to implement the modulo function. Participants of the second group were asked to do the same, however, using the Eclipse IDE with testing signals first and the normal Eclipse IDE second. Fig. 9.5 shows the altered Eclipse IDE with testing displays. Participants were given up to 25 minutes per programming tasks, but no participant needed all of the allocated time slot. After finishing both tasks, the number of written tests were counted

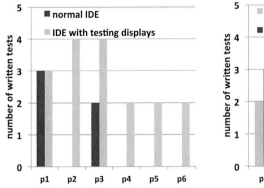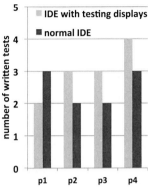

(a) First group, normal IDE first, altered IDE with testing displays second.

(b) Second group, altered IDE with testing displays first, normal IDE second.

Figure 9.6: Being exposed to testing displays gets novices to write more tests (left). Testing displays have a learning effect (right).

and each participant was interviewed, inquiring why or why not they had engaged in test writing.

Results.   Participants solved the first faculty task in 13 minutes and the second modulo task in 18 minutes. Most of the participants did not notice the big icons on the bottom of the altered IDE, even though these were placed prominently (*I did not notice the icons in the bottom.*, *I did not bother with the lower icons as I did not see any value in them. I knew what I had to do, so...*).

Remedy-buttons were mostly overlooked, only three participants clicked on them (*These buttons need to be more eye-catching!*). Clicking these, however, influenced the participant's following behavior positively. *"After clicking these buttons, I noticed that testing seems to be important."* , *"All of these buttons tell me to write tests and commit them."* The researchers take this as a hint to make remedy-buttons more noticeable.

The results of this evaluation suggest that being exposed to testing displays *does* trigger inexperienced developers to write tests. When exposed to testing displays during the second programming tasks, all six participants of the first group began writing tests (cf. Fig. 9.6a). Except for two participants, all students did not engage in test writing when they were working with the normal Eclipse IDE without testing displays. These two participants did have more testing experience (two and three years, *"If possible, I always write tests, even at work."* , *"Writing tests is common practice and I do it whenever I have enough time. At work, though, there is little time for that."*

All other participants reported to not give unit testing any thought when working with the normal IDE (not exposed to testing displays). *"I did not think of JUnit at all. Mostly, I use* `system.out`*. It is very fast."*

One participants reported to have little knowledge with unit testing, which hindered him in engaging in testing. *"I am not familiar with the JUnit environment."*

All in all, testing displays effectively communicated to participants that engagement in testing was demanded. *"The diagrams on the right side requested me to write tests."* , *"I always try to follow the line of least resistance and here I was told that checking my source code could be done the easiest when using unit testing."*

As suggested by the ranking of evaluation 2, those testing displays, which compared the students' performance to other team members' performance, motivated students the most. The testing displays "Test Coverage" and "Test Code Ratio" were especially mentioned by participants. *"This kind of ranking is pushing me, I want to perform better."* , *"All my colleagues are better ranked than me, I wanted to change that."*

However, more implicit testing displays like the "Test Code explorer" had a positive influence as well. It helped participants to find their way around better and gave them an easier access to test code. This lowered the barrier to engage in systematic testing and underlines the importance of easy access to testing resources such test code. *"I haven't used JUnit that much, and so the existing test codes were of big help to me. I have copied them and adapted them to my needs easily."* , *"Using the existing tests, I was able to quickly understand how to test a method using JUnit."*

Having been exposed to testing displays may induce a learning effect. Participants of the second group who were using the altered Eclipse IDE first and a normal one second, were engaging in test writing during *both* rounds (cf. Fig. 9.6b). Participants acknowledged this learning effect. *"Now, I know how testing works."* , *"I have written unit tests in the first round. Naturally, I do it in this round as well."*

9.5.4 Evaluation 4

This fourth evaluation was a replication of the setup of evaluation 3. Its goals was to measure if inexperienced developers would write more tests when exposed to testing displays—only this time, the population was more sensitized towards testing. Five undergraduates in their first Master's semester, one in their final Bachelor's semester participated in this evaluation (one participant had left the evaluation early due to language problems). These students were participating a seminar on current systematic testing techniques (the seminar was called "Testing Today") and had interest in testing. Compared to participants of evaluation 3, these participants had considerable more experience in programming (from four to 10 years) and testing (from three to six years.).

The core setup of evaluation 4 is similar to evaluation 3, using the same Eclipse IDE and same altered Eclipse IDE with testing displays (cf. Fig. 9.2) and the same programming tasks. This time, programming tasks were completed in two rounds simultaneously by all participants. Participants were grouped in two groups. Two participants were asked to work with the normal Eclipse IDE first and with the altered Eclipse IDE with testing displays second. The reverse applies to the second group of four participants.

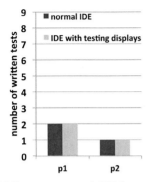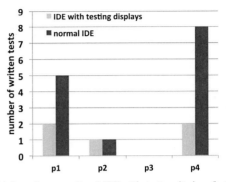

(a) First group, normal IDE first, altered IDE with testing displays second.

(b) Second group, altered IDE with testing displays first, normal IDE second.

Figure 9.7: Effect of testing displays on participants sensitized towards systematic testing inconclusive. Participants engaged in testing nonetheless.

There was no interview at the end of this evaluation, instead participants were asked to fill out a questionnaire. Lastly, the number of written tests were counted.

Results. This time, results are not as clear-cut as in evaluation 3. All participants engaged in test writing, regardless of whether or not they were shown the testing displays. The number of written tests does not change for the first group (two participants, cf. Fig. 9.7a). The second group engaged in test writing more when not exposed to testing signals (cf. Fig. 9.7b) but also engaged in test writing with testing displays. Those participants reported to feel that that the programming task without testing displays (second task) warranted more tests than the first. All in all, results were inconclusive. The researchers suspect that the high sensibility of participants for the activity of systematic testing influenced their testing behavior—making the testing displays ineffective. These participants would engage in systematic testing regardless of testing displays. Compared to the prior populations, they would not need this kind of reminder.

9.5.5 Evaluation 5

The last evaluation was similar to evaluation 1 and evaluation 2. This time, participants were not interviewed but took part in an online questionnaire and—instead of paper prototypes—were shown online pictures of the testing displays. The goal of this final evaluation was to assess how the communicated messages of the testing displays was perceived by inexperienced developers. As a second goal, the number of evaluation participants was increased, strengthening confidence in the effect of testing displays.

In this evaluation, nearly the whole set of attendees of a course on software quality participated. All in all, 35 Bachelor students and one Master student of different fields of study took part in the questionnaire: 28 Bachelor undergraduates in computer science, 7 Bachelor undergraduates in computer engineering, and 1 Master's undergraduate in electrical engineering and information technology. These undergraduates were in different semesters of study, ranging from second semester (two undergraduates) to 7th semester (one undergraduate), with the majority being in their fourth semester (median). All participants except four had completed a lecture on software engineering prior to this software engineering lecture. Programming experience stemmed from university courses and from private projects, with most students having 2 years of programming experience. Testing experience was lower than programming experience (about 1 year).

In July 2015, the last exercise of the software quality course included a link to an online questionnaire (included in the appendix, p. 196). Participation was voluntary and earned participants 10 bonus exercise points. Nearly the whole set of lecture participants enrolled (36 students). The setup for this questionnaire was similar to the setup of evaluation 1 & 2. The questionnaire explained to the participant that she was the newest addition to a software development team and introduced the team members with photos. The participant was shown an overview of the altered IDE (cf. Fig. 9.5) and a bigger picture of each of the six testing displays. The questionnaire asked the participant to:

- describe each testing display shortly (*What do you see?*),

- describe the message perceived by the testing display (*What are you supposed to do? How does that make you feel?*),

- rank all six testing displays by the perceived strength of the call to action,

- comment on each testing display.

Each participant was asked to rate on a five-item Likert scale:[6]

- effectivity of testing displays to invoke more systematic testing in inexperienced developers (*Seeing testing displays influences me to write tests.*), and

- acceptance of testing displays by inexperienced developers (*I would like to have testing displays in my IDE.*).

Text descriptions and text comments on testing displays were qualitatively coded, summarized and are presented below.

Evaluation 5: Results

Generally, testing displays were successful in communicating the team's testing culture. Participants agreed that seeing testing displays would increase their test writing efforts

---

[6]with one being strong disagreement and five being strong agreement

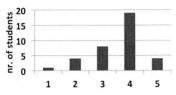

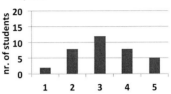

(a) Effect of testing displays on inexperienced developers, self-assessed.

(b) Acceptance of testing displays by inexperienced developers, self-assessed.

Figure 9.8: Inexperienced developers influenced to test more (median is 4). Testing displays' acceptance is inconclusive (median at 3).

(cf. Fig. 9.8a). The median of this distribution is 4 (Likert-item *agree*). However, when it came to install testing displays and using them in their IDE, results were not as clear-cut (cf. Fig. 9.8b). In this population, both extremes emerged: The median of this distribution is 3 (Likert-item *neutral*). Participants want to use testing displays and reject them in nearly equal parts.

> *"Please please write a plugin for testing displays! :-)"* — participant 13, general comment

> *"Most diagrams seem useless to me."* — p14, general comment

Stronger Call-To-Action by Competitive Testing Displays. Similarly to the results of evaluation 1 and 2, some testing displays were judged to have a stronger influence on participants than others. Stemming from students' textual description of the testing displays, the perceived call-to-action (to test more) was strongest with those three testing displays that showed the participant's testing behavior in comparison to other team members. These testing displays are Test Code Coverage (cf. Fig. 9.3b), Test Code Commit (cf. Fig. 9.1) and Test Code Ratio (cf. Fig. 9.3a). Seeing these testing displays, nearly all students recognized that they were being compared to other team members and that their testing effort was below average. This sparked a feeling of competition in them. The other three testing displays did not have this effect on students. Their call-to-action was more implicit to students. These were Test Code Explorer (cf. Fig. 9.4a), Test Documentation (cf. Fig. 9.4c) and Using Test Services (cf. Fig. 9.4b).

> *"One can see the test coverage for the code of each team member. My test coverage is below average, I should write more tests for my existing code before writing new source code."* — p25, about Test Code Coverage

Table 9.2: Ranking of testing displays by effect on participant (sorted by median). The table shows the accumulated number of placements per rank. Bold numbers mark highest numbers (modus).

Testing display	1st	2nd	3rd	4th	5th	6th	Median
Test Code Coverage	**13**	4	12	7			3
Test Code Commits	10	3	**12**	8	3		3
Test Code Ratio	4	9	5	4	**10**	4	3.5
Test Code Explorer	9	2	6	**15**	4		4
Test Code Doc.		7	1	2	**16**	10	5
Using Test Services		11			3	**22**	6

"Being compared to others is a good trigger to write tests. Reminds me of gamification." — p1, general comment

Students' stronger perception of call-to-action of the competitive testing displays is mirrored in their ranking of testing displays (cf. Table 9.2). Students were asked to rank the testing displays by the strength of their influence, from strong (1st place) to low (6th place). As in evaluation 2, testing displays were sorted by the median of this distribution. The three competitive testing displays were ranked with a stronger influence (1st, 2nd, and 3rd place) than the more implicit testing displays: Test Code Explorer, Test Code Ratio, and Using Test Services were ranked last. Apart from the sorting of the three competitive testing displays, the overall ranking is similar to the results of evaluation 2.

Testing Performance Comparison Effective but Risky. Being so openly compared to other team members also introduced a feeling of uneasiness and guilt in students. Students were conscious about their low rating and felt guilty for showing a low score. They did not want to be judged as performing badly or being lazy. It is important to note that participants were not informed whether or not the depicted team members (with better scores) would be shown the same diagrams. If participants were of this impression, they came to it by assumption. At the time of evaluation, it was not yet decided if testing displays would be made accessible to all team members or to the newcomer only.

"The diagram shows that my engagement in testing is below average. This causes negative feelings—the others might think I'm lazy." — p30, on Test Code Coverage

"I am slightly ashamed because I am lagging behind, but at the same time, I feel motivated to do more." — p36, on Test Code Coverage

Interestingly, students did not only compare themselves to team members who were performing better than themselves but also to colleagues who were lagging behind them.

Seeing someone performing worse than themselves also sparked a feeling of uneasiness—but this time directed towards others, resulting in a feeling of unfairness. Of 36 participants, two students questioned why they would be required to increase their workload if some other team member did not perform as much as they did.

> *"[...] My rating is marked with a note to increase my test coverage. I would feel that this is unfair because another team member has a considerably lower test coverage than me! On the other hand, this shows me how to improve my work, which is positive."* — p21 on Test Code Coverage

One student put the general cautiousness into a nutshell: competitive testing displays need a healthy team culture to have a positive effect. Otherwise, performance comparison can quickly poison the working environment. In this regard, further research about the positive and negative effects of testing displays is necessary.

> *"This diagram has the same problem as Test Code Coverage—something like this can only work if the colleagues know each other well and support each other. Otherwise, there is only competitive thinking."* — p29, on Test Code Commits

Role of the Remedy Button. The remedy buttons shown in the diagrams intrigued participants and supported the testing displays' acceptance. Students recognized the diagrams' remedy button and understood it as an offer to help and improve the situation. Often, students felt curios to click it.

> *"Less than 10 % of my code is test code? There is something seriously wrong, I should rectify that immediately! The 'improve'-button motivates me to do so."* — p12, on Test Code Ratio

> *"The button virtually invites me to click it. The diagram encourages to reach a higher test coverage in order to reach the same level as the other developers."* — p6, on Test Code Coverage

Wording of this offer for help is important. By coincidence, the researchers gave each remedy-button of the three competitive testing displays another wording. Latest Test Code Commits had 'Commit Testcode', Test Code Coverage had 'Increase Coverage', and Test Code Ratio had 'Improve'. Each wording was designed to communicate a clear offer for help. While the first two remedy buttons were sometimes understood as demands, the last remedy button ('improve') unwillingly intensified feelings of guilt in two students. Being told to improve made them more aware of their bad performance.

> *"[...] Being compared to my team members makes me feel bad because I am lagging behind. The wording on the button 'improve' makes it worse."* — p22, on Test Code Ratio

Focus on Systematic Testing not immediately clear. Some students had difficulties recognizing the testing focus of the diagrams. Testing displays were shown to them without any explanation about their purpose (to increase testing efforts). Especially those testing displays that used a metric not usually associated with systematic testing were misunderstood. Seven students mistook Test Code Commits for a measure for normal source code commit frequency and two students thought that Test Code Ratio measured normal source code LOC. Interestingly, the one testing display using a testing-related measure (Test Code Coverage) was recognized without fail. It appears that students associate different measures with different contexts. The intended effect (to increase engagement), however, did not changed: for example, students that mistook Testing Code Ratio for a diagram showing source code LOC wanted to increase their source code LOC count.

> *"At the beginning, I haven't noticed that all diagrams focused on testing. For example, I thought that normal productivity was measured."* — p35, general remark

> *"I haven't committed in a while my team members have worked on the [source] code recently."* — p15, on Test Code Commit

Criticizing new Test Measures. While most participants perceived a call to test more from the testing displays, there were also critical voices. Eight students questioned the rationale behind the testing displays Test Code Commits and Test Code Ratio. In their opinion, measuring test code frequency or number of lines of test code was not an adequate indicator of the quality of the involved test code.

> *"In my view, this diagram provides only little meaning. It does not provide any statement about the size or quality of the committed test code. I would concentrate on [Test Code Coverage] instead."* — p20, on Test Code Commit.

> *"LOC is a good statistical number, but it does not provide any statement about the amount of work that went into the commit. [...]"* — p8, on Test Code Ratio.

Students also questioned the idea of comparing LOC of test code with LOC of source code in a 1:1 relation. In their view, this was an over-simplification, which required a more fine-grained consideration.

> *"In my opinion, the amount of test [code] is not meaningful, as there is often less test code necessary for testing a certain amount of source code."* — p21, on Test Code Ratio.

While these eight students rejected the rationale behind these two testing displays, the design of these testing displays was not coincidental. As shown in the empirical study with students (cf. section 4.1), inexperienced developers have the tendency to engage in testing efforts much too late (cf. problem area 1). Test Code Commits is designed to make newcomers commit test code more regularly and engage in systematic testing earlier. Additionally, inexperienced students reported to feel unproductive when engaging in test writing instead of implementing source code (cf. section 4.1 and problem area 3). Being made aware of the usual amount of test code a senior software developer produces can help to counteract this. Test Code Ratio is designed to help newcomers understand the usual amount of test code in relation to source code. While there is potential for improvement for the criticized testing displays, it is also possible that these eight participants were simply not affected by the associated problem areas.

Unexpected Adoption Blockers. Two distinct blockers for adoption emerged. Peculiarly, students complained about the design and level of polished looks. Testing displays were implemented by a Master's student (Jonas Mörschbach) and not done by a professional software developer or designer and as such testing displays looked a little rough. For students, that was a reason to not use them.

> *"[Test Code Coverage, Test Code Commits, and Test Code Ratio] are useful and I would like to have them in my IDE—but I'd like them to look more fancy and polished."* — p18, general remark

The other complaint concerns a perceived waste of IDE screen space. Some students were particularly firm about their screen space and did not appreciate big allocations of space. Each testing display took a lot of space and there is room for optimization. Students, however, did not like to 'waste' space on something that provides relatively little information in return, for example, the big icons of the testing display Test Code Documentation. These icons were static and did not change much.

> *"I'd like it more if the diagrams were not visible constantly in my IDE. I'd like to summon them, when I need them. This way, they use a lot of screen space."* — p5, general remark.

This thought is similar to a strategy that the researchers also propose: smart display. Testing displays are only shown when they are probable to have a positive effect on the newcomer and otherwise they are hidden. This is discussed in more detail on p. 114.

Feedback on Test Code Explorer. Looking at Test Code Explorer (cf. Fig. 9.4a), most students recognized that they were looking at a project file explorer highlighting the test classes. Students understood that the upper window showed the test class tree of the project and the lower window showed the normal project tree of the project. This lead students to comparing the two views and looking for gaps and matches. Intuitively, students wanted to see each source code class matched with a test class—which exposed untested source code classes.

> *"The first thing I noticed is that there are packages without corresponding test code. Such a gap can be risky because defects can slip in more easily."* — p30, on Test Code Explorer.

Not every participant agreed with the re-ordering of the common project file explorer. Four students assessed the two views of Test Code Explorer to be chaotic and unproductive. These students did recognize the prominently exposed test file tree but did not agree on its importance. In their view, tucking all test files away in a normal project file explorer was sufficient and any change would be distracting.

> *"This divided file tree puts a stronger focus on test-related packages. However, I would quickly miss my normal outline and overview and I would try to re-arrange all packages in one shared file tree." —* p6, on Test Code Explorer.

Feedback on Test Code Documentation. Regarding Test Code Documentation, most participants recognized that they were offered project documentation in general (this testing display uses a document icon, cf. Fig. 9.4c) as well as documentation on systematic testing specifically. The big icons were easy to spot and often sparked curiosity. This spawned two opinions in the population. Some students were relieved to have this kind of documentation prominently featured. This reduced uncertainty in them and spared them the trouble of looking for these kinds of docs. Also, they felt that they were able to start working on the project right away, seeing that important docs were already provided to them.

> *"I see that I am being offered tutorials and information on systematic testing. I like that. This way, I can start right away without having to search for it. This saves time." —* p30, on Test Code Documentation.

Other students felt strongly against the big icons and assessed them as a waste of space. In their opinion, this kind of information should be made available less prominently, for example as a list or drop-down menu somewhere in the IDE. Hiding test documentation away, however, is exactly what this testing display tries to fight. If the participating viewer of the testing display is already sensitized towards this kind of documentation, it may feel unnecessary.

Not all students appreciated being offered documentation and a certain bias against reading complex documents emerged. This notions was mixed with a feeling of guilt.

> *"I still don't like to read documentation, it is a hassle. However, I see that it is actually necessary to do so." —* p36, on Test Code Documentation.

Feedback on Using Test Services. This testing display was misunderstood most by participants. Students did associate 'protection' with this big icon, and were curios about its meaning and what 'continuous integration' meant (9 students). Providing a link to an explanation of CI was met with delight because students felt that it was relatively easy to get this information.

However, 12 students (one third of the population) rejected this testing display or did not know what to make of it. Seven students associated the used shape of a shield with other shields found in software, for example, the symbol for an anti-virus software. Such signals, students stated, would ignored regularly and so would this testing display.

"This diagram informs the about the use of continuous integration in this project. The shape of it is odd, I usually associate this shape with firewall software and not something related to software engineering. But it's nice that I to read upon it easily." — p30, on Test Code Documentation.

Regarding this testing display, there is room for improvement and for making its message clearer. This is also reflected in the last place ranking of its call-to-action (cf. Table 9.2). Students suggested to make it more active and to give it more information. The plain and static design was judged to be a waste of space. Most participants stated that they did not know what CI is before encountering this testing display, but being provided with this kind of link nudged many of them to read up on it.

9.5.6 Summary of Five Evaluations

The effects of testing displays on inexperienced developers was extensively evaluated in five evaluations with different setups. These included qualitative evaluations using semi-structured interviews (evaluation 1 & 2) or extensive online questionnaires (evaluation 5) and quantitative evaluations using a cross-design (evaluation 3 & 4). As a population the researchers chose computer science students at the end of their Bachelor studies. These participants were about to enter the engineering working force. As such, they represented the population of inexperienced newcomers well: As seen in two empirical studies, the testing skills that such students exhibit are similar to the testing skills found in newcomers in the industrial onboarding situation (cf. section 4.3).

Student participants agreed that being exposed to testing displays would make them engage in writing more tests (self-assessment, qual. eval. 1 & 5). This perceived call-to-action was confirmed in a quantitative cross-design evaluation with ten students (quant. eval. 3): Being exposed to testing displays made them write more test code than working with a normal IDE. The cross-design of this evaluation also uncovered a possible learning effect: After being exposed to testing displays, participants continued to write more tests, even though they were working with a normal IDE. Due to the small number in participants in these quantitative evaluations, both effects are not statistically significant and can only be seen as indicators. Further and more vigorous quantitative evaluations are needed.

The effect of testing displays on 'test-sensitive' participants (participants primed for systematic testing) was inconclusive. When participants were already sensitized towards systematic testing, there was little effect from testing displays. Eight Master's students from a testing-focused seminar did not show any significant change in their testing behavior and engaged in systematic testing regardless of exposure to testing displays (quant. eval 4).

The perceived call-to-action is stronger with *competitive* testing displays that used traits of social transparency to explicitly show the team's testing efforts to the participants (qual. eval 1 & 5). Testing displays that did not put the participant's testing effort in comparison to other team members emitted a less pronounced call to engage in systematic testing (qual. eval 1 & 5). This effect is also mirrored in students' ranking of the influence they perceive by testing displays (qual. eval 2 & 5).

Exposing participants to other team member's testing efforts and putting them into comparison often created a feeling of competition. While this feeling was motivating to improve their testing behavior to most students, some participants expressed a feeling of guilt and fear to be exposed as under-performing. A small group of participants even pointed out that other team members were performing worse than them, posing the question why they would be required to improve their behavior. This shows that increasing the level of social transparency can introduce motivating competition but needs to be handled with care in order to achieve the wanted effect. Further research into this delicate matter is needed.

Interestingly, some participants had difficulties recognizing new and more uncommon measures for testing effort, such as frequency of test code commits (testing display Test Code Commit, cf. Fig. 9.1) and ratio of test code lines (testing display Test Code Ratio, cf. Fig. 9.3a). A small group of participants even questioned the rationale of the design of these testing displays. These testing displays were engineered after specific testing problems that inexperienced developers are prone to have (cf. section 4.3). The researchers suspect that those participants rejecting these testing displays may not be affected by the testing problems that guided the design of these testing displays.

Lastly, unexpected blockers for adoption of testing displays were uncovered. Students reacted harshly towards the amount of space that some testing displays allocated. While some displays were even judged as a 'waste of space', these displays succeeded in providing testing-related information and sparking curiosity in most participants.

Unexpectedly, some students frowned upon the design of testing displays, assessing it as unprofessional or 'implemented/designed by a student in 10 min.'. The design of testing displays was indeed kept functional, without much polishing. Commercially employed testing displays could easily be re-designed, keeping the core concepts.

All in all, testing displays succeeded in communicating and diffusing the team's testing culture to the participant, increasing her engagement in systematic testing. However, there is still room for improvement.

10 Implementation and Evaluation of Pillar 2

Findings presented in this chapter have been published in a study titled 'Automatically Recommending Test Code Examples to Inexperienced Developers' [123]. The original study was conducted by Raphael Pham, Yauheni Stoliar, and Kurt Schneider. This research team is subsequently called Pham et al. 2015b. In 2015, Raphael Pham presented the original study at the 10th Joint Meeting of the European Software Engineering Conference and the ACM SIGSOFT Symposium on the Foundations of Software Engineering (ESEC/FSE) in Bergamo, Italy. This original study was based on the Master's thesis of Yauheni Stoliar [143], which Raphael Pham proposed and supervised.

10.1 Test Recommender

This study is a concrete implementation the strategy 2 (p. 90). Pham et al. 2015b strategically present useful and contextual test code examples from a project's test suite to newcomers in order to facilitate learning and test writing: They introduce an automatic recommender system that analyzes the changes that the newcomer has made to the source code, called *Test Recommender*. Based on these changes, the recommender system proposes test code (from the set of existing test codes of the test suite of the project) that is most probable to be a suitable basis for a new test code. With an automatic suggestion mechanism for valuable test code, the newcomer is enabled to learn how senior developers write tests and copy it.

To this end, *suitable* test code is defined as: First, the suggested test code must serve as a good basis for the new test, i.e. only a relatively small amount of changes need to be made. The test code suggestion has to take into account the current changes to the production code. Second, the suggested test code shows features of the test framework that the newbie can learn and use.

Main Use Case for the Test Recommender. A new graduate makes changes to production code. When she is done, she triggers Test Recommender by the push of a button in her IDE. Test Recommender analyzes the changes made by the newcomer. Next, it searches through the set of existing tests, looking for test code that is similar to what the newcomer might need in this situation: test code that tests something remotely similar. The Test Recommender window appears and suggests a list of suitable tests, ascending from best suited to marginally suited. Tests not matching the Test

Figure 10.1: Suggesting a suitable example of test code in the IDE of a newcomer.

Recommender's heuristic will not be included. The user browses through the set of tests, choses one and uses it to write her test.

Graphical User Interface of the Test Recommender. Pham et al. 2015b have implemented the approach as an Eclipse IDE Plugin, called *Test Recommender* (see Fig. 10.1). The main view of Test Recommender features two panes. The left pane is informative and explains why this test has been recommended. For the newcomer, this facilitates an understanding of why a particular test has been shown to her. Also, it can give her an idea of where to find other tests and how to approach the search for tests in general.

The right pane shows the recommended test code example and is *browsable*: The newcomer can click through all suggestions using the buttons below the right pane. Each time, the rationale on the left pane and the suggestion is updated. Seeing senior developer's test code in action should give the newcomer an understanding of how such tests can be used. Both the rationale on the left as well as the test code on the right are highlighted. This facilitates a quicker grasp of important parts of the code.

10.1.1 Technical Approach of the Test Recommender

The general rationale for finding a suitable tests is 'suitable test code will use the same types as the current changes to the production code' (types can be classes or primitive data types). For example, a test that covers a certain class will at least use this class to instantiate an object of this class. Going through the set of tests one by one, Test Recommender compares types used in the changes to the types used in each test and ranks these tests accordingly. Two situations emerge:

- At best, the newcomer changes a class that is already covered by a written test case—this test case would certainly refer to this class in test code and it would be suited for adoption.

- At worst, the newcomer introduces a new class, not mentioned in the test suite.

In the latter case, Test Recommender attempts to look for tests in the test suite that cover classes, which are *similar* to the newly introduced class. Similarity is measured as 'located in the same package': Tests for other classes in the same package as the current code changes can be useful as test examples. For example, classes from the package 'view' and tests for classes in the package 'view' have similar instantiation patterns. If the newcomer adds a new view object with no tests, being presented with a test for another, similar view object can help.

A more in-depth description of the technical workings of the Test Recommender can be found in the appendix (cf. p. 14). It is, however, not mandatory.

10.2 Evaluation: Test Recommender

To better understand the impacts of the Test Recommender approach, the researchers performed two evaluations. The first evaluation helped the researchers to validate and correct implementation and design decisions during the development of the Test Recommender system. The researchers wanted to understand whether inexperienced developers agreed with the provided matching and prioritization of suitable test codes and what advantages these developers recognized in using the approach. While the first evaluation was qualitative, the second evaluation was quantitative. It featured a cross-design and helped measure a quantitative effect of using the Test Recommender system.

Two rounds of evaluation have been conducted, using the following configurations.

Evaluation 1: perceived advantages of approach and correctness of matching algorithm, paper prototype, qualitative, 10 Bachelor & Master students.

Evaluation 2: measurable impact on test writing behavior, working implementation, quantitative, 12 Bachelor & Master students.

10.2.1 Evaluation 1

The population consisted of 10 students in computer science (nine) and computer engineering (one) who were just about to get their degrees. These students included four master and six bachelor students. All of these students had been programming during lecture courses of their recent semesters. Their programming experience ranged from one year up to eight years, testing experience ranging from none to up to two years.

At the time of this evaluation, only the search algorithm of the Test Recommender was finished and the researchers used paper printouts of source code. They used the open source project 'Picasso' [1] as a source for real-world production code and test code. The researchers selected a relatively small commit that only edited one class. They removed the developer-provided test code that belonged to these changes from the project's test suite and applied the Test Recommender search approach to the remaining

---

[1] https://github.com/square/picasso

tests. The tool ranked 23 of those tests according to their hypothesized suitability as a 'copy&paste'-template for a newcomer, from high to low. The researchers picked six test code suggestions: two test codes with highest ratings for suitability, two with middle ratings and two with lowest ratings. They were interested in whether these ratings were at least reflected in how students would assess the suitability of these test code suggestions for writing their own test code. Using two tests for each quality level helped to smooth out minor deviations.

Each participant was presented with the source code of the commit (as a printed listing, presented with formatting and syntax highlighting similar to Eclipse's code editor), asked to examine the code and to explain the character of the changes made. The researchers rated their level of understanding: Seven participants were able to explain both of the two main changes to the code while the three explained only one.

Choosing A Suitable Test Code.   After that, each participant was shown the six suggestions for test code. We asked each participant to examine the tests one by one and explain them for better understanding. Each participant was asked to select one of the tests that—according to them—was best suited to be used as a 'template-for-reuse' in this situation, i.e. for copy & paste & adaption. Eight of ten participants selected a test code suggestion from the two top matches. The remaining two participants opted for a middle match.

The researchers asked participants to explain their reasoning behind their selection. The researchers wanted to know what participants were looking for when looking for test code to copy from. Participants preferred test code that used classes that were affected in the changes. Seeing 'how things worked' was important to participants. The main motivation was to see how these objects could be used and invoked: *"That test shows me how to use the constructor of the class used in changes."* One participant decided to go with the a longer test, calling its bigger size an advantage, because *"bigger test shows more"*. However, short and concise style of test code can seem more accessible and less intimidating. One participant selected a middle-matched test code for its shortness, making it *"easy to understand"*.

Perceived Advantages of Using Test Recommender.   Next, the researchers asked the participants to describe briefly what advantages they saw in being presented with test examples. Participants welcomed the concept of test code suggestions as templates (*"It can be directly used as a template"*) over having to write tests from scratch. Test code suggestions helped them to get going with testing, *"It saves my time, I can start right away"*. Would our participants like to use the Test Recommender tool when developing? On a scale of 1 ('absolutely not') to 10 ('definitely yes'), five participants chose rating 8 and four participants chose rating 6. One participant chose rating 7.

Validating Test Recommender's Ranking.   As a final task, we asked the participants to order the remaining five tests according to their perception of usefulness as a template for copying. Unsurprisingly, the tests with no correspondence to the changes (only

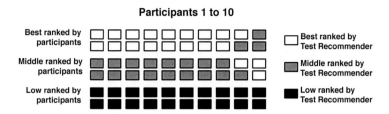

Figure 10.2: Participants' ranking of six test cases according to their usefulness as a copy-template. Each column is one participant's ranking of six test codes.

few classes in common) were quickly ranked last. Fig. 10.2 shows the ordering that participants chose, distinguished in three tiers: Test Recommender predicted white tests to be most useful to newcomers, gray tests had a middle rank and black tests had a very low rating. Overall, the ranking by participants matched the ranking of the Test Recommender. This is most evident when considering low ranked tests—deciding that a test code suggestion is *not* relevant seems easier. As already indicated in the participants' multi-facetted reasoning for selecting the best suited test code suggestion, the ordering differs more regarding better ranked suggestions.

10.2.2 Evaluation 2

In a second evaluation, Pham et al. 2015b studied the effects of using the Test Recommender plug-in quantitatively. The researchers were interested in whether being provided with such a context-sensitive test recommendation would help the newcomers to write tests faster. After all, they would not have to search through the project's test suite themselves. The researchers designed the evaluation as a simple cross-validation and engaged a population similar to the population of evaluation 1. It consisted of 12 soon-to-graduate students in computer science, among them four master and eight bachelor students. Their programming experience ranged from 1,5 to 5 years and testing experience from none to 2 years.

The evaluation was done using a versioned (SVN) Android project that incorporated two carefully curated code changes (several changed lines) in the form of two commits and using the final Test Recommender tool in an Eclipse IDE. The general evaluation setup was as follows—it was repeated twice for each participant: First, the app (a simple library management system) was demonstrated to each participant in order to make her familiar with its functionality. The first set of changes in the source code was highlighted by using the SVN annotate function in Eclipse. Each participant was asked to explain the effects of the code changes using the running app. The researchers rated the level of their understanding based on the quality of the description. All twelve participants were able to describe the implemented functions correctly after reviewing the code changes for less than one minute and 20 seconds.

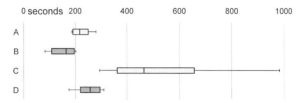

Figure 10.3: Having access to the Test Recommender (TR) enabled students to deliver tests faster, regardless of task difficulty. Group A: easier task w/o TR, Group B: easier task w/ TR, Group C: harder task w/o TR, Group D: harder task w/ TR. Whiskers are the maximum and minimum values.

Second, participants were asked to write a test, which would cover the first set of changes. For better comparability between participants and test results, the researchers provided participants with a clear description of the feature test. Researchers measured the time each participant needed to implement the test.

The population was divided into two groups of six participants each. The first group was given access to the Test Recommender for the first task but not the second task and vice versa for the second group. All participants had free access to project's test suite and internet browser. The second testing task was a little more complex than the first, providing results for the tool under differing conditions. Overall, participants using Test Recommender were able to complete the task faster than participants without it. This is effect is clearer for the second task, which had an increased complexity level: for the first task, participants using the Test Recommender were about one minute (52 sec, median) faster while their lead increased to about three and a half minutes (206 sec, median) for the second test task. Given the small size of our population, the results cannot provide statistical significance.

11 Solution Empirical Study

In 2012, Raphael Pham, Leif Singer, Olga Liskin, Fernando Figueira Filho, and Kurt Schneider conducted a Grounded Theory study, which inspired the tripartite approach (Pham et al. 2012). The goal of this study was to understand the influences of a high degree of social transparency on testing behavior: How did project owners on a social coding site quickly communicate their testing culture (their testing needs) to new contributors and how did these contributors perceive this testing culture?

Working environments with high degree of social transparency influence collaboration between software developers [37]: Developers can see what artifacts other users are interacting with a lot and what they pay attention to, identifying important artifacts and projects. Following discussions and observing how other developers find solutions, developers learn from each other, disseminating technical knowledge.

Pham et al. 2012 interviewed 33 active github.com users and validated their core findings with 569 users using an online questionnaire. Pillar 1 and pillar 2 are inspired by real-world phenomena observed in this study: a degree of high social transparency increases testing engagement, existing test code supports developers in writing their own code and developers heavily rely on it.

The most influential themes of this study are presented here. The original paper is published as "Creating a shared understanding of testing culture on a social coding site" [122] and was presented by Raphael Pham at the International Conference on Software Engineering (ICSE) in San Francisco. An adapted version can also be found in Leif Singer's PhD thesis [139].

11.1 Testing Behavior on a Social Coding Site

Developers active on github.com reported that their testing behavior was indeed influenced by the high degree of social transparency. Users knew that their actions were visible, which made them more cautious of the quality of their contributions to projects. Contributors even specifically added written tests to their code to highlight their qualitative work and the added value of their code.

Effects of Existing Test Code. Being aware of and having access to test code in a project had an especially strong effect on contributors. When users perceived a prominently placed test suite in a project, it communicated to them the impression of an informal guideline to write tests for their own contribution. They felt an implicit demand for tests and engaged in more test writing. Contributors reported to perceive a strong communication of test values and testing culture. Relatedly, when contributors did not find any test suite or any sign of test activity in a project, they assumed that no tests were demanded and did not hand in any.

Technical Support by Existing Test Code. Providing developers with easy access to the existing test code proved very important: Developers used existing tests as a source for education. They heavily relied on "copy & paste & adapt" when writing their own tests. They sought out the existing test code on their own or project owners even pointed them to similar tests to base their own on. Project owners even opened up Skype calls and taught new contributors how to write tests.

Having an extensive test suite in a project increased confidence for exploration and experimentation in contributors. Contributors also felt more confident in their own creations and were less afraid of breaking other users' code.

Communicating Testing Culture. However, not only hard test code and whole test suites communicated a project's testing culture. Other—more indirectly testing-related—signals also communicated the project's testing culture. For example, when a project on github.com uses a continuous integration server, its profile site is adorned with a CI-badge. Users who saw this badge changed their behavior and knew to add tests to their contributions if they wanted them to be accepted by the project owner.

Findings in Context of DOI-Theory. The contributors' behavior of increasing testing activity when being more socially transparent can be put into context of Rogers' Diffusion of Innovations Theory. On github.com, engaging in systematic testing increased the perceived *relative advantage*: Knowing that one's actions are more visible to peers, contributors wanted to decrease their chances of delivering false code. Others wanted to highlight their qualitative work to get their changes accepted into the project.

By providing test suites in their projects and by using easier-to-use test frameworks, project owners decreased the *complexity* of systematic testing perceived by contributors. Project owners actively helped contributors overcome technical issues and knowledge gap, further decreasing the perceived complexity of the endeavor 'systematic testing'. Github.com provides many tools needed in software development in an integrated way (e.g. an issue tracker or a wiki) and allows to start collaborations with a push of a button, lowering many technical barriers to start coding. This increases perceived *trialability* of new technologies: checking out a new project, running test suites with few clicks made testing easier.

Contributors perceived a high degree of *observability* of systematic testing. From simple clues and visible signs of testing activities (e.g. CI-badge), over following discussions about testing, to hard evidence of systematic testing in form of test-related artifacts such as test code, contributors were supplied with many channels of perceiving their peers engaging in systematic testing. This strong observability in combination with *relative advantage* help to overcome a negatively perceived *compatibility*. Contributors not convinced of systematic testing will have trouble getting their contribution accepted while perceiving testing all around them.

12 Related Work

12.1 Industry's View on Testing Education

Practitioners Only Learn Testing on the Job. All over the world, senior developers had to learn systematic testing on the job, not having received formal training.

In 2004, Ng et al. [115] conducted a survey about testing practices in Australia, including questions about developers' formal training in testing. Most practitioners were self-taught in testing practices while half of the respondents reported a lack of expertise as a major barrier for using testing methodologies. Only one third of participants had received formal training in testing. While most companies provided opportunities for testing training to their testing staff, half of the companies did so only on a needs basis.

Also in 2004, Geras et al. [64] extensively surveyed testing practitioners in Alberta, Canada. They found little test automation efforts in general, being limited to unit testing ('integration' and 'system testing' were underrepresented). Only a third of participating practitioners had received testing training. Even in practitioners who specialized in testing practice, (test team leaders) only one fifth of had received testing training.

In 2005, Chan et al. [31] interviewed practitioners in Hong Kong, inquiring practitioners about their formal test training. A third of participants reported to have independent and dedicated testing teams in their project. Only a third of these groups consisted of developers who had *all* received formal training in training while in another third, test-trained members were in the minority (only 20% of the teams). Chan et al. suspected that the test-training situation was even worse in teams of participants without dedicated testing teams. Chan et al. found that smaller companies provided less training courses than bigger companies. Participants reported to be provided with internal and external test training opportunities and courses in-service (about 70%) while 39% or practitioners reported to engage in self-learning. Most practitioners received their test training outside of university, in courses provided to them when they were already in-service.

In 2006, Grindal et al. surveyed practitioners in Sweden [71]. Similar to Geras et al., they found systematic testing underrepresented in their testing behavior and hypothesized that too little test education may be a cause.

In 2010, Garousi et al. replicated the study by Geras et al., again in Alberta, Canada [62]. Test automation efforts had increased, again unit testing was still the dominant form. While one half of participating companies reported to have installed some form of training in testing, less than 20% of participating practitioners (test team leads, developers, process engineers) reported to have received formal test training. Cost and time were found to be barriers for more engagement in test training.

In 2013, Garousi et al. replicated their study from 2010, this time spanning the whole of Canada [63]. They found the situation improved—with a rising awareness for test education—but still problematic. While half of the practitioners had received at least 20h of test training, nearly half of the respondents had not received any training at all. Barriers were—again—costs, time and lack of managerial support.

As early as 2000, Weyuker et al. [153] reported on the role and job position of a software tester at AT&T in North America. They introduce a formal 'Software Test Engineer Professional Development Program' to strategically develop, educate and position testing-focused developer careers. While such focus on systematic testing in software developer careers is very laudable, it appears limited to this company.

Testing Skills of New Hires. From the employers' perspective, practitioners find the lack of practical testing skills in newcomers problematic.

In 2000, while explaining rationale for a dedicated tester's career at AT&T, Weyuker et al. [153] note that they *"found it extremely rare for even the best-educated hires to have had formal testing instruction as part of their academic training.".*

In 2002, researcher Hisham Haddad [72] assessed the skills of 14 newly hired graduates in a small software company in North America, emphasizing the non-generalizability of his non-formal report. Even though the study's focus is on critical thinking and problem solving abilities, the author notes a distinct lack of code testing abilities. They were unaware of the positive impact of systematic testing and practitioners felt compelled to file complaints to upper management about this issue.

In 2010, Simmons et al. [135] interviewed 20 practitioners of Fortune 500 companies in North America about the desired skills in a computer science graduate when applying. While the study focused on the impact of outsourcing development and their questions did not mention testing, practitioners demanded unit testing as a skill for newcomers.

In 2014, Radermacher et al. [128] interviewed 23 practitioners, mostly from North America about the skills of graduates in the interview situation and during training. Practitioners criticized graduates' inability to write usable unit tests, deeming them redundant, sometimes even re-introducing old bugs. They complained about having to train newcomers in using their test platform and writing tests in general. Graduates lacked proficiency in using software tools of a commercial production environment, having had little to no exposure to continuous integration or regression testing software (Jenkins or Microsoft Team Foundation Server). Newcomers have trouble asking for help as they do not want to appear foolish.

However, not all reports on newcomers onboarding at a company criticize the testing abilities of graduates. In 2008, Begel et al. shadowed eight newly-hired graduates at Microsoft [15]. Begel et al. identify five areas of frequent problems: cognition, collaboration, communication, orientation, technical. Newcomers were a little bit isolated from the team and had difficulties finding their way around: Finding the right person to ask for specific questions was a big issue for the new hires. Again, newcomers wanted to be seen as performing well and did not want to reveal deficiencies. Newcomers had little access to easily consumable documentation and expressed the wish for more and more in-depth documentation. They showed good efforts in testing their application and engaged in automated testing. Begel et al. criticize educational capstone projects for being "greenfield" projects (fresh and small projects, without any legacy code base) that do not represent onboarding situations for newcomers. They suggest encounters with larger, pre-existing code bases for students.

Relation to This Thesis. During the interviews for the practitioner study in chapter 4.2, all of the findings cited above came up and were re-confirmed, strengthening their validity. Practitioners whole-heartedly complained about too little test education, recounted to have had very little test education themselves. Just like the studies cited above, participants came from all over the world and from different working environments. The practitioner study of this thesis adds to these studies in the following ways: it firmly re-confirms the continued existence of a distinct lack in testing skills in newcomers and it qualitatively defines it. According to the systematic literature review by Radermacher et al. [127] of 2014, such a qualitative understanding of this skill gap has been missing. This understanding can now be used to design tailored solution approaches (which this thesis provides in chapters 5 to 8).

12.2 Academia's View on Testing Skills of Students

Need for Research into Testing Education. Researchers and educators have long since tried to align software engineering research with industry's needs. Testing has become more and more a focus for research.

In 2005, Taipale et al. [147] conducted a discussion in a focus group of researchers and practitioners to evaluate what improvements were needed most for the discipline of testing. The group agreed on ideas for improving the testing process in general, better testing tool support and an applicable standardization for testing. Curiously, even though the focus group mentions the topic of testing education, this item nor support of newcomers makes it on their final list.

In 2007, Lethbridge et al. [105] compiled a list of challenges for research, education, and industry, advocating a tighter collaboration between industry and academia and a better communicating of industrial realities in education. 'Quality' is a topic that is critical to industry but challenging to motivate students to feel passionate about.

In 2007, Antonia Bertolino [20] presented a roadmap of challenges for the discipline of systematic testing. The proper education of capable testers is a main challenge proposed by Bertolino. She emphasizes education's need to convey basic notions of testing, its limitations and possibilities while staying up-to-date to important advances.

Trying to Understand Practitioners' Testing Skill Requirements. When trying to understand industry's demands in a IT worker's skill set, researchers have turned to coding and analyzing job advertisements [58,59,96,100,106,124]. Although the results of the researchers do touch upon topics such as quality assurance, testing is represented only little. The researchers' results point to specific technological topics such as the use of programming languages (Java, C, ...). Systematic testing, however, is not a specific language but rather an engineering method—and therefore not represented by name but (probably) implied when a job advertisement reads 'programming skills in Java needed'. It could also be that quality assurance methods (or software engineering methods) were not part of the researchers' coding system.

In 2012, Moreno et al. [112] analyzed to what extent two curriculum guidelines for undergraduate degree programs in software engineering (SE2004 [99], GSwE2009 [2]) covered the skills demanded in job profiles as suggested by the industrial consortium Career Space [141]. While they find that required skills in quality assurance and systematic testing are covered by the knowledge guidelines, the researchers note that the extent of these topics is little (only from 3% up to 6% of lecture time) or even optional.

Critique of Traditional Forms of Lecturing. Educational institutions convey the role and value of testing to undergraduates. Traditional forms of lecturing testing are criticized for a lack of effectively enabling students to test in a real-world situation.

Back in 2001, educators Shepard et al. demanded to teach more testing to students *before* letting them enter commercial development [133], presenting a testing-focused course. According to Shepard, *"students today are not well equipped to apply widely practiced techniques [...] they are graduating with a serious gap in the knowledge they need to be effective software developers"*.

Kaner et al. [88] found that traditional forms of lecturing using left students unable to apply their knowledge to real-world examples. After lecturing and extensively practicing domain testing with several courses, students' were asked to write domain test cases for use cases for the software Microsoft PowerPoint but could not transfer their knowledge to real-world applications satisfyingly.

Testing Skills of Students and Graduates. In 2004, Scott et al. conducted a two-part survey about the testing behavior of Information System students when working on industrial projects and practitioners' view of students' testing performance [132][1]. Scott et al. surveyed 48 practitioners from varying company sizes and 160 students in South Africa. Students relied mostly on manual validation using GUI mask inputs and unit tests, neglecting integration or system tests. Over two thirds of practitioners felt that newcomers did not know how to properly test. While students rated their understanding of testing methodologies significantly higher than practitioners did, students reported to feel that the depth of their test training was insufficient.

In 2011, Carver et al. [28] let students test a small program and measured the test coverage when providing them with a coverage tool and without. Without a coverage tool, relying on their intuitive understanding of the effects of their test writing, students were not able to reach 100% coverage. With a coverage tool, students significantly increased their test coverage, but tended to over-assert and produce redundant tests.

---

[1]Even though this study was conducted among Information System students (and not Computer Science students), it had a strong focus on systematic software testing which is why it was included.

The test suites handed in by students were oversized, indicating that students have not internalized effective and efficient test writing.

In 2010, Sudol et al. [145] pin-pointed common misconceptions of students about the work of a software engineer using a forced-choice survey tool. They compared their results with practitioners' views but did not include test-related statements.

In 2015, Beller et al. [18] monitored students' testing activities in a software engineering course. They found that students spent only a fraction of their time testing (4%) and constantly overestimated their own testing effort. Ellims et al. [53] have found similar results in industrial projects: Unit testing is often criticized for its *high perceived costs* while the perceived costs are exaggerated compared to the benefits of testing activities.

In Context of This Thesis. While several studies analyzed the testing skills of students, none provided a comprehensive and qualitative insight into enablers and barriers to systematic testing as perceived by these inexperienced developers. All findings cited above have been confirmed in students study of chapter 4.1, strengthening their validity. This student study, however, goes beyond that and gives a more in-depth understanding of the motivations and problems students had with systematic testing. This provides an opportunity to strategically improve the testing experience for students and newcomers.

12.2.1 Academia's Efforts to Improve Testing Education

Educators have put considerable efforts in integrating systematic testing into curricula and improving testing education—with varying results.

Making Testing Ubiquitous, As Early As Possible. Jones et al. [85–87] present a holistic approach to integrate testing into the curriculum, spread throughout the curriculum with repeating testing experiences for students. They present a framework provide testing experiences in small doses, already in early courses. Several educators [33, 69, 108, 113] take a similar view and advocate to include systematic testing throughout the whole curriculum to facilitate the creation of a testing habit.

Other educators make the case for testing-focused course. Shepard et al. [133] present a testing course with more practical exercises and promising educational results.

Rise of TDD in Education. With the rise of test-driven development (TDD) as a development approach, educators began advocating the integration of TDD into the curriculum [50, 82, 83, 126]. Students were expected to better understand and appreciate systematic testing, reducing forming of bad programming habits. However, the effect of TDD on students is mixed: Edwards et al. [50] used web applications to give students clear feedback on their TDD behavior, which improved their approach to testing. Desai et al. [47], on the other hand, did not find any increase of quality in student code.

Student Capstone Projects for Hands-On Testing Experience. As proposed in the discussion 13 of this thesis, encounters with real-world projects increase the hands-on experience for students and ultimately help graduates to overcome the shock of practice better. Many educators report on cooperation projects with real-world stakeholders, use of industrial projects in university courses and even student developments at companies.

In 2002, Hayes et al. [73] report on a successful student capstone project involving real stakeholders and software used in a medicine context. With a strong focus on software quality and reliability engineering, the software was developed at the university. students were convinced of the *"need to need to build quality in as opposed to testing quality in"* and developed more quality engineering skills than in normal courses.

While providing students with more motivation and real-world requirements, Begel et al. [15] caution that such kind of 'greenfield' projects with no legacy code and only student developers do not reflect industry realities.

In 2011, Garousi et al. [60] incorporated industrial projects into a testing course and let students write test suites for real-world projects with industrial stakeholders. The results were promising with positive long-term effects: students reported to have learned a lot, even benefiting from this knowledge long after the course ended. This collaboration resulted in immediate job offers for students and companies were provided with test code and test suites. Confidentiality and intellectual property were barriers to overcome.

Knudson et al. [95] gained a lot of experience in university-industry collaborations and cautions about distinct differences between student capstone projects done with industry stakeholders at university and cooperation projects with students working on industrial projects at companies. They presents a process to navigate dissimilarities and mitigate pitfalls.

12.3 Systematic Testing in Industry.

There are many reports on industrial software testing, its context, motivators & inhibitors, and lessons learnt. Only a selection is described here to draw an understanding of the role of a software tester in industry.

Berner et al. [19] of the software development company Zuehlke report on experiences when engaging in industrial systematic testing. Similarly, Karhu et al. [90] reported on factors that support or hinder the automation of tests. Among other things, they found the general cost of automation and the cost of training developers in test automation to be a barrier for test automation. Runeson et al. [131] conducted a questionnaire-based survey on unit testing in industry and report on current practices, benefits, and problems of unit testing. They uncover different perceptions of what constitutes a good unit test. Greiler et al. [70] investigate the testing practices in the Eclipse Plug-In community. Michlmayr et al. [110] report on a study that investigated the quality-related practices in a diverse set of open source projects and associated problems.

Beller et al. [17] monitored the testing activities of open source developers through instrumenting their IDE. Developers overestimate their own test efforts considerably, conducting less testing than assumed and test-driven development was not practiced as presented in literature—if at all. LaToza et al. [98] find similar results: although the developers reported to spend about half of their time on fixing defects, unit testing was one of the activities developers spent the least time on. In a systematic literature review, Causevic et al. [30] identified several factors that limit the adoption of TDD in industry, such as higher development time and insufficient experience.

Industrial Requirements for Being a Good Tester. Deak et al. [43] investigated what characteristic traits were required to be a good software tester. Communication skills, programming and technical testing skills were most wished for by practitioners. When comparing qualitative issues of software testers in both traditional waterfall and modern agile development, Deak et al. [42] found motivators and de-motivators when working as testers: testers in waterfall projects felt more stressed while testers in agile projects felt better integrated into their teams. Both studies by Deak et al. feature only a small and non-representative set of participants in Norway.

Kanij et al. [89] investigated which factors affect effectiveness of testing. In a questionnaire-based survey they inquired about the importance of factors such as tools and training, but also more human-centered factors like personality characteristics and experience. They find that, among others, good domain knowledge, experience, and interpersonal skills were considered important.

Beer et al. [12] examined the role of experience in software testing practice: test case design based on experience complementary to requirements' based. Though testing tools exists, they determined that these tools do not take advantage of testers' experience, supporting her in designing a test case based on past testing experience. Sources for testing experience for practitioners were: being involved with previous versions of the software system, fixing defects, engagement in development and maintenance of the software system and working in a similar domain before. Regarding inexperienced newcomers, these sources appear very hard to attain—if not provided systematically in the educational environment (cf. chapter 13).

Perception of Systematic Testing and Being a Tester. The way that inexperienced developers approach testing is influenced by the image of a software tester and the associated prestige or lack thereof. Deak et al. [41] proposes a deeper investigation into the image of software testers in industry. Deak et al. [45] investigate students' perception of the role a tester and asked whether or not they wanted to work as testers later on. The majority of students did not, associating it with boredom. Students interested in testing longed for more practical experience.

12.4 Supporting Newcomers During Onboarding

In 2015, Sebastiano Panichella's [116] thesis supports newcomers in OSS development. Panichella' approach is divided into three parts: helping the newcomer to find the best mentor, helping her to navigate legacy code, and serving generated code summaries for a better understanding. Panichella analyzes mailing lists and other artifacts of communication for important information that could help newcomers. Using this information, his tool YODA can automatically recommend a good mentor to newcomers. Another tool, CODES, mines the same communication information to generate code descriptions from developer communication about specific code parts. This information can help newcomers understand legacy code better.

While both this thesis and Panichella's approach aim to support newcomers in software development environments, there are certain differences. Panichella's approach is tailored to OSS while this thesis approach targets the commercial software industry. Developing in open source projects shares similarities with professional software development, however, there are different dynamics not found in both (for example: working voluntary vs. paid, pressure to lose one's job,...).

This thesis approach is tailored towards systematic testing while Panichella's approach targets general code comprehension. This thesis employs social transparency to establish an awareness for a testing demand and to overcome negative attitudes that have developed due to the nature of testing and shortcomings in education. This is a specialization that Panichella's approach does consider. While both approaches want to ease (test) code comprehension, this thesis approach does not depend on mining developer communication but analyses existing test suites.

Socially Transparent Development Environments. The effects of social transparency and social translucency on human interaction using computers are manifold. The framework of social transparency [144] has been employed to explain a variety of behaviors and situations: Mutual assessment of software developers [137] or competing effects on workers solving micro-tasks in crowdsourcing [78, 91]. Research of social transparency's effect of on software engineering, especially software testing, are rarer.

Dabbish et al. [37, 38] give an overview of how software developers work in a new kind of development environment: On github.com, flexible version control systems (git) are combined with a high degree of social transparency, making artifacts and actions of other users more visible and traceable. This enables developers to see what artifacts other users are interacting with a lot and what they pay attention to, identifying important artifacts and projects. Transferred to the onboarding situation and testing, the newcomer is enabled to 'see' what other developers are doing with the test suite (cf. Testing Displays), judging it to be very important.

Social transparency supports coordination and awareness within teams. Begel et al. [16] report on a newsfeed system that increases project awareness. DeSouza et al. [140] investigate which actions should be presented to whom in such feeds. Selecting specific test-suite-related events to show to the newcomer could help to the effect on the newcomer. The smart display strategy discussed in the discussion part is a first step in this direction (p. 114). None of these studies has examined the effects increased social transparency might have on testing practices.

In his PhD thesis, Leif Singer [139] presents a framework and process to improve the adoption of software engineering practices through persuasive, non-coercive interventions. Singer focuses on the adoption of software engineering practices in general and also suggests to strategically employ social transparency. This thesis, however, has a strong focus on the practice of systematic testing as well as the specific circumstances of the industrial onboarding situation. It is tailored to qualitative insights about barriers to systematic testing from the point of view of newcomers. While Singers's approach could be used to nudge newcomers into engaging more in testing, its abstraction level is considerably higher than in this thesis, leading to a different implementation if applied.

Use of Dashboards. This thesis augments the newcomer's onboarding environment with dashboard-like monitors of testing culture. Dashboards help the developer to develop and maintain a mental model of a project's progress. Treude et al. give an overview of dashboards that foster awareness of a project's status, developer's activities and artifacts [148]. IBM's Jazz [57] aggregates project status and developer activities in configurable dashboards. Tools like FASTDash [21] and SeeSoft [51] work on a shared codebase to gain and maintain awareness of team members' activities (e.g. who is looking at which file, who edited which file). While these tools increase awareness for different aspects of development, Testing Displays focus on awareness of testing activities.

Ranking team members and introducing the element of competition to inexperienced developers can have beneficial impacts on their development behavior. Singer et al. ranked members of a student software engineering project by the number of their commits and rewarded more commits with better badges [138]. This ranking was only visible to the team and led to more frequent and smaller commits, which was desirable.

Dubois et al. propose to research a framework for using gamification in software engineering [48]. They made software development metrics (for example, Test Coverage, #lines of JavaDoc, Code Duplication) of one student software project team visible to another student software project team with promising results.

Recommending Test Code The idea of using existing code examples as a learning aid is not new. Barzilay et al. [9] describe it as an *"act of embedding a code segment from an example into a software system being developed"* and advocate to see it as an activity of software engineering. While staying on the theoretical level, Barzilay et al. suggest an overlay structure to example embedding as a part of code reuse and identify several categories, practices, and possible tool application areas. Although providing many vital examples and explanations [8], there is no mention of example embedding for software testing.

Nasehi et al. [114] did a qualitative study of the most popular answers with examples on stackoverflow.com to gain an understanding what a good code example looks like.

Edwards et al. present an eclipse plug-in, which operates on a set of pre-written code examples, highlighting their occurrences in code [49]. These stand-alone examples are used in real-life code and allow for learning without having to leave the IDE. Similar to Edwards, Test Recommender uses tracing to determine suitable code and operates on previously created content, however this content does not need to be explicitly created for learning purposes—instead, Test Recommender uses content that is already existing (such as the existing test suite).

Hummel et al. introduce "Code Conjurer", a tool that uses queries to search for code examples [79]. Again, "Code Conjurer" operates on a pool of pre-written examples, albeit provided by an external source. Brandt et al. present "Blueprint", an IDE plug-in that provides code examples on demand—including context information for it [22]. It mines regular websites and fetches the descriptions from around the code examples. Only few of few of the attempts to apply example-centric programming mention the writing of software tests as a possible application area. In contrast to Test Recommender approach, both "Code Conjurer" and "Blueprint" require a user written and explicit query and do not provide any insights into the matching decisions to the user. Targeting inexperienced developers operating query-less and offering insights for learning is crucial. Test Recommender limits the search set for test code to the project's own test suite in order to guarantee applicability of the suggested test code. Direct and easy applicability of the test code is important as it reduces frustration and facilitates adoption of the approach among inexperienced developers.

In his PhD thesis, Werner Janjic presented an approach for reuse-based test recommendation [81] by leveraging strategies from software reuse techniques and as well as ideas from code search engines. His work is considerably more focused on an effective test code recommendation experience for the user: While the user types, recommendations for the next line of test code (such as a specific assert-statement) are generated from the set of scanned test codes. In contrast, the Test Recommender implementation is less sophisticated and provides full test code methods to the newcomer (—ultimately, Test Recommender is only one of three parts of this thesis). This however, can be an advantage. Providing test code *context* to the newcomer can help to facilitate understanding of technicalities, for example: the correct use of a test framework feature can be shown in the lines above or below a critical line of test code. This way, the newcomer is enabled to adopt this new test feature. Students in the evaluation rounds of Test Recommender stated to specifically like the *browse*-feature, letting them browse and study an set of related test codes. When dealing with newcomers, rationale and context can be of help.

Recommending Test Tutorials   There is a lot of related work on the use of knowledge bases and knowledge management in context of training newcomers. For example, Dagenais et al. [40] investigate the creation and maintenance of developer documentation and how developers use it to learn in open source environments. However, only test-related publications are discussed here.

Elbaum et al. present a stand-alone web-application BugHunt that students can use to work through interactive test tutorials in a self-paced manner [52]. BugHunt's tutorials cover a set of test techniques, complete with introduction, source code examples and opportunities to enter test code and receive results (cf. Fig. **??**). As the examples are pre-engineered and contained in their complexity, BugHunt can offer interactive help and point the student to issues that keep her from completing the test task.

ButHunt's web-based tutorial-like approach differs to the Test Tutorial approach presented in Pillar 3 in the following ways: BugHunt is designed to teach students certain test-techniques while Test Tutorial is designed to help newcomers overcome specific test-related knowledge and experience gaps in an industrial situation. While BugHunt covers test principles and provides artificial test code examples, Test Tutorial uses *running* test code examples that show off how testing is accomplished in *that* specific situation for the newcomer. As seen in chapter 4.1, inexperienced developers are easily side-tracked. Providing newcomers with a BugHunt implementation would certainly help them in learning how to test, but it would not guarantee that newcomers could apply this knowledge in the real surroundings—technicalities could still hinder them.

BugHunt includes a pre-set set of topics. With BugHunt, the student incrementally builds up testing knowledge while Test Tutorial's approach is more ad-hoc: only those topics are covered that *actually* came up in onboarding. This ensures that practice-relevant questions are addressed and saves the newcomer's time. In onboarding, newcomers bring different skills and different knowledge gaps to the table, having them work through a standardized set of tutorials could be perceived as counter-productive. Here, an approach by Agarwal et al. [3] could help: test tutorial systems that adapt their courseware based on the current knowledge of the student user by maintaining a model of the user's knowledge. This could help avoiding unnecessary lessons and increase the test tutorial's effectiveness in bringing the newcomer up to speed. However, both approaches by Elbaum et al. and Agarwal et al. focus on the educational situation while the test tutorial approach presented here is tailored to the industrial onboarding situation, putting a focus on immediate real-world applicability.

In 2005, Collofello et al. presented Test Trainer Tool, a web-based environment for training computer science students on software testing [34]. Similar to Elbaum's et al. BugHunt, it includes test tutorial instructions and the opportunity to actually enter test code with interactive feedback. Just like BugHunt, it shares the same dissimilarities to the test tutorial approach of this thesis: the choice of test-related topics is not ad-hoc and need-based and the examples are not guaranteed to work in an industrial environment.

12.5 Onboarding of Newcomers

While the onboarding process in open source often is observable, this is not generally true for commercial software companies, reducing the number of publications on it.

Johnson et al. [84], engineers at Google, describes an industrial onboarding process at Google. They advocate ad-hoc learning and refinement of skills on-the-job and present a framework for practice-based learning: They systematically make information accessible to the newcomer for self-participation. Mailing lists and events have intranet-sites and communities of practice for specific topics (knowledge guilds) offer sources for information if needed. Employees make their actions visible (by weekly, quarterly reports) and are encouraged to feel a personal responsibility career development, catering to an entrepreneurial mindset: you have to do it on your own, and you are responsible.

Studying the onboarding of newcomers in open source development, the fundamental role of a capable mentor as well as the newcomer's need for support in that phase becomes apparent. Steinmacher et al. [142] studied the onboarding process in an open source development setting. They describe a catalogue of barriers that newcomers to open source projects face: Newcomers have trouble finding persons—such as mentors—for support. For example, 'Problems with Documentation' often hindered new developers in getting started. Steinmacher et al. conclude that active support while onboarding helps new-comers to contribute to the project more actively. Fagerholm et al. [56] hypothesizes that developers, who were supported during their onboarding phase, have a higher chance to *"be exposed to, select, and perform tasks in a proactive and self-directed manner"*. Supporting onboarding with mentoring seems to be most influential in this regard. Dagenais et al. [39] studied the impacts of a new project landscape on newcomers. They found that *"helpful landscape inhabitants make a key difference to how easy it is for newcomers to find their way and settle in"*.

Von Krogh et al. [152] qualitatively analyzed the onboarding process of one open source project and developed a theory of processes and barriers to becoming a part of the OSS community. Herraiz et al. [76] uncovered differences the onboarding process of volunteer open source contributors and paid, hired contributors to open source projects. While volunteer contributors follow the common onion model [36] and slowly work through different stages of involvement, hired contributors face a much more sudden onboarding and are expected to be productive faster.

Hemphill et al. [74, 75] analyzed the onboarding process in distributed development teams and found that remote new hires are isolated from the rest of the team, not being able to follow what others are doing. Newcomers want to prove themselves but struggle to get noticed by their managers and team members.

Critique About Mentoring. Onboarding is generally easier for the newcomer when being technically supported, in open source development [39] as well as in commercial development. However, as seen in the practitioner study in chapter 4.2, mentoring is also costly. In open source projects, mentorship can bring the newcomer up to speed faster but *"requires a significant investment of time and effort"* [55]. Similarly, Sim et al. [134] consider it as inefficient and disruptive, though very effective in passing on new information to the onboarder. The mentor cannot complete other tasks [46] and the team's productivity suffers.

Improvements to Mentoring. The impact of mentoring on productivity has been eval-uated by several practitioners. Begel et al. [14] approves mentoring if the novice can learn from a mentor acting as a role model. Begel suggests a chat room or mailing lists that novices can use to ask questions openly without fearing to be asking unnecessary questions. One step further, Begel et al. [13] even suggests to preemptively help devel-opers who got stuck using a suggestion system integrated into the IDE. Transferred to onboarding, this could help newcomers when they do not know when or where to ask.

Canforra et al. [26, 27] present an approach to support assigning of mentors to new-comers in open source projects by mining data from mailing lists and versioning systems. They found that the most active member regarding a specific topic is not best suited to act as a mentor.

13 Discussion

Some parts of this discussion are based on discussions in publications [119] and [120].

Generalizability of this Discussion.   There is a whole spectrum of different educational settings and industrial onboarding environments. Some parts of academia are not affected by the problems described in chapter 4—their graduates are equipped with very good testing skills. Successful software companies that have well-established onboarding processes may perceive only little struggles with handling newcomers. There are, however, also parts of academia and industry that are directly affected by a low level of testing skills in newcomers. Astigarra et al. [5] and Garousi et al. [61] discovered that systematic testing is heavily underrepresented in current university curricula and Kaner et. al [88] found that traditional lecture methods left students unable to apply their knowledge in practice. Also, before a software company becomes successful and is able to provide a well-established onboarding process, it would have had to start small and accomplish onboarding with less man-power or budget. Similarly, smaller or differently-focused educational settings may handle testing differently from those parts of academia that are more successful in this regard. This discussion may be of value to these parts of academia and industry.

Contribution of this Discussion.   Proposals in this discussion stem from the many insights in this thesis about graduates' testing behavior and the industrial onboarding process. It provides:

- an analysis of the impact of the 3-pillar approach on researchers, educators and practitioners (section 13.1), and

- a proposal of improvements for academia (section 13.2) for increasing testing skills in graduates, and

- a description of a tighter collaboration scheme between academia and industry (section 13.3).

Importance of the Onboarding Phase.   The actual onboarding phase may seem relatively short and insignificant compared to the lifetime of a software engineer's career. However, if gaps in testing skills are not taken care of early on, they can negatively influence the newcomers progress in becoming a high-quality engineer.

Onboarding is already a stressful situation in which the new hire has to adapt to the company's development culture and processes. Teaching of fundamental engineering practices impacts the onboarding situation negatively: both the teaching load on the practitioner and the learning load on the new hire are higher. This is expensive and frustrates practitioners and smaller sized companies may not be able to afford this.

This Thesis: Solution Proposal for Industry. Practitioners are dissatisfied with the testing skills of newcomers (cf. section 4.2). In this regard, four distinct Problem Areas in the testing skills of inexperienced developers have emerged (cf. section 4.3):

Problem Area 1: Having Trouble Implementing a Test Process.

Problem Area 2: Lack of How-To-Knowledge.

Problem Area 3: Dismissive Testing Attitude.

Problem Area 4: Deterred by High Learning Curves.

This thesis proposes an improvement approach for industry. Chapter 5 through 10 explain, implement and evaluate a proposal for the industrial onboarding phase: systematically increasing the level of observability and trialability while decreasing the perceived complexity of systematic testing for newcomers. According to Rogers' Theory of Diffusion of Innovations [130], such a configuration greatly helps the adoption of the practice of systematic testing. This is achieved by three strategies that are based on these insights while tackling Problem Areas 1 to 4:

Pillar 1: increase social transparency and make actions and testing behavior of others observable to the newcomer.

Pillar 2: provide the newcomer with runnable test code to help getting started when she needs it, decreasing complexity and increasing trialability.

Pillar 3: provide the newcomer with test-related learning materials when she needs them, decreasing complexity and increasing trialability.

13.1 Impact of the Approach of this Thesis

This thesis is located at the intersection between educational institutions, researchers, and practitioners. Its approach impacts the current hiring situation for both companies and newcomers. For researchers, it points in new research directions and for educators, it uncovers potential for improvement.

13.1.1 Impact on Industry.

For industry, this thesis delivers a comprehensive view on the current onboarding situation that newcomers and practitioners face. It touches upon topics that may have been presented in prior studies or that are seen as 'well-known' facts. For example, the use of a wiki where information on company processes and tools is made available (cf.

practitioner study in section 4.2) is a well-known industry practice. However, as this data was found in an empirical Grounded Theory approach, it is presented nonetheless, striving for an inclusive and current presentation of the onboarding situation in this population. While some companies have little problems in onboarding and see only little value in the insights repeated in this thesis, others may find them more insightful. A comprehensive view on current testing-related onboarding issues gives companies a chance to recognize related problem areas. While it is well-known that the update cycle of a wiki can become problematic, it is not guaranteed that affected companies associate this issue with *onboarding* and *testing*. This establishes new perspectives and gives rise to new approaches for improvement.

Financial Aspects of Low Testing Skills. In this thesis, the financial aspects of onboarding and the impact of low testing skills on it remain undefined. While onboarding was perceived as "costly" in the practitioner study of section 4.2, the researchers did not talk about financial numbers for the costs induced by a low level of testing skills and cannot make any statement in that direction. The population of that study was quite diverse and the numbers would have fluctuated greatly, resulting in no definitive answer. It is not clear whether or not these participants (software developers handling the onboarding process) were in the best position to answer financial questions reliably. In the interviews of the Grounded Theory study, it became clear that practitioners perceived the cost of managing these problems during onboarding as *too high* and that they were discontent with the current situation. This qualitative insight presents a good starting point for further research into this area.

Costs of Operating the 3-Pillar Approach of This Thesis

The cost of installing and operating tripartite approach (cf. chapter 5) is difficult to assess in detail. However, its *general impact* on the cost of onboarding is clear:

Hypothesis The approach of this thesis reduces the cost of onboarding.

The three pillars of this thesis are not disruptive in nature. They are not designed to fully replace current onboarding practices, such as mentoring a newcomer. Their goal is to help the newcomer adopt quicker, better and more independently—this way reducing effort and enhancing the overall onboarding phase.

Implementation and Installation Costs. For all three implementation proposals (Testing Displays, Test Recommender, Test Tutorials), there is a cost of implementation of the tools and their installation in the work place. The cost of implementation is relatively small. As shown, Master students were able to implement working prototypes of the concepts. The price of a professional re-implementation would be in known and manageable magnitudes. Installation costs for Test Recommender and Testing Displays is negligible (e.g. as easy-to-download Eclipse plugins). Test Tutorials requires server hardware to serve the test-related learning materials in form of wiki-like tutorial pages—also with negligible costs. Most importantly, all aforementioned costs are all *nonrecurring* and amortize quickly over the long period of using such a three-part system.

No Recurring Costs for Pillar 1 & 2.   Once installed, the first two parts of the three-part system operate with nearly no additional or recurring costs. The strategies of pillars 1 and 2 essentially gather test-related information that is *already* present in the development team and strategically present it to the newcomer: Testing Displays gathers information on team members testing behavior and Test Recommender analyzes the existing test suite. Both strategies (and tools) work automatically and need little input from the mentor or the newcomer. Still, the newcomer is provided with valuable information at the right time, creating an improved onboarding experience and lowering the cost of onboarding: The newcomer is enabled to work more independently and to solve some of her problems on her own, lowering the teaching effort on the mentor. This frees the mentor up for other tasks, increasing productivity compared to normal mentoring. Additionally, the newcomer is supported in adopting the testing culture quicker, thusly becoming a productive member of the team quicker and shortening the overall onboarding phase. As seen in evaluations of both tools, Testing displays makes inexperienced developers engage in testing more (cf. evaluation 3, p. 118) and Test Recommender supports them in writing test code quicker (cf. evaluation 2, p. 135). Translating this boost in productivity for the mentor, the improvement in newcomers' testing behavior as well as the shortened onboarding phase into saved costs, both strategies reduce the cost of onboarding. This claim does not only hold true for the first newcomer using this enhanced onboarding process but for each subsequent newcomer as well.

Recurring Costs for Pillar 3.   Regarding pillar 3, the situation is more complicated to assess. However, the result is the same: Implementing strategy 3 reduces onboarding costs in the long run. The implementation proposed for pillar 3 requires the mentor to provide tailored test-related tutorials with running examples, all linked to the company's code base. Producing such tutorials is costly in time and effort. However, producing them is—again—a nonrecurring cost that amortizes quickly: Not only will the first newcomer (who stumbled across a test-related issue, triggering the creation of the tutorial) benefit from that tutorial, but every newcomer after that can potentially benefit as well. Assuming that newcomers have similar core of questions, the number of tutorials that are required repeatedly should outweigh the number of tutorials that are required only once. Not creating these tutorials would require the mentor to explain these complex issues again and again. This way, the newcomer can work more independently and the mentor can take a more supportive role helping her understand the issue at hand. Again, this frees the mentor up for other tasks, reducing onboarding costs.

Maintaining such a tutorial system and keeping it up-to-date is a recurring cost. This thesis assumes that this maintenance cost is lower than the costs saved by using the three-part system.

Barriers to Realization and Time Frame.

Currently, the 3-pillar approach of this thesis is not yet in use in industry. One barrier for its application is that it is not yet fully implemented.

Strategies of Pillar 1 and 2 have been implemented in running prototypes and first evaluations have been completed with encouraging results. Strategy of Pillar 3 is still theoretical and needs to be implemented in a prototype before the 3-pillar approach can be used in industry. For this last implementation, wiki systems like `dokuwiki`[1] could be used as a basis for prototyping. The intended recommender system for test tutorial pages could be build on top of the implementation of Test Recommender, using its data on changed source code and existing test code for recommending a suitable test suite. Implementation of a Test Tutorial system could be done in the course of a Master's thesis in four to six months, including first evaluations. The whole 3-pillar system could be implemented for a test run in industry in six months, assuming that a suitable industry partner has been found already.

Consequences

The approach of this thesis improves the onboarding experience, impacting involved stakeholders (cf. description of stakeholders in section 5.1) in different ways.

Consequences for the Newcomer. The first benefactor if this approach is the newcomer herself. She is supported in overcoming the 'shock of practice' regarding systematic testing. The approach makes the testing culture more observable and reduces uncertainty about the demand for systematic testing in the newcomer (pillar 1). With little hands-on experience with systematic testing, the approach supports her in engaging in systematic testing and writing test code (pillar 2). The newcomer is supported in overcoming the real-world technicalities of systematic testing. Lastly, the approach supports her in overcoming gaps in test-related knowledge (pillar 3). Overall, the approach helps to reduce a perceived feeling of being overwhelmed with the task of testing and supports the newcomer in becoming a high-quality software engineer.

Consequences for the Mentor. The second benefactor of this approach is the senior developer handling the onboarding process. The approach is designed to help newcomers in overcoming testing-related issues more easily and independently, reducing the efforts for onboarding. It does not fully relieve the mentor role from her tasks but gives her a more *supportive* role. Instead of explaining test-related implementations and solutions to the newcomer herself, she can let the Test Recommender system (pillar 2) and Test Tutorial system (pillar 3) help the newcomer in understanding that test code. If further issues arise, the mentor will still have to explain the issue at hand, but not from scratch: Using the approach of this thesis, the newcomer will already have worked through some parts of the problem.

---

[1] https://www.dokuwiki.org/dokuwiki#

Recommending test code that demonstrates certain testing techniques and implementations to the newcomer is a well-established practice. For the newcomer, these test codes provide crucial information and for the mentor, they are easily identifiable: the senior developer should have a good mental model of the test suite and the tests within— at least the test code she has written herself. In the light of the finding that newcomers are sometimes shy to ask too many questions (cf. section 4.2.2, p. 62), an automated and more independent approach such as Test Recommender lends itself well: having a pool of test code recommendations ready for browsing at one's leisure (automated requests) greatly reduces the barrier for engaging in testing. Asking the mentor for the same amount of test code examples is unfeasible and would probably take up too much time for the mentor.

Even though a mentor can point to 'a very suiting' test code in a second's time, it is not guaranteed that the newcomer will ask for the n'th time or that she will ask at all. Even if requests for test codes arise repeatedly, the strategy of pillar 2 (Test Recommender) helps to alleviate the senior developers such a repeating task. Also, senior developers sometimes move to different projects, departments, or quit working at a company and this kind of knowledge is lost.

Consequences for Management.   The impact for the management role of the software company is limited. The financial impact of the 3-pillar approach is negligible and it promises to shorten onboarding times. From the viewpoint of the management, this is beneficial as it reduces onboarding costs with very little invested costs.

However, it is the management's task to ensure that employees' rights are honored and working conditions are good. In this case, management has to ensure that senior developers agree to the increased social transparency and the more visible testing culture. Management has to establish an opt-in process for using the 3-pillar approach and has to ensure that it is executed correctly.

It could fall into the hands of the management to opt for an anonymized version of Testing Displays (e.g. using smileys and nicknames). For reasons of scope, the effects of different degrees of *personally referencing* team members on the newcomer are not investigated in this thesis. The evaluations of Testing Displays show that personal reference of colleagues (real pictures and real names) do influence inexperienced developers (cf. section 9.5.5, p. 124): Participants mentioned that this personal reference increased the perceived feeling of competition and the associated call-to-action. However, the teams shown to participants were imaginative in nature (there was no actual software development team that the participant was part of). The use of smiley-faces instead of real team members' photos with randomized nicknames—counteracting identification of actually depicted team members—could reap positive results while maintaining a connection to the actual team.

Another approach would be to display a completely imaginative team to the newcomer instead of her team members. This could be combined with the *smart display* strategy, engineering most encouraging testing culture configurations in an ad-hoc manner: The newcomer would be shown Testing Displays that are most encouraging to engage in testing herself, but that do not reflect the current testing culture of the team. However, the effects of this last approach are uncertain and would mark a departure from the initial idea to make the *team's* testing culture more easily adoptable to the newcomer. These two approaches are left for future work.

Consequences for Society. A widely-accepted use of the 3-pillar approach in onboarding would have small but transformative effects on the software engineering society. While the newcomer is supported to master the new onboarding situation more confidently and the mentor is relieved of certain tasks, the tensed relations between academia and industry would be improved in general. Disgruntled expressions of disappointment such as *'Testing is learnt on the job — not at university.'* (cf. section 4.2) would be more rare. Practitioners would not have to deal with low levels of testing skills in graduates in such a direct manner as they currently have to—the 3-pillar approach could help in bridging the gap in testing skills. This would reduce the perceived negative impact of these testing skills on practitioners' view on academia.

The disgruntled expression above implicates that proper testing skills are the product of yearlong experience of working as a software engineer—and that fresh graduates cannot deliver this, which closes job opportunities for them. Using the 3-pillar approach improves the hiring situation for both the potential newcomer and the hiring company. While industry prefers practical experience in applicants, the 3-pillar approach can lessen the negative impact of a lack of hands-on test experience. With the improved 3-pillar-based onboarding process at hand, companies may look more forgivingly on low testing skills in applicants: applicants that would otherwise be rejected could still be considered for hiring. Endowing a systematic way to lessen the effort of handling low testing skills of inexperienced developers upon industry can act as a 'door-opener' for many fresh graduates on the job-market. This can help graduates land job positions that were unattainable before. This changes the dynamics of current hiring processes in favor of fresh graduates and inexperienced developers and widens the hiring options for companies.

There is not always room for choice when hiring. Especially smaller companies can benefit from using the 3-pillar approach: even though they *want* testing expertise, they make due with low testing skills of inexperienced developers (cf. Fig. 4.7, statement 11, p. 66). Qualified testing experience is hard to find (cf. Fig. 4.6b, statement 5, p. 66) and hiring testing experts is more expensive than training newcomers. This way, the hiring situation for these smaller companies is relieved in some degree. Even though they often have to deal with low level of testing skills, onboarding is less effortful and newcomers' testing behavior is improved quicker.

13.1.2 Impact on Education.

While the 3-pillar approach focuses on the onboarding phase, the prior phase—education— can benefit greatly from the findings in this thesis. Testing skills of fresh graduates are discussed in detail (cf. section 4.1) and related to practitioners' views (cf. section 4.2). The gap in graduates' testing skills and industry's expectations is openly discussed and the educational situation is analyzed in detail for possible causes for this situation, employing Rogers' Diffusion of Innovations Theory [130] (cf. chapter 3). This plethora of qualitative insights and the theoretical analysis can help to guide many improvements in current testing education.

Solving Hard Problems. For example, educators could focus in specific improvements for very concrete problems. In the empirical student study, participants had considerable trouble in engaging in automated GUI testing efficiently and correctly (cf. section 4.1.2, p. 51). Correct use and differentiation between unit tests, integration tests and system tests was difficult for participants, resulting in mostly engagement in unit testing (cf. section 4.1.4, p. 53). Here, more technical training in testing frameworks (e.g. GUI testing) and more opportunities for application of higher-level testing techniques could improve the situation.

Solving Systemic Problems. Besides such concrete problems, this thesis uncovers obstacles pertaining to the way systematic testing is taught. Student participants reported to feel that working on pre-prepared test exercises did not give them a feeling of accomplishment when engaging in systematic testing. They only felt accomplished when testing in a real project environment (cf. section 4.1.2, p. 46). Insights like these opens potential to re-think the way test-related exercises are presented, influencing the attitude that graduates form about systematic testing. Here, the theoretical analysis of the way systematic testing is taught in context of Rogers Diffusion of Innovations [130] is helpful (cf. chapter 3) and can guide the design of new teaching approaches: The perceived low relative advantage and the deceitfully low complexity present opportunities in improving testing education. The low observability of other students' successes in applying systematic testing is problematic and should be improved.

Increasing Focus on Testing. Generally, the findings presented in this thesis point to the need for a stronger focus on systematic testing in computer science education. Nowadays, systematic testing takes only a little place in curricula. Educational institutions can expand lecture programs and put more emphasis on practical training. A first and more concrete step in this direction is given in form of the practical testing-focused course model proposed in section 13.2.1. Such practical course models help to elevate importance of the topic of systematic testing while maintaining focus on principles and keeping an eye on current technical implementations. Interestingly, fixing all testing-related problems identified in this thesis might have the potential to make the 3-pillar approach obsolete.

Increasing Hands-On Experience. Generally, graduating at a university should not implicate little hands-on experience with testing—even if there is no real-world industry project at hand. If there are no industry projects, open source projects provide easy access to practical experiences. Particularly GitHub has seen a rise in educational applications [155]. Herein lies a chance for universities to promote open source engagement in students, integrating open source development into lectures [4], and facilitating early contact with real-world projects.

13.1.3 Impact on Research.

The 'shock of practice' that newcomers endure when they enter the working force is an important research topic, concerning research, academia and industry alike. For researchers, the findings of this thesis give opportunity to focus on mitigating the current 'shock of practice' for newcomers even further: New and better approaches for an uplifting and effective onboarding experience could be researched, focusing on making this transition smoother for the newcomer, more effective and efficient.

Supporting Inexperienced Developers Warrants Strong Impact. Inexperienced developers benefit greatly from any new form of support and helping them to be productive faster and to work with more confidence will positively influence their success in industry. Supporting the most inexperienced members of the software engineering community in applying fundamental engineering principles correctly from the beginning has considerable impact on the practice of software engineering. Supporting the base of the community warrants a greater practical impact than supporting the best developers in becoming even better, simply for reasons of scale.

Operationalizing Social Transparency Further. Another potential research area is the directed use of social transparency. While the core effects of increased social transparency have already been uncovered (cf. chapter 11), this thesis found that its operationalization calls for further research. As seen in the evaluations of Testing Displays (cf. evaluations in section 9.5), care needs to be taken when making the efforts of other team members visible to the newcomer. Feelings of competition or pressure can backfire and reduce the wanted effect of increasing test efforts. The proposed strategy to display only encouraging Testing Displays (smart display strategy, cf. section 9.4, p. 114) is a first step in that direction. Further research on this delicate matter and a more fine-grained adjustment is necessary.

Lifting Limitations of This Approach. Other potential research directions arise from the limitations of the 3-pillar approach presented in this thesis. The 3-pillar approach demands some form of testing culture to communicate it to the newcomer. New research approaches could focus on communicating a healthy testing culture to the newcomer in a team without any, effectively establishing a testing culture from scratch. For example, only small modifications would be necessary to increase the competitive edge of the Testing Displays approach: the project lead could set a test code coverage goal and Testing Displays could monitor the 'race' to the goal, rewarding the winner. As mentioned before, such a competitive approach needs to be handled with care.

Similarly, both strategies of pillar 2 & 3 rely on test code within the project and *limit* their approach to test code *of* the project. This is due to the fact that an easy-to-accomplish execution of these test codes is a fundamental part of the 3-pillar approach—inexperienced developers are easily side-tracked, for example, by transfer effort of un-executable test code examples (cf. student study in section 4.1.2, p. 50). Relaxing this limitation and opening the approach for search in internet code databases or open source projects can improve its effectivity by magnitudes. For example, Barzilay [8] suggests example recommendation using internet databases. For reasons of scope, these opportunities were not explored any further.

The current state of the 3-pillar approach itself provides opportunity for further research and continuation of this work. Many evaluations have been performed, however, a final evaluation in a real-world onboarding context is missing. Further, this can only be achieved if the strategy of pillar 3 is implemented first.

Inspire Similar Research Endeavors. Lastly, this thesis hopes to inspire further research endeavors employing a similar qualitative and practice-affine approach. Rogers' Theory lends itself well for analyzing the lack of application of preventive innovations and ideas and uncovering possible causes. Researchers could re-use it to analyze other preventive practices in software engineering that—ideally—should be practiced on a regular basis but are not. Developing an effective and healthy documentation habit when coding or systematic refactoring are just some examples. Here, the Grounded Theory research methodology helps to develop a clear and true-to-practice picture of the situation—which may sometimes differ from education's and academia's view.

13.2 Proposal for Improvements in Academia

While the focus of this thesis lies on the industrial onboarding phase, this thesis thoroughly analyzes today's educational testing situation and uncovers causes for low testing skills of fresh graduates. In this section, these insights are used to present improvement proposals for the current testing education.

Prepare Students for Onboarding. The onboarding situation and the changes that newcomers will have to accommodate could be made a part of the software engineering curriculum. Newcomers are overwhelmed by the new tasks demanded from them (cf. practitioners study in section 4.2). Such insights as 'newcomers being too intimidated to ask their mentors for help' or the newcomers' struggle with outdated wikis could be made a subject of discussion in software engineering courses. Being explicitly prepared for this situation can help to lessen the impact of the new environment.

13.2.1 Providing More Practical Experience With Focus on Testing.

Industry puts emphasis on technical implementations rather than on principle-knowledge and practitioners are disappointed by the technical know-how of newcomers (cf. section 4.2). However, following industry's wishes blindly is not in academia's best interests. Technical implementations in industry change quickly and are subject to trends and fast innovation cycles. Letting that guide the education of software engineers can bring by unforeseen consequences[2]. The divide between principle and actual implementation is important. But, seeing that industry moves fast and academia having an interest in graduates to work efficiently in this environment, this divide needs constant curation.

A two-phased course model could help to approach the problem of elevating graduates testing skills to industry's needs while maintaining academic independence: a *dedicated* and *practical* course on systematic software testing, targeting two goals:

- students understand the underlying principles of systematic testing first, gaining principles-knowledge.

- students are confronted with writing tests in a real-world environment early on and learn how to overcome real-world testing problems, gaining and expanding how-to-knowledge.

Part 1: A Dedicated Course on Testing. Software testing is part of software engineering courses at universities, but courses focusing *solely* on testing activities remain rare. There is a distinct need for a *dedicated* course on systematic software testing in today's software engineering curriculum: For students it is difficult to learn and apply the practice of systematic testing *simultaneously* to other software engineering activities and often systematic testing is the first activity to be left out (cf. Problem Area 1). During the 4-month development project of the study in section 4.1, students struggled with practicing systematic testing as they had to concentrate on learning how to collaborate in a software development project. They were busy learning team-based development, gathering and documenting requirements, designing, and implementing their software. This left them no time to learn testing practices at the same time. Just as they had been taught programming before, these findings suggest that there is a need for a purely testing-oriented course that lets students focus on this part of software development.

Similar to exercises accompanying engineering lectures nowadays, this dedicated course targets to convey the principles of systematic testing. Testing techniques can be exercised in small groups of students, supervised by a lecturer. At this stage, it is important to strip the learning experience from distracting technicalities or implementation details of systematic testing. Lecturers can base such a dedicated testing course on existing test-related exercises and expand on new testing topics from there.

Part 2: A Practical Course on Testing. As the second part of this testing course, students should practice systematic testing in a real-world setting, putting emphasis on two aspects:

- students are pushed to apply the theoretical testing knowledge that they have gained in the first part of the testing course, and

---

[2]For example, technologies like Adobe Flash go in and out of fashion, but the engineering community would not want a whole generation of software engineers being trained solely in how to work with Adobe Flash.

- students work on a real software project (provided by industry) and are confronted with testing-related technicalities early on.

This part of the testing course accompanies the development of an industrial project and puts students in the role of dedicated testers. To lower barriers and to facilitate communication and diffusion about testing techniques, students are paired and implement tests in a pair programming manner. The lecturer of this course acts as a coach for testing technicalities and guides students through different testing phases (for example, considering testability at design time, actual test implementation before or at implementation time). Students experience the project's development through the viewpoint of an actual software tester.

Working on a real-world project positively influences students' view on systematic testing and improves their general attitude towards it (cf. Problem Area 3). Students value the feeling of accomplishment when finding defects in an actual project, but do not feel this in lecture exercises (cf. section 4.1.2, p. 46). Lecture exercises[3] are isolated, focusing only on the principles of testing techniques. They lack a project to give these techniques context. Solving such testing exercises does not communicate a high relative advantage, however, practicing systematic testing in the context of an actual project does—actual defects are found and subsequently removed.

Introducing a real-world project context must be done with care and in a controlled manner. Overloading the student with technicalities can quickly distract from the actual testing task. Distracting technical issues not pertaining to the testing task at hand should be excluded. This differentiates this practical course from an internship or an educational software development project, making it a middle path. For example, going through a requirements and design phase or maintaining a mysql user database before starting to test is not expedient for practicing systematic testing. However, learning how to setup and use features of a test framework is.

The target of this course is to help students build up a technical knowledge of *actually* practicing systematic testing while maintaining a manageable workload for the student. This technical knowledge helps her in overcoming similar technical barriers when onboarding. While, it is not guaranteed that she will encounter just the same testing framework, her hands-on experience should prove beneficial. This will help her in mastering this new situation more quickly and reduce feelings of being overwhelmed.

In current software engineering curricula, there are already efforts for providing students with hands-on experience in systematic testing. Software testing courses focused on practicing testing in open source projects [4], classic student software projects [107] such as in the study of section 4.1, or project-based collaboration with industry partners [24] are some examples of these efforts. It is not clear whether the majority of educational institutions is able to offer these kinds of industrial collaborations. Regarding the latter two examples, there is no particular focus on systematic testing. As mentioned before, this may result in students being overwhelmed with other engineering tasks (cf. study in section 4.1).

---

[3]such as used in the first part of this testing course

13.3 Collaboration between Academia and Industry

As a premise for the proposed practical testing course, academia is in need of a constant flow of model commercial projects. Give students a fairly current impression of testing in industry, the subject project for the testing course needs to be updated regularly.

These projects must fulfill certain requirements to serve as educational material. Their implementation of testing techniques should not be opposite to what is taught in class, the techniques used in the project should not be outdated, and so on[4]. A manageable (e.g. in size, etc), presentable project representing common industrial practice is needed.

This re-occurring need for current model projects could spawn a collaboration between academia and industry: Software development companies could submit presentable real-world projects as model projects and academia could establish a database of projects with "good testing practices, as applied in industry". Software companies in the vicinity of the university could participate and have their projects dissected by students—giving them a spotlight to show their high-quality standards and attract potential newcomers. Sometimes, companies make their products available as open source in order to show off their high quality standards and attract capable contributors [122].

Sharing these "best testing practices of commercial software projects" globally online can potentially create a *common body of model testing projects* and diffuse best practices in the software engineering community. Sharing onboarding practices and testing-guidelines between companies is not an uncommon practice. The company Airbnb shared their guidelines for newcomers about using javascript and how to test it[5] and other companies can base their own guidelines on it. Such a common body of model testing projects would make the discovery of advantageous testing practices more systematic and easier. While academic conferences report on industrial experiences and produce proceedings, attending such conferences is of little interest to smaller companies and sometimes these proceedings are hidden behind paywalls. Entry fees are relatively high and small teams are unable to afford the downtime of a team member. Access to and participation in this common body of model testing projects could help these companies in improving their quality assurance efforts and in attracting newcomers. As seen in the practitioners study (cf. section 4.2), these smaller companies are struggling with low testing skills the most.

This collaboration would offer both academia and industry a low-barrier opportunity to diffuse living software engineering practice into the curriculum while maintaining a focus on academia's principles. Other forms of collaborations with industry, such as internships, are harder to come by: Software companies are busy with day-to-day business and a collaboration with educational institutions may not seem lucrative—the industrial side is usually paying for the collaboration. Collaborations between university and industry partners often pursue a certain research question but do not focus on day-to-day business. The software company may not trust a student to work on a commercial product. While regular and long-time collaboration with software companies are most

---

[4]The compilation of a comprehensive list of quality attributes is left to future work.

[5]https://github.com/airbnb/javascript#testing

effective in conveying real-world testing experience to students, they represent a bigger commitment and require a certain company size. Smaller companies—while being most affected by the lack of testing skills—may not be able to provide this.

13.4 Transferability of the Approach of this Thesis.

The approach presented in this thesis is specific to the discipline of systematic testing. It is not suited to be applied—without changes—to other engineering disciplines that newcomers may struggle with (e.g. implementing code). The approach has been tailored to the attributes of testing and testing problems of newcomers: Internalizing, training and becoming proficient in systematic testing techniques differs from becoming proficient in coding and implementing. Testing is *preventive* in nature while implementing is *productive*. This is why this approach, among other things, dedicates a strong focus on overcoming soft inhibiting factors (attitude-, motivation-related) in newcomers (pillar 1) which possibly not be a focus when engineering an approach to get inexperienced developers to engage in implementing more. Another facet of this attribute of testing is that newcomers often feel *unproductive* when engaging in test writing (cf. chapter 4.1). Even senior developers reported to feel unproductive when having to write tests [109]. The discipline of implementing source code is not generally associated with this connotation. As this approach tries to overcome this feeling of unproductiveness in newcomers when writing tests, it is not trivially applicable to another software engineering discipline.

All implementations of this thesis' approach and strategies are focused on testing. The testing displays in chapter 9 are tailored to the discipline of testing. During the course of designing these testing displays, an individual GQM-approach was used to find suitable aspects of activities for representing a team's testing culture, for example 'average source code coverage by test code' (cf. Mörschbach's Master Thesis [111]). If one's goal was to represent 'code writing culture', these aspects would differ. The Test Recommender presented in chapter 10, is tailored to testing: its input is a written test suite and it operates on written test code methods.

14 Conclusion

Contributions of this Thesis

The gaps in computer science graduates' skills and industry's expectations have long been a busy research topic. In 2013, Radermacher et al. [127] systematically analyzed 30 years of software engineering literature and identified testing skills as one of the most problematic knowledge deficiencies in fresh graduates. Even though industry has complained periodically about this lack of testing skills, Radermacher et al. note that there has been very little descriptive information about the actual *extend* of newcomers testing skills.

Confirmation and Qualitative Understanding. In this thesis, the current state of newcomers' testing skills is assessed and industry's need for better testing skills is reiterated. Beyond this reconfirmation, this thesis delivers a comprehensive and qualitative understanding of newcomers' testing behavior, from both the graduates' and the practitioners' perspectives. In two extensive Grounded Theory studies, the enablers and inhibitors of systematic testing for inexperienced developers and practitioners' struggles with such developers are investigated.

Theoretical Analysis and Goal Setting. Using Everett M. Rogers' Theory of Diffusion of Innovations [130], the educational situation of inexperienced developers is analyzed, providing an understanding of how the practice of systematic testing is perceived by them when being first introduced to it. This uncovers deficiencies in traditional lecture settings as well as attributes of systematic testing that hinder its adoption, validating and enriching the understanding of real-world phenomena observed in newcomers' testing behavior. This analysis is then expanded to the industrial onboarding situation, providing insights into the testing-related struggles of newcomers in this new environment. Employing the terms and predictions of Rogers' theory, strategic improvements are formulated to facilitate a quick adoption of systematic testing practices by inexperienced developers in the onboarding situation.

Solution Strategies. Drawing from real-world observations combined with theoretical background, a three-part approach is engineered with the goal of supporting newcomers in adopting systematic testing practices in the industrial onboarding setting and in overcoming the 'shock of practice' as quickly as possible. The newcomer's awareness for the prevailing testing culture of the development team is raised and she is supported in overcoming testing related technical barriers, e.g. in writing test code. Bigger testing knowledge gaps are closed with a tailored test tutorial system that provides testing-related principles-knowledge and how-to-knowledge where needed.

The strategies of the three-part approach of this thesis draw from real-world insights of the testing behavior of active practitioners collaborating on modern social coding sites. The social transparency framework is employed as well as ideas from the fields of code recommendation, example-based programming and knowledge management.

Implementation and Evaluation. The first two parts of the tripartite approach have been implemented in working Eclipse IDE plugins and evaluated in multiple rounds of evaluations and experiments with computer science students nearing their graduation. The Testing Display plugin inserts dashboard-like diagrams into the newcomer's IDE, providing an understanding of the testing efforts in her new team. In evaluations, a rise of test writing activity was observed. The Test Recommender plugin serves the newcomer with a browsable set of example test code at the push of a button, facilitating a "copy & paste & adapt" strategy for writing new test code. Participants were enabled to write test code quicker and used the suggested test code examples to learn how to write tests in that particular project.

Limitations & Future Work.

While the tripartite approach of this thesis is based on real-world observations of practitioner-focused research and thereby trying to adapt to practitioners' realities, its evaluation is limited. The individual strategies have been evaluated with students in an educational setting. While the testing skills of soon-to-be graduates are assumed to be very similar to the skills of newcomers in onboarding, the lack of a final evaluation is a limitation. Companies wanting to implement the tripartite approach have to judge its applicability in their settings individually. Relatedly, implementation of the third strategy—a context-sensitive and automatic Test Tutorial Recommender—is missing.

This thesis assumes an existing testing culture in team that the newcomer is onboarding to. Herein lies potential for improvement of the approach: Helping newcomers in adopting healthy testing cultures of *other* development teams—essentially establishing a testing culture in her own team—appears promising. Whether the *other* development team needs to be real or can be virtual (simulated) and which visible testing clues and configurations promise best adoption rates are only some research questions.

There is a strong emphasis on containing the search space to the current project space when looking for practical test code recommendations and test tutorials. This limitation ensures *direct applicability* of the recommendations and—as seen in this thesis—services newcomers' need for easy transfer of examples. Relaxing these limitations can open up the solution space and make both recommendation mechanisms more powerful. For example, test code could be searched in similar open source projects. Other researchers have made advancements in the mining of software discussion boards such as `stackoverflow.com` for good code examples or comprehensive API documentation (cf. Nasehi et al. [114] or relatedly Parnin et al. [117]).

Curriculum Vitae

Raphael Pham
born on April 10th 1987 in Berlin, Germany

Education	
02/2011–10/2016	PhD Student in Computer Science, Leibniz Universität Hannover, Germany
10/2005–01/2011	Diploma in Mathematics with Focus on Computer Science, Leibniz Universität Hannover, Germany
10/2003–05/2005	Abitur (general eligibility of university admission), Erich Kästner Gymnasium, Laatzen, Germany

Professional Experience	
since 08/2016	Software Engineer at Daimler TSS, Berlin, Germany
02/2011–02/2016	Researcher at Software Engineering Group, Leibniz Universität Hannover, Germany
03/2006–03/2008	Student Tutor at Software Engineering Group, Leibniz Universität Hannover, Germany

Appendix

Grounded Theory

This thesis leverages findings from three extensive empirical studies (cf. chapters 4.1, 4.2, and 11). All of these studies were conducted using qualitative and systematic research methodology Grounded Theory, which is often used in social science. This section gives a short overview[1] of this research methodology.

General idea of Grounded Theory.

In 1965, sociologists Barney Glaser and Anselm Strauss conducted the first Grounded Theory study [66], leading to the promotion of Grounded Theory [67] as a research methodology in 1967. The idea of grounded theory is to keep an open mind and to not enter a population with a predetermined research question. The general goal is to let most important questions of the population emerge from insights into the population's motives and actions. This is done using qualitative research methods such as repeatedly interviewing the population and incrementally adapting and building a theory of the population's motives and behavior. This allows for an unbiased analysis of a population's most important problems in practice.

Rationale for Grounded Theory Methodology in Empirical Studies.

The Grounded Theory methodology is well-suited to qualitatively model a practical problem complex of a population. This is a common endeavor in social sciences. Using this qualitative method, "softer", hard-to-grasp, and human-related problems can be outlined. Such knowledge can be used as a basis for engineering solutions, which help this population in overcoming these problems. This is demonstrated in this thesis: The problems that inexperienced developers have with systematic testing are qualitatively defined from different perspectives (undergraduates and newcomers, practitioners handling the onboarding process) and based on this knowledge, a software engineering solution is presented.

Software engineering is conducted by humans collaborating in teams and as such the toolset of social science lends itself for researching some problems related to software engineering. For the empirical research in this thesis, the Grounded Theory methodology was chosen mainly for two reasons:

---

[1]For a more in-depth explanation of the approach, see [67] or [32], and for a practical in-depth application of Grounded Theory in the field of software engineering, see [77].

- it provides an unbiased approach without pre-defined research questions, thusly allowing the researcher to keep an open mind, and

- it emphasizes an affinity to practice: the insights gained are very practical problems of the population under research.

With regard to the empirical research in this thesis, these attributes came into play as follows: Researching the problems and inhibitors that kept students from systematic testing (cf. chapter 4.1) demanded an unrestricted and qualitative approach that would uncover the most important factors as well as many factors as possible. This served to get a very practical picture of the situation that was as complete and saturated as possible. These reasons lead to using the Grounded Theory methodology when researching the impact of social transparency on the testing behavior of users on a social coding site (cf. chapter 11). In both cases, the research group had very little prior experience with the practical problems of the populations.

When researching the practitioners' view on testing skills of newcomers (cf. chapter 4.2), the unbiased approach of the Grounded Theory methodology was even more important. One overarching research question for the researchers was whether or not similar problems to the ones found in undergraduates would emerge—e.g. whether or not the problems of undergraduates carry over to the onboarding situation (they do, cf. section 4.3). Here, the Grounded Theory methodology helped to gather the set of *actual* problems that practitioners have with the testing skills of newcomers instead of the set of problems that the researchers were looking for.

Short Overview of Grounded Theory Methodology.

In this section, a condensed overview of the process steps of the Grounded Theory methodology is presented. This serves as an description of the *usual* research processes applied in the three empirical studies in this thesis (disregarding minor deviations that may have been necessary).

Data Gathering. In the first step, data from the chosen population was gathered. Usually, a first online questionnaire was sent to the population, gathering first data and inviting to participate in online interviews (conducted using Microsoft's Skype). Participants who agreed were interviewed by different researchers, using a semi-structured interview guide. These interviews were recorded with consent. The interview guide was kept flexible to allow the researcher to dive deeper into more pressing topics of the interview participant. The interview guide was iteratively adapted between interviews to reflect saturation of certain topics and to allow gathering of more data on unsaturated topics. During the whole data gathering process and continuing on for the rest of the Grounded Theory process, the researchers would make notes about insights and revise and adapt these notes according to newly gained insights. This continuous step is called *memoing*.

Transcribing and Data Preparation. After the data gathering phase, the collected data was transcribed for easier access and handling. Reading and skimming text files is easier than accessing audio recordings quickly. This step was sometimes done with the help of external assistants, such as paid undergraduates.

Open Coding. With the data prepared, researchers set out to uncover emerging hypotheses and relationships. To this end, the data was *open coded* as a first step. *Key points* in the narrative of the interviews were identified and coded using short codes. For example, key points were decisive statements of participants, their opinions, description of important situations and context, and so on, that—piece by piece—helped to get a picture of their situation. In that sense, a key point was regarded the smallest unit of data without taking its statement out of context.

This coding activity is called *open* coding because it was not guided by topics or themes and all key points identified are coded. While open coding, researchers constantly compared new emerging codes to existing codes in order to identify similarities or to pinpoint important differences. The Grounded Theory methodology calls this *constant comparison method*. It extends to every step of the methodology that involves identifying the emergence of a new concept.

Before open coding began, however, the researchers went through a normalizing step: Several researchers coded the same interview data simultaneously, compared their resulting codes, and discussed them until agreement was reached. This served to gain a uniform coding system from several collaborating researchers, established a similar understanding, and helped to retain an open mind and identify potential bias.

Concepts, Subcategories, Core-Category Leveraging the insights from memos and aggregating codes, higher level concepts emerged—concepts that were important to the population and have validity only in this population. Higher level concepts helped the researchers to understand the struggles of the population from different perspectives, for example: what mechanisms prevailed in the population, what problems they have, and how they coped with them. Again, aggregating and abstracting these concepts, sub-categories and one core category emerged. The core category describes the main problem or main theme of the population and connects all sub-categories. According to Glaser, the core category *"accounts for a large portion of the variation in a pattern of behaviour"* [65]. At this point, *selective coding* followed: the remaining data was coded with the new category model in mind and added to these categories until saturation was reached.

Fig. .1 shows the arranging of codes to help the emergence of subcategories and a core-category.

Emergence of the Grounded Theory. Throughout the whole process, researchers noted and gathered memos to highlight interesting findings and connections between emerging themes, describing preliminary insights, and hypotheses about the population's behavior. In a step called *sorting*, these memos were sorted and related to the

Figure .1: Data (white cut out text snippets) coded (yellow post-its), arranged into concepts and categories (red and blue post-its). Photo from Grounded Theory study about testing problems of undergraduates, cf. chapter 4.1.

categories found in the data. This helps to develop a theory connecting data, emerged concepts, and categories into a Grounded Theory. Glaser proposes some helpful theoretical frameworks to guide forming of this theory (for example, the Six C's: causes, contexts, contingencies, consequences, covariances, and conditions; or Process: stages, phases, passages) of which the use is voluntary.

Validation of Findings The Grounded Theory methodology emphasizes the emergence of a theory *from the population's data* and not vice versa. As such, the generalizability of this theory is low—it is only valid for the actual population that has been questioned. To heighten confidence in the developed Grounded Theory, the researchers extracted main concept of the Grounded Theory and validated them with a larger part of the population, which has not been questioned yet. This was usually done using online questionnaires: main concepts of the Grounded Theory were formulated as statements, presented to participants, and participants were asked to agree or disagree with these statements on a five-item Likert scale with the option to leave comments. For example, in the case of the empirical studies presented in this thesis, these final validation rounds comprised of 539 active open source developers (cf. chapter 11) and 698 commercial software practitioners (cf. chapter 4.2).

Triangulation of Testing Culture

The German Duden defines the term culture in a product-oriented way: Culture emerges as a characterizing product, created by a society as a symbol for their level of sophistication at a specific moment in time.

> **Definition A** *Culture* is the entirety of the characterizing intellectual, artistic, and creative contributions of a community to a specific domain during a specific era.

> Gesamtheit der von einer bestimmten Gemeinschaft auf einem bestimmten Gebiet während einer bestimmten Epoche geschaffenen, charakteristischen geistigen, künstlerischen, gestaltenden Leistungen. (translated from German)[2]

This definition emphasizes that culture is specific to a group of people at a specific point in time. Culture is defined as an artifact that they create in collaboration, e.g. when working and living together as a community.

However, in context of this thesis, this approach of defining "testing culture" is too focused on it being an artifact or a product. Being an artifact indicates something that can be gained but indicates little guiding power. Other sources define culture in a more dynamic way that emphasizes it being a "way of how to get things done".

> **Definition B** *Culture* is the way of life, especially the general customs and beliefs, of a particular group of people at a particular time.[3]

> **Definition C** *Culture* is the ideas, customs, and social behavior of a particular people or society.[4]

Again, culture is defined as something a specific group of people share at a specific point in time. Here, however, the "way of life" and customs are included, as well as the social behavior. These definitions award the term culture the power to describe *how* this particular group behaves.

For this thesis, a mix of all three definitions is used to define "testing culture" for a software development team. This definition includes the idea of culture being an artifact that the whole team produces and shares as well as it providing guidance on how to achieve certain things. This way, the newcomer is enabled to adopt it and rely on it for guidance.

> **Definition** *Testing Culture of a Software Development Team* is the team's way of engaging in systematic software testing, the entirety of the team's testing-related ideas and customs, and associated social behavior during a software development project.

This definition of testing culture helps members of the team to decide what testing behavior they will tolerate and what testing behavior they will reject. It explains *what* it means to be engaging in systematic testing as a member of this team and *how* to do it. This way, the expression of the "newcomer adopting the team's testing culture" expresses that the newcomer starts to behave as the rest of the team.

---

[2]http://www.duden.de/rechtschreibung/Kultur#Bedeutung1b, retr. 11 March 2016.

[3]http://dictionary.cambridge.org/dictionary/english/culture, retr. 11 March 2016

[4]http://www.oxforddictionaries.com/definition/english/culture, retr. 11 March 2016

Testing Skills of Newcomers

In this section, the research process of the practitioner study in section 4.2 is explained in detail. Additionally, the coding system used in this Grounded Theory study is described.

Procedure. The findings of this study result from a multi-step data collection process. From July 2014 to October 2014, two online questionnaires were sent out to 2,500 members of the hosting site GitHub[5]. Users were selected based on whether they were recently active on the site, had made their email address public, and whether they had set an organization in their profile, targeting professional developers.

For better understanding and deeper insights, Pham et al. 2014b interviewed 22 professional software developers via Skype calls. These semi-structured interviews lasted about half an hour. During the interview phase, the researchers constantly compared insights to data from earlier interviews and textual answers from questionnaires. This iteratively refined the data collection process. Between interview sessions, the interview guide was to reflect newly gained insights and the researchers wrote memos to highlight interesting findings and connections between emerging themes.

The Grounded Theory model presented in this paper has two data sources: textual answers obtained from the two online questionnaires, and a set of transcribed interview recordings. Two researchers, working in close cooperation, identified key points in the interviews. Two random interviews were used as a baseline: each researcher identified key points in them independently and their results were compared. Transcripts and textual data and key points were open coded until the researchers identified the core category *'Practitioner's View of Testing Skills on New Hires'*, at which point selective coding followed. Codes were grouped, leading to the emergence of concepts (such as different onboarding strategies). These were either attributed to subcategories[6] or the core category (for example, a subcategory was *'Coping Strategies'*). Lastly, a third questionnaire was created for a final validation by a 698 practitioners.

Questionnaires Design. In this study, three online questionnaires were sent out, two while constructing the Grounded Theory model and one for validation purposes. The first questionnaire was exploratory in nature and served to provide a first understanding of the practitioner population and its concerns. After analyzing the first results, the questions in the second questionnaire were refined to get a better understanding of emerging themes and environmental attributes, such as the *educational origin of the new hire* or the *size of the company*.

The second questionnaires contained two different kinds of questions: questions about the respondent's situation—to give the researchers a better picture of who they were talking to—and open questions about their experience with newcomers. Pham et al. 2014b asked whether they were satisfied with the testing skills of new hires and, if there were any problems, what was perceived as problematic exactly. Between "yes" and

---

[5]https://github.com

[6]These categories are reflected as Subsections of section 4.2.2, which presents the main findings.

"no", the population was given the option of a textual answer. These textual answers were analyzed and counted towards "yes" and "no" where applicable. Ultimately, 10 ambiguous responses were removed.

The respondents' situation was assessed regarding *company size, criticality of their product* and the *level of sophistication* of the organization's testing process: whether it was done manually or automatically, systematically or not. For better context, a more in-depth textual description of the testing process was requested. The questionnaire also asked how closely the respondent worked with new hires.

Data Collection. In July 2014, the first questionnaire was sent out to 500 active GitHub users who had been active in June 2014, had made their email address public, and had filled in the *organization* field in their public user profile. Pham et al. 2014b received 72 answers by mid-July. Data from respondents who did not come in contact with new hires or who did not develop software professionally and commercially (e.g., pet projects) were removed. 54 responses remained. Of those, 28 respondents agreed to be contacted for interviews and were invited, but none enrolled. In July 2014, the improved second questionnaire to 2,000 active users was sent out, excluding the previous 500 users. Pham et al. 2014b received 237 answers by the end of August 2014. After data clean-up, 170 responses remained. Of 109 participants who left contact information, 22 enrolled for semi-structured interviews via Skype call.

Coding System

This section contains the coding system that was developed in the study in section 4.2. Each category contains concepts, which themselves contain codes. Codes are described in more detail. The abbreviation *NH* is used for the term 'new hire'.

Core Category: Practitioner's Views on Testing Skills

What are the main views of practitioners who handle the onboarding of newcomers? They have expressed stark views about newcomers' testing skills and their testing education. Topics of general criticism, testing experience and testing attitude emerged.

Concept: General Views and Expectations. The expectations of practitioners are not met—testing skills are criticized. Practitioners have come to the conclusion that testing cannot be learnt in education, coining the expression 'Testing is learnt on the job—not at university'.

Code	Description
more interest in programming than testing	Practitioners reported on a imbalance in new hires' curiosity regarding testing and programming; new hires had practiced more programming than testing and felt more engaged in programming than testing.
finding testing skills	Practitioners had difficulties finding applicants with well-developed testing skills.
real testing practice	Practitioners expressed disbelief that testing could be learnt in a university—testing skills were only developed when engaging in real and commercial projects. Also: practical-relevant testing skills were not taught in a university setting.
testing knowledge	New hires had gaps in fundamental testing knowledge, for example the distinction between integration and system tests.

Concept: Lack of Experience.   Practitioners noticed a lack of experience in newcomers when it comes to testing. This lack has impacted the testing behavior of newcomers in the onboarding situation in different ways: Engaging in test writing is problematic and—taking a bigger perspective—the role of testing appears unclear.

Code	Description
hands-on experience	New hires showed deficiencies in actually writing test code. They did not know how to write it or what to test. Practitioners had problems using these tests in production.
test process	New hires had very little understanding or experience with the overall test process. The role of testing in the development process was unclear.
newbies after all	Some practitioners were forgiving for newcomers' lack of proficiency in testing, after all, these were inexperienced developers.
quick learners	Some newcomers were quick learning when it came to testing, pleasing practitioners.

Concept: Testing Attitude.   With little hands-on experience with testing, newcomers have developed little appreciation for the practice of testing. Their attitude appears mostly dismissive.

Code	Description
neglect testing	New hires would even suggest to not test at all, surprising practitioners.
programming over testing	Between programming and writing tests, newcomers would chose programming.
no benefit from testing	Some newcomers saw very little benefit in testing. They did not find it useful and could not relate to its benefits.

Category: Practitioner's Views on Testing Education

The impact of low testing skills in graduates has given practitioners a negative impression of testing education. Disappointment and anger are mixed into their views.

Concept: Testing neglected in Education   From their expression on testing skills of fresh graduates, practitioners feel that testing is not taught at universities enough.

Code	Description
testing not taught at universities	Practitioners were under the impression that the topic of testing was not covered in university studies, at least that is what they gathered from handling graduates in onboarding.
testing not important at universities	Practitioners were under the impression that the topic of testing was not given the importance in education that it deserved.
I myself haven't learnt about it	Some practitioners recounted that they themselves had not learnt testing during their studies. Some mentioned that the topic of testing was optional, entirely skippable.

Concept: Testing Education not Appropriate for Practice.   Some practitioners criticized the way testing was taught and wished for a more practice-relevant way of teaching it.

Code	Description
testing taught too theoretical	Testing exercises were deemed to be far too theoretical and oversimplifying, resulting in test training not suited for real-world use.
testing education outdated	Practitioners criticized that if testing was taught, outdated topics were covered.

Category: Coping Strategies

Practitioners have clearly recognized the lack of testing skills in newcomers. They have devised different coping strategies for handling it and for aligning it with industry reality.

Concept: Low-Effort Strategies These strategies demanded very little intervention by the practitioners. However, its effectivity in supporting the newcomer varied.

Code	Description
no onboarding	Some companies have no onboarding process at all, letting newcomers overcome their problems alone.
ease-in testing onboarding	Newcomers are allowed to manually test and get accommodated with test automation over time.
environmental properties	External factors influenced newcomers in their testing behavior. When working in testing-intensive teams, they started to test as well. Guidelines, short and concise how-tos helped new hires in overcoming uncertainties and problems.

Concept: Semi-Active Strategies A common pattern was to rely on the newcomer in asking for help and providing it in an ad-hoc manner, making this a semi-active strategy: the newcomer has to identify gaps and ask for help and the mentor has provide support. Specifically assigned senior developers worked as mentors and helped the newcomer whenever she needed it.

Code	Description
mentoring	Most common, practitioners reported on mentoring as their current onboarding strategy.
NH asks for questions	New hires are expected to ask questions when they do not understand something or have problems. 'Just let them ask' was a popular onboarding strategy.
NH imposing	For newcomers, asking a senior developer for help—especially regarding fundamental techniques—is problematic. They are aware that other team members are busy and they do not want to impose.

Concept: Active Strategies Fully active strategies took newcomers in and boosted their testing skills until alignment with company requirements was found. Often, the lack of testing skills was met with a dedicated onboarding process in which the newcomer learnt how to test from scratch.

Code	Description
bootcamp	When available, newcomers were sent to dedicated training camps, focused on aligning their skills with the company's demand.
cross-pollination	Often, newcomers were put into teams according to their skill set and the lack thereof, facilitating a transfer of knowledge. This was also done with senior developers and newcomers.
implement small internal project	Newcomers were given small projects for internal use and little outside impact. They had to apply the company development process for this small project to get acquainted with this process.
working on (small) commercial project	Newcomers worked on (commercial) projects with external impact, but only smaller ones.
working on company product	Newcomers worked on the commercial product of the company straight-away, mostly on a non-critical task, such as maintenance or bug-fixing.
working on fresh project	Under the supervision of the mentor, the newcomer started a fresh project with no legacy code to deal with. Dealing with legacy code was deemed to difficult at that stage and boring.

Category: Impact of Low Testing Skills.

Having to elevate a newcomer's testing skill during onboarding has different impacts: costs are increased and the hiring behavior of practitioners changes.

Concept: Costs of Teaching Testing Anew. When mentoring, a senior developer cannot fully take care of all her tasks. This way, the team's productivity is lowered during onboarding.

Code	Description
companies want quick learners	Some practitioners preferred to work only with quick-learning newcomers.
mentoring is costly	Practitioners reported that mentoring took a great deal of their time. They perceived a clear decrease of productivity when mentoring. Especially small teams had problems dedicating a whole team member for mentoring.

Concept: Raising the Hiring Bar. The lack of testing skills has impacted the hiring situation for both the newcomer and the practitioner. For some companies, it is not longer reasonable to hire inexperienced developers because of the training costs. Even though testing skills are hard to find and more expensive, these companies look for testing-experienced candidates.

Code	Description
pay more for testing skills	Companies have begun to reject newcomers and instead look for better trained senior developers, simply because they do not want to train newcomers in testing.
testing in interviews	Practitioners reported to deliberately include testing tasks in interview situations to assess a candidates' testing skills early.
hiring problem	Former newcomers and graduates reported to see a gap: coming from university, graduates have little experience but this experience is demanded by potential employers.

Testing Displays Evaluation

In this section, all three questionnaires are presented that that were used to evaluate practitioners' view on newcomers' testing skills (cf. section 4.2, p. 4.2). The order of questionnaires reflect their chronological order (three questionnaires), the last one being the validation questionnaire providing the results discussed in section 4.2.3, p. 4.2.3.

Edit this form

Testing Skills of New Hires

Hi there, thank you for taking the time to complete our survey!

We are Raphael Pham [http://www.raphaelpham.de] from the University of Hannover in Germany and Leif Singer [http://leif.me] from the University of Victoria in Canada. We're researchers trying to understand how newly hired developers are onboarded at companies.

Please do not fill out the survey if you are not a professional working as or with software developers.

First, we want to understand your working environment a little better and need some context. Please think of your workplace and your current software development project(s).

Your GitHub username
Please remove if you'd rather not have us know.

[   ]

How big is the company you are currently working at?
A rough estimate is sufficient.

○ I am not working at a company at this time.

○ 1 - 20 employees

○ 21 - 100 employees

○ 101 - 500 employees

○ more than 500 employees

If our software product fails, ...

○ human lives are in danger.

○ business stops running and money is lost.

○ it is not the end of the world.

Do you systematically test your software product?
You may choose multiple answers.

☐ Yes, we test manually.

☐ Yes, we test automatically.

☐ No.

☐ Other: [   ]

What does your testing process look like?
This is optional but would help us understand how you deal with testing.

[   ]

New Hires and Testing

Now, please focus on new hires that just started to work as software engineers for the first time. For example, this could be (not limited to) newly graduated computer science students or similar groups.

How close do you work with new hires?
You may choose multiple answers.

☐ I am in charge of recruiting developers.

☐ I am developing software together with new hires.

☐ I am training new hires to work in our company.

☐ I am not in contact with new hires.

☐ Other: [   ]

Are you satisfied with the testing skills of new hires?

○ Yes.

○ No.

○ Other: [   ]

Do you see any problems with the testing skills of new hires?

If you see any problems -- how does your company deal with them?

If you see any problems -- why are they important to your company?
E.g. what is their cost or impact?

A new hire arrives at your company. What happens next?
What does onboarding look like at your company?

Closing

Thank you for taking the time to complete our questionnaire!

Your email address
We will only email you again if you check one of the boxes below.

Is it OK for us to contact you for a short interview?
☐ I'd be up for that!

Do you want to be notified of the results of our study?
☐ Yes, please!

Do you have any other comments?
This is of course optional.

Submit

Never submit passwords through Google Forms.

Edit this form

Testing Skills of New Hires

Hi there, thank you for taking the time to complete our survey!

We are Raphael Pham [http://www.raphaelpham.de] from the University of Hannover in Germany and Leif Singer [http://leif.me] from the University of Victoria in Canada. We're researchers trying to understand how newly hired developers are onboarded at companies.

Please do not fill out the survey if you are not working as or with professional software developers.

First, we want to understand your professional working environment a little better and need some context. Please think of your workplace and your current software development project(s).

Your GitHub username
Please remove if you'd rather not have us know.

☐ _____

Do you develop software?
Please check all that apply

☐ Yes, professionally

☐ Yes, I contribute to open source projects

☐ Yes, I maintain one or more open source projects

☐ Yes, I work on my own pet projects

Where are you located?
The name of your country is sufficient.

☐ _____

How many total employees work at the organization you're currently working for?

◯ I am not working at an organization at this time

◯ I am self-employed

◯ 1 - 9 employees

◯ 10 - 19 employees

◯ 20 - 49 employees

◯ 50 - 249 employees

◯ 250 or more employees

Roughly, how many of those employees are working on software development in some sense?

◯ 0% - 20%

○ 20% - 40%
○ 40% - 60%
○ 60% - 80%
○ 80% - 100%

In short, what kind of product is your organization developing?
Describe the most important product.

If your software product fails, ...

○ human lives are in danger.

○ business stops running and money is lost.

○ it is not the end of the world.

Does your organization test its software product systematically?
You may choose multiple answers.

☐ Yes, we test manually in a systematic manner.

☐ Yes, we test automatically in a systematic manner.

☐ We test manually, but it's not systematic.

☐ We test automatically, but it's not systematic.

☐ We don't test.

☐ Other:

What does your testing process look like?
This is optional but would help us understand how you deal with testing.

New Hires and Testing

Now, please focus on new hires that just started to work as software engineers for the first time. For example, this could be (not limited to) newly graduated computer science students or similar groups.

Where do your new hires come from, mostly?

○ University

○ Other:

How closely do you work with new hires?
You may choose multiple answers.

☐ I am in charge of recruiting developers.

☐ I am developing software together with new hires.

☐ I am training new hires to work in our company.

☐ I am not in contact with new hires.

☐ Other: [   ]

Are you satisfied with the testing skills of new hires?

◯ Yes.

◯ No.

◯ Other: [   ]

Do you see any problems with the testing skills of new hires?

If you see any problems with testing skills -- how does your company deal with them?

If you see any such problems -- why are they important to your company?
E.g. what is their cost or impact?

A new hire arrives at your company. What happens next?
What does onboarding look like at your company?

[text box]

Closing

Thank you for taking the time to complete our questionnaire!

Your email address
We will only email you again only if you check one of the boxes below.

[text field]

Is it OK for us to contact you for a short interview?

☐ I'd be up for that!

Do you want to be notified of the results of our study?

☐ Yes, please!

Do you have any other comments?
This is of course optional.

[text box]

Submit

Never submit passwords through Google Forms.

Powered by

This content is neither created nor endorsed by Google.

Report Abuse · Terms of Service · Additional Terms

Edit this form

Testing Skills of New Hires

Thanks so much for taking the time to help us in our research!

– Raphael Pham, Stephan Kiesling, and Kurt Schneider from the University of Hannover, Germany
– Leif Singer from the University of Victoria, Canada

Your GitHub username
Please remove if you'd rather not have us know.

[   ]

Do you develop software?
Please check all that apply

- ☐ Yes, professionally
- ☐ Yes, I contribute to open source projects
- ☐ Yes, I maintain one or more open source projects
- ☐ Yes, I work on my own pet projects

Where are you located?
For example the name of the country.

[   ]

How many total employees work at the organization you're currently working for?
Feel free to skip if you don't know.

- ○ I am not working at an organization at this time
- ○ I am self-employed
- ○ 1 - 9 employees
- ○ 10 - 19 employees
- ○ 20 - 49 employees
- ○ 50 - 99 employees
- ○ 100 - 149 employees
- ○ 150 - 199 employees
- ○ 200 - 249 employees
- ○ 250 - 999 employees
- ○ 1000 or more employees

What domain or field is your most important product or service in?
A short answer is fine.

[   ]

Does your organization test its software product(s) systematically?

You may choose multiple answers.

☐ Yes, we test manually -- in a systematic manner.

☐ Yes, we test automatically -- in a systematic manner.

☐ We test manually, but it's not systematic.

☐ We test automatically, but it's not systematic.

☐ We don't test.

☐ Other: [_____]

New Hires at your Organization

Now please focus on new hires that just started to work as software developers or a similar position for the first time.

For example, this could be (but not limited to) recently graduated computer science students or similar groups.

Where do your new hires come from, mostly?

○ University

○ Industry

○ Online "Coding Schools" / MOOCs

○ Offline "Coding Schools" (intensive but relatively short programs)

○ Other: [_____]

How closely do you work with new hires?
You may choose multiple answers.

☐ I am in charge of recruiting developers.

☐ I am developing software together with new hires.

☐ I am training new hires to work in our company.

☐ I am not in contact with new hires.

☐ Other: [_____]

When new hires arrive, we onboard them by ...
You may choose multiple answers.

☐ sending them to a programming boot camp.

☐ assigning them a mentor for asking questions.

☐ pair programming with senior developers.

☐ lecturing them from scratch.

☐ we have no onboarding process, the new hire begins to work straight away.

☐ the new hire works on non-critical stuff.

☐ Other: [_____]

Are you satisfied with the testing skills of new hires?

○ No.

○ Yes.

○ Other: [   ]

New Hires and Testing

Below, we present you with a couple of statements. Please rate them reflecting your personal experience and opinion. Each statement can be rated from left to right using the following scale:

1 = I strongly disagree.
2 = I disagree.
3 = Neither disagree nor agree.
4 = I agree.
5 = I strongly agree.

Note: Feel free to skip statements that do not apply to your situation.

Testing is learnt on the job, not at universities.

           1   2   3   4   5

Strongly disagree ○ ○ ○ ○ ○ Strongly Agree

In hiring, we're having trouble finding software developers that meet our needs.

           1   2   3   4   5

Strongly disagree ○ ○ ○ ○ ○ Strongly agree

Software testing education at universities meets industry needs.

           1   2   3   4   5

Strongly disagree ○ ○ ○ ○ ○ Strongly agree

New hires rely on manual trial & error and do not write test code.

           1   2   3   4   5

Strongly disagree ○ ○ ○ ○ ○ Strongly agree

In hiring, we're having trouble finding software developers that have acceptable testing skills.

           1   2   3   4   5

Strongly disagree ○ ○ ○ ○ ○ Strongly agree

When new hires *do* write tests, they are limited to unit testing.

           1   2   3   4   5

Strongly disagree ◯ ◯ ◯ ◯ ◯ Strongly agree

New hires lack technical knowledge to write tests in the real-world.
For example, mocking objects, connecting to databases, etc.

     1   2   3   4   5

Strongly disagree ◯ ◯ ◯ ◯ ◯ Strongly agree

Software testing as taught at universities is pragmatic enough.

     1   2   3   4   5

Strongly disagree ◯ ◯ ◯ ◯ ◯ Strongly agree

The lack of testing skills in new hires is problematic for us. We do not have enough resources for onboarding.

     1   2   3   4   5

Strongly disagree ◯ ◯ ◯ ◯ ◯ Strongly agree

Testing is an integral part of software development.

     1   2   3   4   5

Strongly Disagree ◯ ◯ ◯ ◯ ◯ Strongly agree

We cannot afford new hires with good testing skills. That is why we accept inexperienced newcomers and train them ourselves.

     1   2   3   4   5

Strongly disagree ◯ ◯ ◯ ◯ ◯ Strongly agree

New hires regard testing as a process that is not part of actual software development.

     1   2   3   4   5

Strongly disagree ◯ ◯ ◯ ◯ ◯ Strongly agree

New hires see no benefit in writing tests and regard it as extra work.

     1   2   3   4   5

Strongly disagree ◯ ◯ ◯ ◯ ◯ Strongly agree

When new hires are put in a team with developers who write tests, they will start testing quickly.

1 2 3 4 5

Strongly Disagree ○ ○ ○ ○ ○ Strongly agree

The lack of testing skills in new hires is overcome easily. We have enough resources for onboarding.

1 2 3 4 5

Strongly disagree ○ ○ ○ ○ ○ Strongly agree

Testing is something that is separate from actual software development.

1 2 3 4 5

Strongly Disagree ○ ○ ○ ○ ○ Strongly agree

We avoid newcomers because we have little resources to train them.

1 2 3 4 5

Strongly Disagree ○ ○ ○ ○ ○ Strongly agree

Closing

Thank you for taking the time to complete our questionnaire!

Do you want to be notified of the results of our study?

☐ Yes, please!

Your email address
We will only email you again only if you checked the box above.

Do you have any other comments?
Optional of course.

Submit

Never submit passwords through Google Forms.

Powered by   This content is neither created nor endorsed by Google.

Testing Displays - Final Evaluation Questionnaire

In this section, the questionnaire is presented (next page) that was used to evaluate Testing Displays with a whole student course on software quality (cf. section 9.5, p. 9.5).

Edit this form

Studie zur Selbstbeschreibungsfähigkeit

Hallo,

toll, dass du an dieser Studie zur Selbstbeschreibungsfähigkeit teilnimmst! Deine Daten werden anonym behandelt und alle Umfrageergebnisse werden nur anonym veröffentlicht. Damit wir dir die sechs Bonuspunkte zuweisen können, brauchen wir jedoch deinen Vor- und Nachnamen.

Diese Studie darf nur einzeln bearbeitet werden --- eine Gruppenarbeit ist nicht möglich.

Bitte nimm an dieser Studie nur teil, wenn du ernsthaft einen Beitrag leisten möchtest --- ausgedachte oder Quatsch-Antworten werden das Ergebnis der Studie ungenau machen.

Vielen Dank,
Das Fachgebiet Software Engineering

* Required

Dein Vor- und Nachname zum Zuweisen der Bonuspunkte.
Die Teilnahme an dieser Studie wird mit 6 Bonuspunkten belohnt.

Start der Umfrage

Stell dir vor, du hast dein Studium erfolgreich beendet und fängst als Software Entwickler bei einer bekannten Software-Firma an.

Dein Team stellt sich vor --- du selbst hast einen blauen Rahmen:

http://www.se.uni-hannover.de/pub/Image/Umfrage/Team.pdf

Du arbeitest mit einer neuartigen Eclipse IDE:

http://www.se.uni-hannover.de/pub/Image/Umfrage/Overview.jpg

Betrachte diese Diagramme

Nun schaue dir bitte die folgenden sechs Diagramme genauer an (Links sind unten).

Beschreibe für jedes Diagramm in ein bis drei Sätzen, welche Botschaft es dir vermittelt. Das kann zum Beispiel sein:
- Was siehst du?
- Was sollst du tun?
- Welche Gefühle ruft es in dir hervor?

Diagramm 1
http://www.se.uni-hannover.de/pub/Image/Umfrage/Diagramm1.png

Diagramm 2
http://www.se.uni-hannover.de/pub/Image/Umfrage/Diagramm2.png

Diagramm 3
http://www.se.uni-hannover.de/pub/Image/Umfrage/Diagramm3.png

Diagramm 4
http://www.se.uni-hannover.de/pub/Image/Umfrage/Diagramm4.png

Diagramm 5
http://www.se.uni-hannover.de/pub/Image/Umfrage/Diagramm5.png

Diagramm 6
http://www.se.uni-hannover.de/pub/Image/Umfrage/Diagramm6.png

Ordne die Diagramme nach der Stärke ihrer Botschaft (absteigend von stark nach schwach).
Deine Antwort sollte aus sechs Zahlen, die durch Kommata getrennt sind, bestehen.

Die oben gezeigten Diagramme bringen mich dazu mehr Tests zu schreiben. *

1   2   3   4   5

Starke Ablehnung ○ ○ ○ ○ ○ Starke Zustimmung

Ich hätte gern diese Diagramme in meiner IDE.

1   2   3   4   5

Starke Ablehnung ○ ○ ○ ○ ○ Starke Zustimmung

Hast du einen Kommentar zu den gezeigten Diagrammen?

Wie erfahren bist du im Software Engineering?

Was studierst du?
z.B. Informatik, technische Informatik, Mathematik,...

Studierst du im Bachelor- oder schon im Master-Studiengang?
○ Bachelor
○ Master
○ Other:

Bestandene Vorlesungen
☐ Software-Technik

☐ Java

Im wievielten Semester bist du?

○ 1

○ 2

○ 3

○ 4

○ 5

○ 6

○ 7

○ 8

○ 9

○ 10

○ Other: [_____]

Wie lange programmierst du schon...

Wir möchten wissen, wie viel Erfahrung du im Programmieren hast. Bitte gib deine Antwort in Jahren an. Eine ungefähre Antwort reicht aus.

Wenn du keine Erfahrung darin hast, kannst du die Felder auch leer lassen.

... privat?

[_____]

... für die Uni?

[_____]

... gegen Bezahlung (als Arbeit)?

[_____]

... für Open Source Projekte?

[_____]

Wie lange testest du schon...

Wir möchten wissen, wie viel Erfahrung du im Testen hast. Bitte gib deine Antwort in Jahren an. Eine ungefähre Antwort reicht aus.

Wenn du keine Erfahrung darin hast, kannst du die Felder auch leer lassen.

... privat?

[_____]

... für die Uni?

... gegen Bezahlung (als Arbeit)?

... für Open Source Projekte?

Ende der Umfrage

Willst du über die Ergebnisse der Studie benachrichtigt werden?

☐ Ja, gerne!

Möchtest du gern an weiteren Umfragen teilnehmen?

☐ Ja, gerne!

Unter welcher E-Mail-Adresse können wir dich erreichen?

Submit

Never submit passwords through Google Forms.

Powered by

This content is neither created nor endorsed by Google.
Report Abuse - Terms of Service - Additional Terms

Test Recommender Technical Steps

In this section, the technical steps of finding and recommending the best test code to the newcomer are explained. The following steps illustrate how Test Recommender works:

Step 1: Identify changed lines of code. First, Test Recommender needs to identify the changes made to the project without any interaction from the user. It leverages information of the versioning system (in this case, subversion). It compares the changed code base to the last commit in order to find which lines of code have been touched.

Step 2: Extract Change Set. Second, it searches the set of changed lines for classes used and distinguishes findings into three categories:*Project classes* are user written, more unusual and point to a stronger connection to the test code (if found there as well). *Non-project classes* are part of the core libraries of the programming language and are more common, such as `String`. These reside somewhere in the packages of the programming languages. *Primitive data types*, such as `int` are fundamental building blocks of the programming language and have no specific package location. The set of project, non-project classes, primitive types and their package locations make up the so-called *change set.*

Step 3: Extract Test Sets. Third, Test Recommender analyzes the test suite in a similar manner to the change set, i.e. extract project classes, non-project classes, and used primitive data types of *each* test. This results in a so-called *test set* for each test.

Step 4: Match Change Set to All Test Sets. Fourth, in the matching step, Test Recommender compares the *change set* to each *test set*. This matching takes into account five categories of findings:

1. Matches in project classes: the strongest indicator for suitability— the candidate test uses the same user-written classes as the current changes.

2. Similarity of project classes used in the change set and project classes used in the test set: do project classes used in the test originate in the same package as the current changes to the production code?

3. Matches in non-project classes. Similar to step 1 but the classes originate outside the project, be it the core library of the programming language or any 3rd party library.

4. Similarity in non-project types: see step 2, but with non-project classes.

5. Exact match in primitive types: the least significant match indicator—a test uses the same primitive types as the current changes. Our similarity concept will not work for primitive data types as they are fundamental building blocks of the programming language and have no specific package location.

Bibliography

[1] A. Abran, P. Bourque, R. Dupuis, and J. W. Moore. *Guide to the software engineering body of knowledge-SWEBOK*. IEEE Press, 2001. 2

[2] R. Adcock, E. Alef, B. Amato, M. Ardis, L. Bernstein, B. Boehm, P. Bourque, J. Brackett, M. Cantor, L. Cassel, et al. Curriculum guidelines for graduate degree programs in software engineering. 2009. 142

[3] R. Agarwal, S. H. Edwards, and M. A. Pérez-Quiñones. Designing an adaptive learning module to teach software testing. In *ACM SIGCSE Bulletin*, volume 38, pages 259–263. ACM, 2006. 149

[4] E. B. Arie van Deursen, Alex Nederlof. Teaching software architecture: with github! http://avandeursen.com/2013/12/30/teaching-software-architecture-with-github/, 2013, retrieved: 24.08.2015. 159, 162

[5] T. Astigarraga, E. M. Dow, C. Lara, R. Prewitt, and M. R. Ward. The emerging role of software testing in curricula. In *Transforming Engineering Education: Creating Interdisciplinary Skills for Complex Global Environments, 2010 IEEE*, pages 1–26. IEEE, 2010. 2, 13, 25, 151

[6] J. M. Atlee, R. J. LeBlanc Jr, T. C. Lethbridge, A. Sobel, and J. B. Thompson. Software engineering 2004: Acm/ieee-cs guidelines for undergraduate programs in software engineering. In *Proceedings of the 27th international conference on Software engineering*, pages 623–624. ACM, 2005. 3

[7] A. Bandura and D. C. McClelland. Social learning theory. 1977. 85

[8] O. Barzilay. Example embedding. In *10th SIGPLAN symposium on New ideas, new paradigms, and reflections on programming and software*, pages 137–144. ACM, 2011. 147, 160

[9] O. Barzilay, O. Hazzan, and A. Yehudai. Characterizing example embedding as a software activity. In *ICSE Workshop on Search-Driven Development-Users, Infrastructure, Tools and Evaluation*, pages 5–8. IEEE Computer Society, 2009. 147

[10] V. R. Basili. *Software modeling and measurement: the goal/question/metric paradigm*. Computer science technical report Series. Maryland Univ., College Park, MD, 1992. 107

[11] V. R. Basili and D. M. Weiss. A methodology for collecting valid software engineering data. *Software Engineering, IEEE Transactions on*, SE-10(6):728 –738, nov. 1984. 107

[12] A. Beer and R. Ramler. The role of experience in software testing practice. In *Software Engineering and Advanced Applications, 2008. SEAA'08. 34th Euromicro Conference*, pages 258–265. IEEE, 2008. 145

[13] A. Begel. Help, i need somebody! *Supporting the Social Side of Large Scale Software Development*, page 59, 2006. 150

[14] A. Begel and B. Simon. Novice software developers, all over again. In *Proceedings of the Fourth international Workshop on Computing Education Research*, pages 3–14. ACM, 2008. 150

[15] A. Begel and B. Simon. Struggles of new college graduates in their first software development job. In *ACM SIGCSE Bulletin*, volume 40, pages 226–230. ACM, 2008. 1, 140, 144

[16] A. Begel and T. Zimmermann. Keeping up with your friends: function foo, library bar.dll, and work item 24. In *Proc. of the 1st Workshop on Web 2.0 for Software Engineering*, Web2SE '10, pages 20–23, New York, NY, USA, 2010. ACM. 146

[17] M. Beller, G. Gousios, A. Panichella, and A. Zaidman. When, how, and why developers (do not) test in their ides. 2015. 144

[18] M. Beller, G. Gousios, and A. Zaidman. How (much) do developers test? In *Software Engineering (ICSE), 2015 IEEE/ACM 37th IEEE International Conference on*, volume 2, pages 559–562. IEEE, 2015. 143

[19] S. Berner, R. Weber, and R. K. Keller. Observations and lessons learned from automated testing. In *Proceedings of the 27th international conference on Software engineering*, pages 571–579. ACM, 2005. 144

[20] A. Bertolino. Software testing research: Achievements, challenges, dreams. In *2007 Future of Software Engineering*, pages 85–103. IEEE Computer Society, 2007. 141

[21] J. T. Biehl, M. Czerwinski, G. Smith, and G. G. Robertson. Fastdash: a visual dashboard for fostering awareness in software teams. In *SIGCHI Conf. on Human Factors in Computing Systems*, pages 1313–1322, 2007. 147

[22] J. Brandt, M. Dontcheva, M. Weskamp, and S. R. Klemmer. Example-centric programming: integrating web search into the development environment. In *SIGCHI Conference on Human Factors in Computing Systems*, pages 513–522. ACM, 2010. 148

[23] E. Brechner. Things they would not teach me of in college: What microsoft developers learn later. In *Companion of the 18th Annual ACM SIGPLAN Conf. on Object-oriented Programming, Systems, Languages, and Applications*, OOPSLA '03, pages 134–136, New York, NY, USA, 2003. ACM. 1

[24] B. Bruegge. Teaching an industry-oriented software engineering course. In C. Sledge, editor, *Software Engineering Education*, volume 640 of *Lecture Notes in Computer Science*, pages 63–87. Springer Berlin Heidelberg, 1992. 13, 162

[25] D. J. Byrne and J. L. Moore. A comparison between the recommendations of computing curriculum 1991 and the views of software development managers in ireland. *Computers & Education*, 28(3):145–154, 1997. 2

[26] G. Canfora, M. Di Penta, S. Giannantonio, R. Oliveto, and S. Panichella. Yoda: young and newcomer developer assistant. In *Proceedings of the 2013 International Conference on Software Engineering*, pages 1331–1334. IEEE Press, 2013. 150

[27] G. Canfora, M. Di Penta, R. Oliveto, and S. Panichella. Who is going to mentor newcomers in open source projects? In *Proceedings of the ACM SIGSOFT 20th International Symposium on the Foundations of Software Engineering*, page 44. ACM, 2012. 150

[28] J. C. Carver and N. A. Kraft. Evaluating the testing ability of senior-level computer science students. In *Software Engineering Education and Training (CSEE&T), 2011 24th IEEE-CS Conference on*, pages 169–178. IEEE, 2011. 1, 142

[29] L. Cassel, A. Clements, G. Davies, M. Guzdial, R. McCauley, A. McGettrick, B. Sloan, L. Snyder, P. Tymann, and B. W. Weide. Computer science curriculum 2008: An interim revision of cs 2001. 2008. 3

[30] A. Causevic, D. Sundmark, and S. Punnekkat. Factors limiting industrial adoption of test driven development: A systematic review. In *Software Testing, Verification and Validation (ICST), 4th International Conference on*, pages 337–346, March 2011. 145

[31] F. Chan, T. Tse, W. Tang, and T. Chen. Software testing education and training in hong kong. In *Quality Software, 2005.(QSIC 2005). Fifth International Conference on*, pages 313–316. IEEE, 2005. 139

[32] K. Charmaz. *Constructing grounded theory*. Sage, 2014. 169

[33] H. B. Christensen. Systematic testing should not be a topic in the computer science curriculum! In *ACM SIGCSE Bulletin*, volume 35, pages 7–10. ACM, 2003. 143

[34] J. Collofello and K. Vehathiri. An environment for training computer science students on software testing. In *Frontiers in Education, 2005. FIE'05. Proceedings 35th Annual Conference*, pages T3E–6. IEEE, 2005. 149

[35] R. Conn. Developing software engineers at the c-130j software factory. *Software, IEEE*, 19:28–29, 2002. 1

[36] K. Crowston and J. Howison. The social structure of free and open source software development. *First Monday*, 10(2), 2005. 150

[37] L. Dabbish, C. Stuart, J. Tsay, and J. Herbsleb. Social coding in github: transparency and collaboration in an open software repository. In *Computer Supported Cooperative Work, CSCW*, pages 1277–1286. ACM, 2012. 137, 146

[38] L. Dabbish, C. Stuart, J. Tsay, and J. Herbsleb. Leveraging transparency. *Software, IEEE*, 30(1):37–43, 2013. 146

[39] B. Dagenais, H. Ossher, R. K. Bellamy, M. P. Robillard, and J. P. De Vries. Moving into a new software project landscape. In *Proceedings of the 32nd ACM/IEEE International Conference on Software Engineering-Volume 1*, pages 275–284. ACM, 2010. 150

[40] B. Dagenais and M. P. Robillard. Creating and evolving developer documentation: understanding the decisions of open source contributors. In *Proc. of the eighteenth ACM SIGSOFT Intern. symposium on Foundations of software engineering*, FSE '10, pages 127–136, New York, NY, USA, 2010. ACM. 148

[41] A. Deak. Understanding the influence of social and technical factors testers in software organizations. In *Software Testing, Verification and Validation (ICST), 2013 IEEE Sixth International Conference on*, pages 511–512. IEEE, 2013. 145

[42] A. Deak. A comparative study of testers' motivation in traditional and agile software development. In *Product-Focused Software Process Improvement*, pages 1–16. Springer, 2014. 145

[43] A. Deak. What characterizes a good software tester?–a survey in four norwegian companies. In *Testing Software and Systems*, pages 161–172. Springer, 2014. 145

[44] A. Deak and G. Sindre. Analyzing the importance of teaching about testing from alumni survey data. *Norsk informatikkonferanse (NIK)*, 2013, 2014. 2

[45] A. Deak, T. Stålhane, and D. Cruzes. Factors influencing the choice of a career in software testing among norwegian students. *Software Engineering*, page 796, 2013. 145

[46] T. DeMarco and T. Lister. Peopleware: Productive people and teams. *Dorseth House*, 1987. 150

[47] C. Desai, D. S. Janzen, and J. Clements. Implications of integrating test-driven development into cs1/cs2 curricula. *ACM SIGCSE Bulletin*, 41(1):148–152, 2009. 143

[48] D. J. Dubois and G. Tamburrelli. Understanding gamification mechanisms for software development. In *9th Foundations of Software Engineering, ESEC/FSE*, pages 659–662, 2012. 147

[49] J. Edwards. Example centric programming. *ACM SIGPLAN Notices*, 39(12):84–91, 2004. 147

[50] S. H. Edwards. Using test-driven development in the classroom: Providing students with automatic, concrete feedback on performance. In *Proceedings of the International Conference on Education and Information Systems: Technologies and Applications EISTA*, volume 3, 2003. 143

[51] S. G. Eick, J. L. Steffen, and E. E. Sumner, Jr. Seesoft - a tool for visualizing line oriented software statistics. In *Software Engineering, IEEE Transactions on*, pages 957–968, 1992. 147

[52] S. Elbaum, S. Person, J. Dokulil, and M. Jorde. Bug hunt: Making early software testing lessons engaging and affordable. In *Software Engineering, 2007. ICSE 2007. 29th Int. Conf. on*, pages 688–697. IEEE, 2007. 148

[53] M. Ellims, J. Bridges, and D. Ince. The economics of unit testing. *Empirical Software Engineering*, 11(1):5–31, 2006. 143

[54] T. Erickson and W. A. Kellogg. Social translucence: an approach to designing systems that support social processes. *ACM transactions on computer-human interaction (TOCHI)*, 7(1):59–83, 2000. 9

[55] F. Fagerholm, A. S. Guinea, J. Münch, and J. Borenstein. The role of mentoring and project characteristics for onboarding in open source software projects. In *Proceedings of the 8th ACM/IEEE International Symposium on Empirical Software Engineering and Measurement*, page 55. ACM, 2014. 150

[56] F. Fagerholm, P. Johnson, A. S. Guinea, J. Borenstein, and J. Munch. Onboarding in open source software projects: A preliminary analysis. In *Global Software Engineering Workshops (ICGSEW), 2013 IEEE 8th International Conference on*, pages 5–10. IEEE, 2013. 150

[57] R. Frost. Jazz and the eclipse way of collaboration. *Software, IEEE*, pages 114–117, 2007. 147

[58] M. Gallivan, D. P. Truex III, and L. Kvasny. An analysis of the changing demand patterns for information technology professionals. In *Proceedings of the 2002 ACM SIGCPR conference on Computer personnel research*, pages 1–13. ACM, 2002. 141

[59] M. J. Gallivan, D. P. Truex III, and L. Kvasny. Changing patterns in it skill sets 1988-2003: a content analysis of classified advertising. *ACM SIGMIS Database*, 35(3):64–87, 2004. 141

[60] V. Garousi. Incorporating real-world industrial testing projects in software testing courses: Opportunities, challenges, and lessons learned. In *Software Engineering Education and Training (CSEE&T), 2011 24th IEEE-CS Conference on*, pages 396–400. IEEE, 2011. 13, 144

[61] V. Garousi and A. Mathur. Current state of the software testing education in north american academia and some recommendations for the new educators. In *Software Engineering Education and Training (CSEE&T), 2010 23rd IEEE Conference on*, pages 89–96. IEEE, 2010. 3, 13, 25, 151

[62] V. Garousi and T. Varma. A replicated survey of software testing practices in the canadian province of alberta: What has changed from 2004 to 2009? *Journal of Systems and Software*, 83(11):2251–2262, 2010. 139

[63] V. Garousi and J. Zhi. A survey of software testing practices in canada. *Journal of Systems and Software*, 86(5):1354–1376, 2013. 140

[64] A. M. Geras, M. Smith, and J. Miller. A survey of software testing practices in alberta. *Electrical and Computer Engineering, Canadian Journal of*, 29(3):183–191, 2004. 139

[65] B. Glaser and A. Strauss. *The Discovery of Grounded Theory: Strategies for Qualitative Research*. Observations (Chicago, Ill.). Aldine de Gruyter, 1967. 54, 171

[66] B. G. Glaser and A. L. Strauss. *Awareness of dying*. Transaction Publishers, 1966. 169

[67] B. G. Glaser and A. L. Strauss. *The discovery of grounded theory: Strategies for qualitative research*. Transaction Publishers, 2009. 169

[68] R. L. Glass, R. Collard, A. Bertolino, J. Bach, and C. Kaner. Software testing and industry needs. *IEEE Software*, 23(4):55–57, 2006. 1

[69] M. H. Goldwasser. A gimmick to integrate software testing throughout the curriculum. In *ACM SIGCSE Bulletin*, volume 34, pages 271–275. ACM, 2002. 143

[70] M. Greiler, A. v. Deursen, and M.-A. Storey. Test confessions: a study of testing practices for plug-in systems. In *Proc. of the 2012 Intern. Conf. on Software Engineering*, ICSE 2012, pages 244–254, Piscataway, NJ, USA, 2012. IEEE Press. 144

[71] M. Grindal, J. Offutt, and J. Mellin. On the testing maturity of software producing organizations. In *Testing: Academic and Industrial Conference-Practice And Research Techniques, 2006. TAIC PART 2006. Proceedings*, pages 171–180. IEEE, 2006. 139

[72] H. Haddad. Post-graduate assessment of cs students: experience and position paper. *Journal of Computing Sciences in Colleges*, 18(2):189–197, 2002. 1, 140

[73] J. H. Hayes. Energizing software engineering education through real-world projects as experimental studies. In *Software Engineering Education and Training, 2002.(CSEE&T 2002). Proceedings. 15th Conference on*, pages 192–206. IEEE, 2002. 13, 144

[74] L. Hemphill and A. Begel. Not seen and not heard: Onboarding challenges in newly virtual teams. 150

[75] L. Hemphill and A. Begel. How will you see my greatness if you can't see me? *Ann Arbor*, 1001:48103, 2008. 150

[76] I. Herraiz, G. Robles, J. J. Amor, T. Romera, and J. M. González Barahona. The processes of joining in global distributed software projects. In *Proceedings of the 2006 international workshop on Global software development for the practitioner*, pages 27–33. ACM, 2006. 150

[77] R. Hoda, J. Noble, and S. Marshall. Developing a grounded theory to explain the practices of self-organizing agile teams. *Empirical Software Engineering*, 17(6):609–639, 2012. 40, 169

[78] S.-W. Huang and W.-T. Fu. Motivating crowds using social facilitation and social transparency. In *Proceedings of the 2013 conference on Computer supported cooperative work companion*, pages 149–152. ACM, 2013. 146

[79] O. Hummel, W. Janjic, and C. Atkinson. Code conjurer: Pulling reusable software out of thin air. *Software, IEEE*, 25(5):45–52, 2008. 147

[80] J. Iivari. Why are case tools not used? *Communications of the ACM*, 39(10):94–103, 1996. 11

[81] W. Janjic. Reuse-based test recommendation in software engineering. 2014. 148

[82] D. Janzen and H. Saiedian. Test-driven learning in early programming courses. In *ACM SIGCSE Bulletin*, volume 40, pages 532–536. ACM, 2008. 143

[83] D. S. Janzen and H. Saiedian. Test-driven learning: intrinsic integration of testing into the cs/se curriculum. In *ACM SIGCSE Bulletin*, volume 38, pages 254–258. ACM, 2006. 143

[84] M. Johnson and M. Senges. Learning to be a programmer in a complex organization: A case study on practice-based learning during the onboarding process at google. *Journal of Workplace Learning*, 22(3):180–194, 2010. 149

[85] E. L. Jones. Software testing in the computer science curriculum–a holistic approach. In *Proceedings of the Australasian conference on Computing education*, pages 153–157. ACM, 2000. 143

[86] E. L. Jones. Integrating testing into the curriculum—arsenic in small doses. *ACM SIGCSE Bulletin*, 33(1):337–341, 2001. 143

[87] E. L. Jones and C. L. Chatmon. A perspective on teaching software testing. In *Journal of Computing Sciences in Colleges*, volume 16, pages 92–100. Consortium for Computing Sciences in Colleges, 2001. 143

[88] C. Kaner and S. Padmanabhan. Practice and transfer of learning in the teaching of software testing. In *Software Engineering Education & Training, 2007. CSEET'07. 20th Conf. on*, pages 157–166. IEEE, 2007. 142, 151

[89] T. Kanij, R. Merkel, and J. Grundy. A preliminary survey of factors affecting software testers. In *2014 Australasian Conference on Software Engineering (ASWEC 2014)*. IEEE CS Press, 2014. 145

[90] K. Karhu, T. Repo, O. Taipale, and K. Smolander. Empirical observations on software testing automation. In *Software Testing Verification and Validation (ICST), International Conference on*, pages 201–209, April 2009. 144

[91] P. Kinnaird, L. Dabbish, S. Kiesler, and H. Faste. Co-worker transparency in a microtask marketplace. In *Proceedings of the 2013 conference on Computer supported cooperative work*, pages 1285–1290. ACM, 2013. 146

[92] B. Kitchenham. Procedures for performing systematic reviews. *Keele, UK, Keele University*, 33(2004):1–26, 2004. 1

[93] B. Kitchenham, D. Budgen, P. Brereton, and P. Woodall. An investigation of software engineering curricula. *Journal of Systems and Software*, 74(3):325–335, 2005. 2

[94] B. Kitchenham and S. Charters. Guidelines for performing systematic literature reviews in software engineering. Technical report, Technical report, EBSE Technical Report EBSE-2007-01, 2007. 1

[95] D. Knudson and A. Radermacher. Software engineering and project management in cs projects vs."real-world" projects: A case study. In *Proceedings of the IASTED International Conference*, volume 669, page 38. 13, 144

[96] P. J. Kovacs and G. A. Davis. Determining critical skills and knowledge requirements of it professionals by analysing keywords in job posting. *Issues in Information Systems*, 9:95–100, 2008. 141

[97] R. Kraut, M. Burke, J. Riedl, and P. Resnick. Dealing with newcomers. *Evidence-based Social Design Mining the Social Sciences to Build Online Communities*, 1:42, 2010. 10

[98] T. D. LaToza, G. Venolia, and R. DeLine. Maintaining mental models: A study of developer work habits. In *28th International Conference on Software Engineering (ICSE)*, pages 492–501. ACM, 2006. 144

[99] R. J. LeBlanc, A. Sobel, J. L. Diaz-Herrera, T. B. Hilburn, et al. *Software Engineering 2004: Curriculum Guidelines for Undergraduate Degree Programs in Software Engineering*. IEEE Computer Society, 2006. 142

[100] C. K. Lee and H.-J. Han. Analysis of skills requirement for entry-level programmer/analysts in fortune 500 corporations. *Journal of Information Systems Education*, 19(1):17, 2008. 141

[101] T. C. Lethbridge. A survey of the relevance of computer science and software engineering education. In *Software Engineering Education, 1998. Proceedings., 11th Conference on*, pages 56–66. IEEE, 1998. 2

[102] T. C. Lethbridge. The relevance of education to software practitioners: Data from the 1998 survey. *School of Information Technology and Engineering, University of Ottowa, Ottowa (Canada), Computer Science Technical Report TR-99-05*, 1999. 2

[103] T. C. Lethbridge. Priorities for the education and training of software engineers. *Journal of Systems and Software*, 53(1):53–71, 2000. 2

[104] T. C. Lethbridge. What knowledge is important to a software professional? *Computer*, (5):44–50, 2000. 2

[105] T. C. Lethbridge, J. Diaz-Herrera, R. J. LeBlanc Jr, and J. B. Thompson. Improving software practice through education: Challenges and future trends. In *Future of Software Engineering, 2007. FOSE'07*, pages 12–28. IEEE, 2007. 141

[106] C. Litecky and K. Arnett. An update on measurement of it job skills for managers and professionals. *AMCIS 2001 Proceedings*, page 371, 2001. 141

[107] D. Lübke, T. Flohr, and K. Schneider. Serious insights through fun software-projects. In T. Dingsøyr, editor, *Software Process Improvement*, volume 3281 of *Lecture Notes in Computer Science*, pages 57–68. Springer Berlin Heidelberg, 2004. 13, 162

[108] W. Marrero and A. Settle. Testing first: emphasizing testing in early programming courses. In *ACM SIGCSE Bulletin*, volume 37, pages 4–8. ACM, 2005. 143

[109] A. N. Meyer, T. Fritz, G. C. Murphy, and T. Zimmermann. Software developers' perceptions of productivity. In *Proceedings of the 22nd ACM SIGSOFT International Symposium on Foundations of Software Engineering*, pages 19–29. ACM, 2014. 164

[110] M. Michlmayr, F. Hunt, and D. Probert. Quality Practices and Problems in Free Software Projects. In *Proc. of the First Intern. Conf. on Open Source Systems*, pages 24–28, 2005. 144

[111] J. Moerschbach. Visualisierung von testsignalen in der ide zur sensibilisierung für automatisiertes testen. Master's thesis, Leibniz Universität Hannover, Fachgebiet Software Engineering, 2015. 105, 107, 114, 164

[112] A. M. Moreno, M.-I. Sanchez-Segura, F. Medina-Dominguez, and L. Carvajal. Balancing software engineering education and industrial needs. *Journal of Systems and Software*, 85(7):1607–1620, 2012. 142

[113] M. C. Murphy and B. Yildirim. Work in progress-testing right from the start. In *Frontiers In Education Conference-Global Engineering: Knowledge Without Borders, Opportunities Without Passports, 2007. FIE'07. 37th Annual*, pages F1H–25. IEEE, 2007. 143

[114] S. M. Nasehi, J. Sillito, F. Maurer, and C. Burns. What makes a good code example?: A study of programming q&a in stackoverflow. In *Software Maintenance (ICSM), 2012 28th IEEE International Conference on*, pages 25–34. IEEE, 2012. 147, 166

[115] S. P. Ng, T. Murnane, K. Reed, D. Grant, and T. Chen. A preliminary survey on software testing practices in Australia. In *Australian Software Engineering Conference (ASWEC)*, pages 116–125, 2004. 139

[116] S. Panichella. Supporting newcomers in software development projects. In *Software Maintenance and Evolution (ICSME), 2015 IEEE International Conference on*, pages 586–589. IEEE, 2015. 145

[117] C. Parnin, C. Treude, L. Grammel, and M.-A. Storey. Crowd documentation: Exploring the coverage and the dynamics of api discussions on stack overflow. *Georgia Institute of Technology, Tech. Rep*, 2012. 166

[118] R. Pham. Improving the software testing skills of novices during onboarding through social transparency. In *Proceedings of the 22nd ACM SIGSOFT International Symposium on Foundations of Software Engineering*, pages 803–806. ACM, 2014. i

[119] R. Pham, S. Kiesling, O. Liskin, L. Singer, and K. Schneider. Enablers, Inhibitors, and Perceptions of Testing in Novice Software Teams. In *22th Foundations of Software Engineering, FSE*, 2014. i, 13, 39, 40, 151

[120] R. Pham, S. Kiesling, L. Singer, and K. Schneider. Onboarding Inexperienced Developers: Struggles and Perceptions Regarding automated testing. In *Software Quality Journal*, Software Quality Journal. Springer Science+Business Media New York 2016, 2016. ii, 54, 151

[121] R. Pham, J. Mörschbach, and K. Schneider. Communicating Software Testing Culture through Visualizing Testing Activity. In *7th International Workshop on Social Software Engineering (SSE 2015)*, SSE 2015. ACM, 2015. 9, 105

[122] R. Pham, L. Singer, O. Liskin, F. Figueira Filho, and K. Schneider. Creating a shared understanding of testing culture on a social coding site. In *International Conference on Software Engineering (ICSE)*, pages 112–121. IEEE Press, 2013. i, 61, 106, 137, 163

[123] R. Pham, Y. Stoliar, and K. Schneider. Automatically Recommending Test Code Examples to Inexperienced Developers. In *Proceedings of the 10th Joint Meeting of the European Software Engineering Conference and the ACM SIGSOFT Symposium on the Foundations of Software Engineering (ESEC/FSE 2015)*, ESEC/FSE 2015. ACM, 2015. ii, 131

[124] B. Prabhakar, C. R. Litecky, and K. Arnett. It skills in a tough job market. *Communications of the ACM*, 48(10):91–94, 2005. 141

[125] G. Premkumar and M. Potter. Adoption of computer aided software engineering (case) technology: an innovation adoption perspective. *ACM SIGMIS Database*, 26(2-3):105–124, 1995. 11

[126] V. K. Proulx. Test-driven design for introductory oo programming. *ACM SIGCSE Bulletin*, 41(1):138–142, 2009. 143

[127] A. Radermacher and G. Walia. Gaps between industry expectations and the abilities of graduates. In *Proceeding of the 44th ACM technical symposium on Computer science education*, pages 525–530. ACM, 2013. 1, 141, 165

[128] A. Radermacher, G. Walia, and D. Knudson. Investigating the skill gap between graduating students and industry expectations. In *Companion Proceedings of the 36th International Conference on Software Engineering*, pages 291–300. ACM, 2014. 140

[129] S. A. Raghavan and D. R. Chand. Diffusing software-engineering methods. *Software, IEEE*, 6(4):81–90, 1989. 11

[130] E. M. Rogers. *Diffusion of Innovations*. Free Press, 5th edition, 2003. 4, 12, 14, 15, 16, 17, 18, 19, 21, 22, 23, 25, 26, 27, 30, 31, 38, 152, 158, 165

[131] P. Runeson. A survey of unit testing practices. *Software, IEEE*, 23(4):22–29, July 2006. 144

[132] E. Scott, A. Zadirov, S. Feinberg, and R. Jayakody. The alignment of software testing skills of is students with industry practices- a south african perspective. *Journal of Information Technology Education*, 3:161–172, 2004. 142

[133] T. Shepard, M. Lamb, and D. Kelly. More testing should be taught. *Communications of the ACM*, 44(6):103–108, 2001. 142, 143

[134] S. E. Sim and R. C. Holt. The ramp-up problem in software projects: A case study of how software immigrants naturalize. In *Software Engineering, 1998. Proceedings of the 1998 International Conference on*, pages 361–370. IEEE, 1998. 150

[135] C. B. Simmons and L. L. Simmons. Gaps in the computer science curriculum: an exploratory study of industry professionals. *Journal of Computing Sciences in Colleges*, 25(5):60–65, 2010. 140

[136] L. Singer. *Improving the Adoption of Software Engineering Practices Through Persuasive Interventions*. PhD thesis, Gottfried Wilhelm Leibniz Universität Hannover, 2013. 85

[137] L. Singer, F. Figueira Filho, B. Cleary, C. Treude, M.-A. Storey, and K. Schneider. Mutual assessment in the social programmer ecosystem: An empirical investigation of developer profile aggregators. In *Proc. 2013 Conf. Comput. Supported Cooperative Work*, CSCW '13, pages 103–116, NY, USA, 2013. ACM. 63, 146

[138] L. Singer and K. Schneider. It was a bit of a race: Gamification of version control. In *2nd Workshop on Games and Software Engineering, GAS*, pages 5–8, 2012. 147

[139] L.-G. Singer. *Improving the adoption of software engineering practices through persuasive interventions*. Lulu. com, 2013. 11, 137, 146

[140] C. Souza and D. Redmiles. The awareness network: To whom should i display my actions? and, whose actions should i monitor? In L. Bannon, I. Wagner, C. Gutwin, R. Harper, and K. Schmidt, editors, *ECSCW 2007*, pages 99–117. Springer London, 2007. 146

[141] C. Space. Curriculum development guidelines: New ict curricula for the 21 st century, designing tomorrow's education. *Luxembourg: Office for Official Publications of the European Communities*, page 50, 2001. 142

[142] I. Steinmacher, I. S. Wiese, T. Conte, M. A. Gerosa, and D. Redmiles. The hard life of open source software project newcomers. In *Proceedings of the 7th International Workshop on Cooperative and Human Aspects of Software Engineering*, pages 72–78. ACM, 2014. 149

[143] Y. Stoliar. Beispiel-basierte unterstützung der erstellung von automatisierten softwaretests. Master's thesis, Leibniz Universität Hannover, Fachgebiet Software Engineering, 2015. 131

[144] H. C. Stuart, L. Dabbish, S. Kiesler, P. Kinnaird, and R. Kang. Social transparency in networked information exchange: a theoretical framework. In *Proc. of the ACM 2012 Conf. on Computer Supported Cooperative Work*, CSCW '12, pages 451–460, New York, NY, USA, 2012. ACM. 9, 146

[145] L. A. Sudol and C. Jaspan. Analyzing the strength of undergraduate misconceptions about software engineering. In *Proceedings of the Sixth international workshop on Computing education research*, pages 31–40. ACM, 2010. 143

[146] S. Surakka. What subjects and skills are important for software developers? *Communications of the ACM*, 50(1):73–78, 2007. 2

[147] O. Taipale, K. Smolander, and H. Kälviäinen. Finding and ranking research directions for software testing. In *Software Process Improvement*, pages 39–48. Springer, 2005. 141

[148] C. Treude and M.-A. Storey. Awareness 2.0: staying aware of projects, developers and tasks using dashboards and feeds. In *32nd Int. Conf. on Software Engineering, ICSE*, pages 365–374, 2010. 147

[149] A. Tucker. A model curriculum for k–12 computer science: Final report of the acm k–12 task force curriculum committee. 2003. 3

[150] A. B. Tucker, R. M. Aiken, K. Barker, K. B. Bruce, J. T. Cain, S. E. Conry, G. L. Engel, R. G. Epstein, D. K. Lidtke, M. C. Mulder, et al. *Computing curricula 1991: report of the ACM/IEEE-CS Joint curriculum task force*. ACM, 1991. 2

[151] F. Van Latum, R. Van Solingen, M. Oivo, B. Hoisl, D. Rombach, and G. Ruhe. Adopting gqm based measurement in an industrial environment. *Software, IEEE*, 15(1):78 –86, jan/feb 1998. 107

[152] G. Von Krogh, S. Spaeth, and K. R. Lakhani. Community, joining, and specialization in open source software innovation: a case study. *Research Policy*, 32(7):1217–1241, 2003. 150

[153] E. J. Weyuker, T. J. Ostrand, J. Brophy, and R. Prasad. Clearing a career path for software testers. *Software, IEEE*, 17:76–82, 2000. 140

[154] S. Xiao, J. Witschey, and E. Murphy-Hill. Social influences on secure development tool adoption: why security tools spread. In *Proceedings of the 17th ACM conference on Computer supported cooperative work & social computing*, pages 1095–1106. ACM, 2014. 11

[155] A. Zagalsky, J. Feliciano, M. D. Storey, Y. Zhao, and W. Wang. The emergence of github as a collaborative platform for education. In *Proceedings of the 18th ACM Conference on Computer Supported Cooperative Work & Social Computing, CSCW 2015, Vancouver, BC, Canada, March 14 - 18, 2015*, pages 1906–1917, 2015. 158